FINDING OWL CANYON

A Novel by

REX OLSEN

Dedicated to Grandsons

Justin, Gabe, and Josh

They will find their own Owl Canyon

Chapter One

BY MOONLIGHT

The fat New Mexico moon dropped blue shadows by a score of flat-topped adobes scattered along the curved road. Some buildings leaned on others; some stood alone like bad teeth in an old man's smile. An owl floated silently across the moon and came to rest in Mesa de Luna's only tree.

Thumps and muffled shouts burst through a flung-open plank door. Lamp light outlined Elwood Renfroe, desperately hopping in a tight circle with trousers pulled up to his knees. The half-empty pant legs flapped like a scarecrow in a whirlwind.

Elwood's long shadow shot across the street as he hopped from the door, cleared the boardwalk, and collided, belly high, with the horizontal pole of a hitch rack. He folded over, spun once, and landed flat on his back. Gasping, El heard the plop of various articles of clothing he'd have to find in the dim light before he could escape to his hidden horse. Only strangers used the hitch rack in front of Ruby Lee's.

The plump, naked body of Ruby Lee Ahearn filled the doorway as she hurled hat, boots, and insults after him. Lamplight shone through her flying hair.

"You beanpole bastard," Ruby yelled. "Next time, you pay first." El heard the door slam before coins rained into the dust.

"Mule-headed woman," El grumbled, scrambling to what he thought was the dark shape of his shirt, but which turned out to be dried horse dung. "Ain't fair," he muttered as he crawled in a different direction and found his vest and one of his boots. "Stores give credit. Saloons give credit—sometimes. But she's too high and mighty to do a man a favor until payday."

'Payday' was a doubtful term. El hadn't held a steady job since the Southern Pacific Railroad hired him to cut trees for trestles. They'd taken him up the Pecos to the slopes above Gabaldon, shown him the type of Ponderosas they wanted, gave him an axe and a can of paint and left him to his work. He was to mark, cut, trim, and skid the trees to the river before the end of spring runoff. The SP would pick them up downstream.

When, after two weeks, no logs floated into view, SP officials visited the work site where they saw hundreds of paint-marked trees. They found El sleeping under one of his targets. His axe was stuck in the side of another. His horse was tethered to a third Ponderosa, and his grub box and frying pan rested under a fourth. It looked as if he'd taken up residence instead of cutting down trees. They woke him and asked him what he was doing.

"Gettin' ready," he replied. "You said mark before cutting."

"We didn't ask you to paint the whole goddamn forest. You've marked enough wood to build a railroad to California! When did you plan to begin?"

"Just a couple more days," El replied. "I need to hunt a deer or two so's I'll have plenty of food when the hard work starts."

The visitors shook their heads, paid him for his time, kept the axe, and sent him on his way. Two years had passed and El was at peace with the experience.

The morning before his visit to Ruby Lee he'd rounded up a few Flying-W strays for Bus Wiley, but Bus hadn't asked him to, and didn't offer to pay. Bus hadn't even seemed grateful, possibly because they had been almost within sight of his ranch buildings and weren't really lost, if one wanted to put a fine point on it.

They were more like *loose*, it seemed to El as he thought back, but they had looked good bunched up in the ranch yard where they milled apprehensively, bawling like lost souls. Bus had elbowed the door open. He'd gripped a mug in one hand and a straight razor in the other. With his lower face lathered and wearing his red union suit, he looked like a drawing of Santa Claus El had seen in a child's picture book.

"Elwood, what the hell are you doing?"

"Brought some strays," El replied, narrowly eyeing the razor.

"They look like the ones I saw yesterday, grazing on bunch-grass the other side of that hill, exactly where I put 'em." He pointed past El with the razor.

El leaned back in the saddle. "Well," he said as he scratched his chin, "I thought you might need some help. Line ridin'. Or whatever."

"I do not. Now move those goddamn cows out of my yard or I'll have to clean my boots every time I go outside."

El had estimated the chance that Bus might pay him later as slim, but the possibility had given him courage to listen at Ruby Lee's back wall after night fell. When he didn't hear bed springs, he'd walked around and knocked on the only door.

Ruby Lee, optimistic about human nature, had let him come in and undress. Thirty minutes later she'd wished she owned a hat shop, but she knew she'd get over it and could look for the coins in the morning. She'd learned to scoop and shake dust through a big tin flour sifter. Sometimes she found coins she hadn't even thrown. She preferred to do it early when she was less likely to draw a crowd.

"Big dumb bastard," she fumed. She'd probably let him in again, but next time she'd count the money first.

El scratched his stubble of beard and wondered how to find his hat when it sailed out of the shadow beside the next door pool hall and slid to a stop at his feet.

"Well," a voice said, "it appears you've ruined it for all of us. At least, tonight you have." Then, after a chuckle, "But I wouldn't have missed the show. Would you, Moose?"

"Ruined what?" El replied, while hurriedly trying to match buttons and corresponding holes without much success.

"You sure put Ruby Lee off her feed," Rozier Wells said as he stepped into the moonlight. Lean and of medium height, he was nearly a head shorter than El. His even teeth gleamed in a broad smile. "And I was just going to visit her for what might be the last time. Now, she'll probably shoot at me." Roz removed his Stetson and smoothed moonlit blond hair before putting it back on.

"Where'd you learn to spin like that," Moose Banner asked mildly as he approached El, boardwalk creaking with each step. The top of Moose's prematurely bald pate formed bright contrast to his dark shirt and vest.

At first glance strangers were apt to conclude Moose was too big and pleasant-looking to worry about. He had a cherubic face with rosy cheeks, a sweet smile, cleft chin, baby-blue eyes, and wisps of soft brown hair around the sides of his head. A few newcomers had thought it might be safe to insult him as he sat on a special stool in Gus Swanson's Billiard Emporium. They usually came to their wits outside the pool hall's double doors, wondering that anyone that big could move so fast.

"Now, Moose, I just lost my balance for a minute, is all."

"Lost your dignity, and about two bits, the way I heard it," Roz said with a wide grin.

"Roz Wells, you can g-go," El stammered, "you kin' see Ruby tomorrow, or you kin' go without for all I care."

"Can't," Roz replied, still smiling. "We might be leaving tomorrow."

"For where?" El said, turning to one, then the other.

"For O-re-gone, the land of milk and honey. Where you pan nuggets while your cows grow fat. Cows, kids, whatever you're raising."

"*Oregon*, for crissake," Moose muttered. "Say it right."

"Oregon?" El replied. "Why are you two going to Oregon?" He glanced at Moose who was pushing the hitch rack back and forth to see how loose El had made it.

"Because," Roz answered, "as you know, there ain't a goddamn thing to do in this dried-up town. There's no work, and land's so poor you wouldn't buy it even if you had the money which you can't earn anyhow." He stopped to breathe.

"That's true," Moose agreed. "And we'd like to see some new country, perhaps where one can enjoy a little more culture than is available in this vicinity." Moose liked words such as vicinity and locale. He read all kinds of books. He enjoyed showing what he'd learned, although he didn't expend too much energy getting to the bottom of difficult concepts. He liked the *what* of things more than the *why*.

"I don't know as Mesaluna's so bad, other than bein' a little dry," El said. He'd heard from old-timers there once was a year-round stream in the dry river bed. Cottonwood trees had lined the bank where now only one remained. Some of the oldest and deepest wells were failing. He didn't like to think about it.

"In Oregon," Roz said, "you can homestead land that sees a drop of rain now and again, unlike this god-forsaken place where plants only grow where you piss."

"Don't mind him," Moose said. "He's peevish and particularly crude tonight, probably on account of spoilt plans, which you had a good deal to do with. Anyway, he's right. You can homestead tall-grass country up there. All you have to do is find it. I have a Great Northern Railroad circular, printed just six months ago. It tells about the Puget Sound area and homestead land. Plenty of rain. Trees everywhere. Good soil, too, although it didn't say anything about gold, Roz."

"And he read it to me," Roz added, "and I know a good thing when I hear one. You don't have to go getting all excited because you aren't going with us."

"Can if I want to," El replied while picking a piece of gravel from his elbow.

"Well, what I want to know is, are you going through Denver City?" Ruby asked through a crack in the door.

"Jesus, Ruby Lee," El exclaimed. "Don't go startlin' us like that." El drew himself to his full height and brushed at his unevenly buttoned fly.

"You go to hell, you hoe handle. It wasn't your idea, anyway." She opened the door. Somehow she had listened and dressed at the same time. "Well, what about it? Are you going to Denver City, or aren't you?"

"I expect so," Moose replied, "unless we wanted to go through Apache country, which we don't. We'll ride up the Mora River to Sabinoso, probably to Wagon Mound or Fort Union, on to Raton Pass or maybe over to Bent's Fort, then north to Denver, and so on. Any other way would be foolish."

"And we ain't foolish," El added.

"I'll reserve judgment," Ruby said. "When? When are you going?"

"Soon as we can, but we'd like to get paid first," Moose said.

"Wouldn't we all," Ruby replied, glancing at El. "Moose, Roz, I got to get out of here. This is no place for a genuine business woman. It keeps getting smaller, and I'm getting smaller with it. There's nothing to think about. Besides, I'm going to starve to death, trying to be a friend to the likes of that fool," she said, jerking a thumb at El, who stiffened and stood as tall as possible.

"Aw, settle down, you bony-butted-bastard," she added. "I guess it isn't your fault. Anyway, I'm not mad anymore."

"Well then, Ruby Lee," Roz began. "I'm wondering if you might…"

"*Not* till we settle who's going where. And I think I *am* going if anybody does. Unless you boys would like to square accounts, so to speak." She looked directly at Roz.

There was silence until Roz turned and said, "Goddamn it, Moose, you and I have to talk. We can't take those two along," he whispered as they stepped back into the shadow. "It'd slow us down. And they don't have any money."

"Neither do we."

"But they'd be fighting all the time. And they'd make so much noise every Indian on the plains would know where we were. I'd like to keep my hair, not that you'd be concerned about such a thing."

It was true that Moose had very little hair, although he was only a few years older than Roz. He was fond of saying mental activity made it hard for hair to catch a hold. That, he'd often said, was probably why Roz had so much of it.

"Still might not be a bad idea."

"Give me one good reason," Roz replied.

"I'll give you several. First, they say El can smell Indians a mile away, and I heard Mad Water's been acting up. Second, he can cook. You don't cook worth a damn, and I don't plan to start. Plus, he plays the harmonica, which would be nice, when it's safe.

"And," he continued, "it's Oregon, not O-re-gone. I fail to understand how you can name damn near every prostitute in New Mexico Territory, but you can't pronounce the name of a place without muckin' it up so bad my ears ring. Sometimes you offend my sensibilities, Roz. I swear you do. As to Ruby Lee, it amazes me you aren't saddling a horse for her already. You're over here so often I thought for a while you lived here."

"Moose, Moose, you're hurtin' my feelings," Roz replied, without changing expression. He walked over to where El and Ruby Lee stood, carefully not looking at each other. "We'll see," he said. "Moose is thinking on it."

He picked El's hat from the ground, brushed off some dirt, and handed it to him. Ruby yanked it from El's hand, whacked it twice against the door frame, dislodging a cloud of dust, and whomped it on his head. She turned, and slammed the door behind her. They all heard the bolt. Ruby was closed for the night.

The owl, safe in his cottonwood, turned large yellow eyes and watched faint paths from nearby buildings to the refuse piles behind them. He needed to eat. Fields and alleys once provided ample voles and mice. Now there were few. The owl usually waited for dawn when geckos moved to trash piles seeking early flies. Sometimes he caught the small lizards. Some days he went hungry.

His mate had died the previous winter for reasons he didn't understand. Soon he would also, unless he risked the unknown. Relying solely on body fluids of prey, he was growing lean and weak. His choices were to stay and hunt the diminishing food supply, or move to the Pecos River an hour's flight east, where other raptors fiercely guarded their territories. He dimly remembered the river banks lined with slender willows and lacy tamarisk only half as high as his cottonwood. He'd be exposed, harried by crows and other birds. But the experience of countless owl generations told him he had no choice, that the time for waiting was done. He called once softly, spread his wings as he dropped from the branch, and sailed silently toward the moon, the river, and risk.

Chapter Two

ALCALDE

Pablo Manuel Luis Borrega pressed his thin shoulder against the rough adobe wall, listening while his young wife bathed his uncle in the room on the other side of the open window. Her voice was low and musical, warm as corn syrup; his uncle's, thick with desire. Pablo's knees ached from squatting on the tiled landing under the sill, but he endured the pain. He had to know.

"Ahhh," said his uncle, Juan Diego Borrega de Ancho, the *Alcalde* of Albuquerque and chief magistrate of the surrounding county. "Just a little more warm water, *cara*."

As the water splashed, Pablo slowly eased to one knee while being careful to stay out of sight.

"That feels good. Yes, *very* good. A little more soap. There. Now both hands, but slowly, slowly," murmured Juan Diego.

Pablo swallowed, thought he might become ill. He remembered his wife's hands, smooth and supple. He turned and looked down the outside stairway. Moving would create noise, noise that might get him hurt, or even killed. He needed a drink, but he'd wait.

"*Como este*'?" Rosalinda asked in a sultry purr, the voice Pablo had heard in the early months of their marriage.

"Speak English, like I told you."

"*Si*—I mean, yes, *Patrón*. Like that?"

"Exactly. Now squeeze, but just a little. I want to talk with you. Don't stop unless I tell you."

"Yes, I—undestand."

Pablo thought of his uncle's broad hairy chest and dark skin, his jet-black hair and eyes, a handsome man with a cruel twist at his mustachioed mouth. He was the only law in Albuquerque and for many miles around. He was older, stronger, and much more determined than Pablo had ever been.

"You could take off your dress."

"Then I might need *tres manos*—ah—three hands." She giggled.

"You have something much better. Warmer—now listen to me. You know the Sandia mine is closing, no?"

There was silence. Pablo assumed she had nodded. He, too, had been told the mine would shut down, and the next day's silver shipment would be the last. He'd ride guard as usual on the Dos Osos stage as it headed east. He'd heard that Rosalinda stayed in his uncle's hacienda during the nights that he, Pablo, completed the long, uncomfortable two-night trip from Albuquerque to Mesa de Luna. Another guard, a *gringo* named Roz Wells, would continue to Tucumcari where the Dos Osos connected with the Butterfield Stage. In Mesa de Luna Pablo would switch to the west-bound stage, ride two nights back to Albuquerque—and Rosalinda would refuse to come to his bed when he returned.

"Pablo will be the guard on the stage. Like always. *Comprende*?"

"*Si*. I mean, yes."

"But he will not come back. Not this time."

"No-o?" Pablo heard the mocking note in her lilting, one-word answer. He swallowed. Perspiration beaded his forehead.

"No, *Cara*. The shipment is a large one. I will send also two riders, two of my trusted men."

Pablo knew he was no longer one of his uncle's 'trusted men'. It had been different when Pablo first came to the *Alcalde's* attention. Son of the *Alcalde's* younger sister, Pablo was summoned, at age eighteen, to be one of

Juan Diego's inner council, male relatives by blood or marriage who would do exactly as his uncle dictated. Pablo, had been a favorite—until he'd brought his voluptuous young wife to live in the hut on his uncle's compound.

Rosalinda, now seventeen and two years younger than himself, had come from a dirt-poor goat farm outside of Corrales. She had seemed excited about Pablo's proposal of marriage, and she had been passionate in the first months, until she saw his uncle with his fine home and fine things. Slowly she had changed, and then his uncle began to distance himself from Pablo. Lately Juan Diego always seemed anxious for Pablo to leave, and it was whispered that he had been seen in Pablo's hut, alone with Rosalinda while Pablo traveled. Then Rosalinda began to spend most of her time in the big house, even when Pablo was at home. Pablo had found that drinking *mescal* helped dull the pain and let him sleep—sometimes.

"The silver will not get to Tucumcari, *cara.* Not even to Mesa de Luna. Pablo will not get there either," his uncle said smoothly. "He will die a brave man in my service, trying to protect the silver. He will fail, of course."

"And the others?"

"I need them. I do not need Pablo. *Comprende*?"

"Ah," she said. "And I…?"

"And *we* will blame the fools who operate the Mesa de Luna stage stop. Those gringos, Wells and Banner. We will catch them and hang them, and say that they hid the silver and we could not find it." *Except for my gift to the governor*, he thought.

"*Pero*—I mean but..."

"But what?"

"But, what will become of me?"

"You? You will have anything you want."

"Anything? Jewelry? This *hacienda*?"

The purring, sultry tone had come back. It is over, Pablo realized. No turning back. No more hope.

"Anything, *Cara*. But, enough questions. Pour a little more water and get in here with me. There is room for two, and I am growing tired of your hands."

"You are growing, *certamente*'."

"So, what will you do for me?"

"Shall I, you know...?"

"Yes. You can talk to me later."

Splashing water masked the sound of Pablo creeping silently down the stairs, retching at the corner of the hacienda. He remembered Rosalinda in their wedding tub, ripe breasts floating; eyes half-closed, lips parted, steam curling her dark hair. The memories made his head hurt and blurred his vision. By the time he'd finished bending over and wiping his mouth on his soiled white sleeve, he had started to form a plan. His uncle, Juan Diego, was correct. One way or another, Pablo would never return to Albuquerque.

Chapter Three

WAITING FOR RAIN

Ruby kept a Doctor Barnwell's Dietary Tonic calendar on her wall. She drew a diagonal line through each day before having breakfast. The last line, made that morning, bisected Tuesday, August 14, 1875. She would have written "Rain" had there been any. There had been none for over a year. She sat and opened her slim account book to the Elwood Renfroe page, wrote a figure, summed the column, and underlined the total twice before closing the cover.

Ruby sighed as she brushed her long red hair. Times had been better. She'd heard that settlers who had come to the area in the 1830s and '40s had found adequate rainfall for growing food and animal fodder. Small lakes had dotted the area, and streams ran year-round. The surrounding plains had provided grass for grazing. In the 1850s, rainfall became sporadic. In the '60s rainfall dropped to a fraction of the amount received two decades earlier. By the '70s there was almost none. Crops failed, and range forage was depleted by lack of moisture as well as over-grazing. Settlers drifted away in search of work and better land. Mesa de Luna residents continued to pull up stakes and move on. A few more of Ruby's friends were planning to leave before summer's end. She looked at her book of accounts thoughtfully, then straightened her shoulders, rose to her feet, and went out into the early sunlight. The clear sky promised heat. Her first step dusted her shoes.

Roz and Moose were waiting until payday, and waiting made each day seem more trivial. There wasn't enough to do, and too much idle time.

"Roz, you forgot to buy cornmeal for crissake," Moose said to the inert form in the pole-and-rope bed in the corner. "You said you were going to, and you didn't. Now all we have is tortillas, and they're dried out. Roz!" He rattled a chair's legs on the plank floor. "Roz, get up and talk to me."

Pigeons in the loft began cooing when Moose rattled the chair, as they always did when anyone made noise in the rooms below.

One night, after drinking a bottle of tequila with a whore at Henry's, Roz had brought her to his bed. As she began to explain her system of pricing, she got the hiccups, and the pigeons began to coo. First, she thought

Roz was mocking her. Then she decided they might be ghosts and Roz couldn't convince her to stay.

"Even if they *are* birds," she'd said, "they give me the creep–hic–creeps." Roz had been trying to get rid of them since, with no success.

"Roz, wake up."

"Morning," Roz yawned. "How'd you sleep?"

"I'm talking about cornmeal, Roz. I was going to make cornbread, and we don't have anything to put on tortillas even if they weren't hard a stove lids."

"Let's go wake up Henry," Roz replied. "Get us some salt meat and biscuits, or whatever he has."

Henry Atwater owned the Cantina Escondido, which served food and whisky whenever Henry was awake. He didn't keep regular hours. He opened when someone woke him by pounding on the cantina's door. He closed when everyone left at night. He didn't have a clock and didn't want one.

Henry liked to cook, pour, and talk. He didn't clean. If customers wanted to sweep out cigar butts or pick up empty bottles, they were welcome. Henry even stepped out of the way. Otherwise, things stayed where they fell.

Everyone trusted Henry, and most people liked him. He was reliable and predictable. He wore the same clothes nearly every day. He even slept in them. "I can open up faster," he explained.

Short and bowlegged, Henry had long arms that reached almost everything in the cooking and bar area. He exhibited an odd kind of efficiency. He didn't do anything not directly related to cooking, pouring, or talking, and he could do all those at once.

It seemed to Roz that Henry should have enjoyed the Mexican culture more than he did, or at least should have accepted it peacefully. Henry had named the saloon the Escondido, which meant "little hidden place", where he served *posole* and *refritos*, not to mention *tequila*. He played a Spanish guitar, although some said not well, and he kept a big Mexican saddle out back by the corral. He owned two horses, named Paco and Monkeybuns. Almost everything Henry saw, ate, or touched had a name that originated in the Spanish language. Still, he criticized Mexican government, weather, habits, and dress, and talked proudly about an England he had never seen.

One day Roz asked him why, if he disliked Mexico so much, did he serve mostly Mexican food and flavor whatever wasn't Mexican with *jalapenos*. "Because it's Spanish, is why," Henry had retorted, "and that's a whole different thing."

"Henry, you don't know Spanish from spinach, nor your ass from a chimney flue."

That made Henry mad, and whenever he got mad, he leaned back as though it might make him taller. He blinked and puffed out his whiskered cheeks like an angry badger. But he just kept talking about England and said he was going to London as soon as he could afford to travel. Roz didn't think he'd ever get out of New Mexico Territory, much less to London, which to Roz seemed almost as far away as the moon.

Roz was still lying in bed with his hands behind his head, trying to think how to rid the loft of pigeons, when he said, "Why, Moose, one time I met an old mule-skinner down in Natkitoches who lived on tortillas and nothing else."

"Nagidoches," Moose muttered.

"He told me any other food upset his stomach. Sixty years old, maybe more. Healthy as you or me. Met him coming out of Luella's, and three whores were waving goodbye."

"Roz, that isn't possible."

"Why not? Three ain't so many."

"That's not what I mean. The human body needs fruits. Or vegetables. Like oranges. Did you know that sailors have to have oranges?"

Roz rolled his eyes and looked at the ceiling.

"Or limes." Moose said.

"Limes," Roz replied evenly. "I know about limes, Moose."

"Anyway, that's why they call the English sailors 'Limeys.'" Moose said coming to the point he'd wanted to make. "They have to have limes. Were you aware that . . ."

"Moose, I just realized I won't have to worry about those damned pigeons. Not after we're out of here."

Moose sighed and said, "Get up. Let's go to Henry's."

"I'll buy cornmeal later. Probably should get a large sack," Roz replied as he sat up and reached for his boots.

"What if we were on the trail?" Moose said. "You can't be hauling a large sack of meal on horseback."

"We could if we had a wagon. But I don't know where we're going to get one."

"Only two people around here have a wagon the size we'd need," Moose replied. "Bus Wiley. And Henry. Neither of them will sell and they don't owe us anything, so I don't know where we'd find a wagon this side of Santa Fe. We can't afford a good one, anyway. We're going to have to ride and live off the land like other folks."

"You say *afford* like you had some money. How much do you have, if you don't mind my asking?"

"A little I saved while you were getting rid of yours in the back room of the Escondido. Beats me how your brains migrate to your pants whenever you get some cash."

Henry sometimes rented the small lean-to on the back of the cantina to whores new to town. The problem was that it was on the south side, and it got so hot in summer and so cold in winter that business fell to nothing except in April, May, and October. Henry wouldn't provide a stove, thinking sooner or later some drunken cowboy would set the roof on fire.

"Moose, we all got our passions. You like your books, while I need the real thing now and then."

"Those are good words for you, Roz. Seems 'now and then' means just about all the time."

"I wouldn't argue," Roz replied, "specially when I'm hungry. Which I am." He stood up and stomped his feet into his boots, which set the pigeons into a fresh round of protests, then hitched his suspenders over his shirt. He raised his arms and stretched. A large blue fly buzzed in and out of a shaft of sunlight. Granny Schneider's rooster crowed in an abrupt, strangled manner.

Roz yawned, considering the merits of rooster strangulation while reaching for his hat under the bunk.

"I can't wait for you this morning. I'm going to Henry's. You can come or not. Suit yourself," Moose said.

"Of course I'll come. I'm starved," Roz said with a grin, but Moose was already out of the door.

Roz watched Moose's broad back diminish as he stepped up the sandy road to the Escondido. Roz stopped on the porch, stretched, settled the hat more comfortably, and ambled at a leisurely pace.

As he passed the cottonwood tree he noticed a scabby, black-and-white tomcat chewing on the decapitated body of a bull snake. The snake was a bit mangled, and Roz figured the horses had stomped it.

If Granny Schneider's hogs had caught it they would have eaten it. The cat must have found it in the stock pens and ate the head first.

As Roz approached, the cat snarled and dragged the snake away through the dust under the tree. It made an interesting track, little cat feet on either side of a groove. Roz began to consider what he could tell Moose about it if he showed him the tracks. Like maybe he had seen a strange animal, half cat and half snake, walking under the tree. Or maybe a cat-like critter with a lizard's tail, so long it dragged the ground.

The trouble with Moose was that he was always in a hurry and he missed interesting sights, like the dried owl pellets under a bare branch of cottonwood. Roz knew the owl perched on the branch and coughed up hair and skin of previous meals. He'd seen the owl several times, outlined against the stars as he walked back from Ruby Lee's.

Moose might not know about owl pellets. Roz dropped one in his shirt pocket, planning to put it by Moose's plate when he joined him for breakfast. Moose would have to ask what it was, and Roz would enjoy telling him something he didn't know. If he didn't.

Moose was standing by the front door of The Escondido. "Come on," he said. "I could eat the balls off a pool table."

"Thanks for waiting," Roz replied. "And for the entertaining image. You can buy."

Chapter Four

POINT OF ROCKS

Pablo yawned. He hadn't slept for two days, and he knew he had to be careful with the *mescal* jug. Too much, and he might pass out. Too little, and he'd shake. His red-rimmed eyes blinked as the rattling Studebaker coach neared the narrow pass. Point of Rocks was named for the ridge of boulders rearing up on both sides of the track like the backbone of a buried beast. Pablo squinted at the rocks dancing in wavering heat, doubling their image under a mid-day sun that beat down like hammers on brass. The boulder ridge split white-rimed alkali flats studded with blue-green sage and agave.

Vicente Cordoba and '*Puerco*' Barranca rode silently by Pablo's side of the stage, Cordoba on a nervous, sweat-slicked bay mare, and Barranca on a strong, line-back dun gelding. Pablo hunched on the oaken seat to the right side of old Moses Avila, the driver, who held four reins in each of his gnarled hands while spitting streams of tobacco juice over the side.

Pablo glanced at Vicente. *This will be the place*, he thought, *when we reach the rocks*. His hands began to tremble. He lifted the earthenware jug by his feet and took a long draught. *Mescal* cooled the fire in his belly and quieted the restless fingers in his brain. He looked from the corners of his eyes. Vicente glared at him, not blinking. *Puerco* snuffled. His chronic sinus problem had marked him with his nickname. *Puerco* meant 'pig' in Spanish, and his sloping forehead and broad flat nose enhanced the image.

Pablo thought he might have been able to shoot Cordoba and Barranca in the back. He'd wanted to, and there had been opportunities, but he found he could not kill men that way, no matter who they were, no matter what they intended to do. They'd have to make the first move. Two days and nights he had waited, and now they were almost within sight of Mesa de Luna. It had to be at Point of Rocks. They would try to kill him as soon as they got there.

Pablo put the jug into the space by his feet and picked up the carbine, as he always did when nearing the pass. It would be expected. The point was the most dangerous spot on the Albuquerque-Tucumcari road.

"Drop it, *Amigo*," Vicente said, a narrow smile showing black teeth. He held a revolver aimed at Pablo's head. Barranca pulled a saddle gun from its scabbard.

Pablo had thought Vicente would say that, or something like it. He tried to act confused. "*Porque*?" he replied. "Why?"

"Do as I tell you, *bufón!*"

Pablo ignored being called a fool. Slowly he lowered the carbine and reached for the revolver hidden in his boot, hoping Vicente couldn't see his shaking hands.

"Moses!" Vicente shouted. "Stop the horses."

"Ho-up!" Moses said, hauling back the lead team's reins. "Ho!"

"Now," Vicente said, waving his pistol at Pablo's head as the teams halted, "throw down the box."

"What?"

"The silver box, *idiota*! *Rapidamente!* Moses, you old fool, you help him."

Moses' mouth fell open. He swore. rose from the seat, and reached for the handgun in his belt. Vicente shot him in the face. Moses toppled over the front of the foot well and landed in the dust behind the left wheel horse. The horse lunged. Vicente fired at Pablo and missed as the coach lurched. Vicente's horse began to spin. Puerco Barranca grunted and leveled his carbine. Pablo pulled the trigger without aiming. His .40 caliber bullet caught

Barranca in the middle of the forehead. Puerco pitched to the ground by Vicente's rearing, wheeling mount.

Vicente tried to turn in the saddle and aim at Pablo. Pablo's second shot raised dust on Vicente's pant leg. Blood sprayed on the saddle's fender and stirrup. Pablo's third shot splintered the cantle of Vicente's saddle and whined away into the rocks. Vicente's horse whirled. Pablo aimed, but the mare straightened and tore up the track as if devils chased her. Vicente screamed obscenities and tried to hang on to the saddle horn. His revolver fell to the road in a puff of dust. Vicente and his horse didn't slow until they were out of sight.

Pablo shivered, and then vomited. He took another pull at the *mescal* jug, and climbed down from the creaking stage, his boots finding the top of the wheel, the hub, and solid ground. Harness jingled. A horse stomped impatiently. Pablo's trembling hands wiped stinging sweat from his eyes. Moses was dead. Barranca, also. Pablo removed his hat, slapped it on his leg to remove sweat from inside the band, and put it back on. All was quiet for the first time in many hours.

Pablo gripped the side of the coach, telling himself he had to think, to plan carefully, and that he was in danger until he was out of New Mexico territory. His uncle would try again. The *Alcalde* had many men who did what he asked. He, Pablo, would be accused and killed; shot "while trying to escape", or hanged in a public place for "attempting a robbery". His uncle might forget his plan to kill the Mesa de Luna relay station managers: he might be satisfied to say that Pablo alone had done it, or he might hang all three. Pablo decided he'd warn Wells and Banner. It could work to his advantage. He needed their help.

Pablo straightened. Carefully, he walked to Barranca's horse that stood watching, staying close to the stage horses. The dun, white-eyed, allowed him to grasp the reins.

"*Gracias Dios*," Pablo said under his breath while crossing himself with his free hand, thankful the saddle horse hadn't run after Vicente's bay. He tied the dun to the rear wheel and retrieved Vicente's revolver, a new navy colt that didn't seem damaged, but was already heated by the sun. He palmed it back and forth until it cooled, then stuck in under his belt and walked back to the coach. "*JesuCristo*," he muttered, wiping his brow with his sleeve.

He thought for a few more minutes, then released the stage horses from their harness. They moved away from the dead bodies, nostrils flaring, white around their eyes. The dun nickered at them from the back of the stage. The teams stopped, not sure what to do. They had not known complete freedom in their lives.

Pablo checked the men's pockets and Moses' bedroll. He gathered a number of coins and bills and decided it wasn't stealing; the dead men wouldn't need money wherever they were going.

Vicente would probably live, and his uncle would send a posse of armed men with instructions to recover the silver and make sure Pablo would never speak of the attempted robbery. Vicente would be among them, unless his injury was too severe to allow him to ride.

Climbing back up to the boot, he wrestled the heavy strong-box to the edge and tipped it over the side. It landed with a thump, spooking the teams. They ran a few more yards before stopping. He carried his jug to the leather-covered storage compartment at the back of the stage and lifted his bedroll. He tied the jug and bedroll behind the dun's saddle. Then he uncoiled Barranca's lariat, wondering if it might have been intended for hanging him, but decided not. There wasn't a tree between Point of rocks and Mesa de Luna, twenty miles away. He'd have been shot and buried, or left for the buzzards.

He placed a slip knot on one of the box's handles, dallied around the saddle horn, climbed on the dun, and urged it to drag the box several hundred yards to a spot where he could scoop sand with his hands and partially bury the box. The dun flinched, but didn't bolt when he shot the lock off. Taking six of the 100-ounce silver bars, he placed them in his saddle bags by the spare change and bills that had belonged to the dead men. He looked at the remaining silver, a fortune, then closed and covered the box with rocks so it couldn't be seen. He marked it with a dark red stone near the cairn. He'd know where to find the box, if he ever had a chance to come back and look.

Pablo rode back to the coach, tied the dun again, broke off a piece of sagebrush, and carefully brushed out the tracks from the coach to the place where he'd hidden the silver. He gathered the firearms, re-mounted, then rode back and forth among the rocks on the other side of the trail where he hoped searchers would suppose he'd buried the bullion. Finally, he urged the dun toward Mesa de Luna with the teams trailing behind. He walked the horse briskly, not running because the dun had to cover many miles, probably hundreds, before Pablo would be safe.

First, he thought, I will warn Roz and that big fellow who runs the station. Maybe they will leave and I'll go with them, but we must go before Juan Diego sends armed men. He'll send the best he can find.

Pablo Borrega urged the dun forward and shivered in spite of shimmering heat waves making lake-images at the blurred horizon. Far above, in a rising thermal, black wings soared over Point of Rocks and the burden of the sand.

Chapter Five

BREAKFAST

Ruby sat inside the Escondido, blowing on a saucer of coffee. El hunched over the only other table, chin on his hands while he stared pensively at the back of Ruby's head. Henry was cooking breakfast, scratching his undershirt, pouring thick, black coffee, and complaining about an armadillo that had run out of his privy while Henry was preparing to go in. El and Ruby weren't interested.

"Hi, boys," he said to Moose and Roz as they opened the door. "What do you think a goddamn armadilla' would be doin' in my outhouse in the middle of the night?"

"What were you doing in there, yourself?" Roz asked as he sat down by El.

"I don't want to talk about that," Moose interrupted. "I need coffee and something to eat. What are you fixing this morning, Henry?" he asked, as he took a chair by Ruby Lee who nodded and kept blowing on her saucer.

"Damn, Ruby Lee," Roz said. "You keep puckering up and blowing on that coffee, and I'm likely to get restive."

"Ignore him," Moose said as Ruby glanced up, turned directly toward Roz, and made an effort to blow small waves without spilling any.

"Nice to see you last night," Roz said, turning to El. "I heard Ruby Lee done you a good turn." El looked like he might move to the bar, but thought better of it.

"Roz," El said, "we're goin' to be travelin' together. Seems like we ought to try to get along."

"*Might* be traveling together. Anyway, we need a wagon or a buckboard, as you should know."

"Don't worry about that," Ruby said as she put the saucer down. "I'll take care of the wagon."

"For crissake, Ruby," Moose exclaimed. "You don't have a wagon."

"I will before the sun sets," she replied. Henry shot a nervous glance in her direction. "And don't ask," she added, as Roz's opened his mouth.

"This is no time to be fooling," Roz said.

"I'm not. Now leave me alone."

Henry brought four plates of corn tortillas and sausage, with a pickled onion on each plate.

"Jesus, Henry. What is this?" Roz asked as he chewed on a resilient bite.

"Best there is. Ain't you ever heard of *Cabrito*?"

"Cruickshank's goat?" Moose asked. "Is this Cruickshank's goat? Why, that goat's as old as I am."

"And prettier. Or he was," Roz said.

"I haven't seen Cruickshank's goat since Tuesday." Moose said. The problem with a small town, he thought, was that there weren't many things to see, and one tended to see them too often. If the least thing changed, everybody knew it.

"I bought him Tuesday and sold him to you today," Henry cackled.

"What day is it?" El asked, as Moose put his fork down.

"It's Friday, you old…" Ruby started to say 'old goat' and then said "old fart," instead. "Goat" didn't seem right under the circumstances.

"Well, that's okay then," El said. "Goat meat'll keep seven or eight days if you hang it right."

"Which I did," Henry replied.

"*Cabrito*!" Roz snorted. "I think *cabrito* is made out of *young* goats. Otherwise, nobody would ever have recommended it."

Roz had a way of saying things that made it difficult to respond. When people didn't know what to say, they usually ignored him. This sometimes upset him because he thought people didn't take him seriously, which at least half the time they didn't.

"Henry," Roz said, "why don't you take that wanted poster down off the wall? Makes me nervous havin' John Wesley Hardin watch me eat breakfast. Besides, that's an ugly picture. It's drawn so bad we wouldn't know him if he walked in here. Why don't you get a picture of a pretty girl? That's something I'd enjoy lookin' at."

"You bring me a picture and I'll put it up. As to John Wesley, I think it's interesting that the more people you kill the more you're worth. Old John Wesley's worth more than this bar and two others like it."

"Can't argue with that," Roz said, sipping his coffee.

Moose looked at El, who sat by the window. It would be good to have El with them if they ever managed to get started. El was lazy in some ways, yet he was a tireless rider and a much better shot than any of them. He had two good horses he'd brought to Mesa de Luna. He owned a .50 caliber Sharps buffalo gun with a long barrel and peep sights, as well as other firearms. He refused to discuss how he'd obtained the horses and guns, saying he didn't even want to think about it, much less explain. El was efficient, even graceful, outside or on horseback. He was clumsy and uncomfortable indoors.

El's natural senses were keen. He had excellent eyesight and ears like a bat, which, Moose realized, they actually did resemble. El's head was mostly protuberances. He had a long nose turned down at the tip. He had spiky red hair and freckles. His red and white mustache flowed from his lip back to his ears as though he was going somewhere quickly, although he rarely did. His ears stuck out just like a bat's, and they were pink in the middle. When Moose looked at El's ears, with the window directly behind them, he thought he could see light coming through them the way he had seen light through a baby's fingers. El's pale eyes had a far-away, over the horizon, look.

Moose enjoyed his company and didn't tease him as Roz did. He thought Roz took unfair advantage at times. When El had returned from the railroad trestle cutting job, he'd told them, "You know, there was trees all over the place," while glancing at the only tree in Mesa de Luna. "And one day I saw a bird knockin' on one of those trees. It was black and white with a red head."

“A red-headed woodpecker,” Moose had said. Then Roz began to laugh.

“Well, what’s so funny about that?” El had asked.

“It occurs to me, you’re a red-headed peckerwood,” Roz crowed.

“That ain’t a damned bit funny, Rozier,” El had said, and then went on with his story.

Moose preferred to be kind to him. “How’s your belly where you hit that pole?”

“I meant to jump over it. But on account of my pants—and my hands not bein’ free, well, you know how it is,” and El continued to chew reflectively.

El was slow to rile. It was almost impossible to make him really angry. About the only thing that angered him was to accuse him of lying or trying to mislead someone. On the rare occasions that he did get mad he was dangerous. But to tease him, or suggest that a bath wouldn’t be wasted on him didn’t bother him at all.

He was unlike Roz, who didn’t mind stretching the truth, particularly for entertainment. When one of his statements was challenged he’d just smile and change the subject.

Moose, whose real name was Morris Royale Banner, wondered how he looked to others. He knew he couldn't see himself clearly. He supposed he was as smart, or smarter than the next person. He knew he liked to impress, and he guessed it was because he'd had trouble making friends as a child. He'd been much bigger than others his age and had been teased because of it.

He'd kept to himself while growing up, reading books so he'd have interesting companions, fun adventures if only in his mind. He'd avoided conflict, but one day, coming home from school, he was stopped and roughed up again. This time it was in front of his mother's rooming house and he saw her at the window. His shame made him lose control. He hit his chief tormenter so hard the bully landed on the other side of a picket fence. Moose had rubbed his smarting knuckles against his pants and stared at his adversary's broken mouth in wide-eyed wonder. He was tried by bigger and rougher boys two or three times after that, with the same result.

When he was eighteen he was six-foot-four and weighed 240 pounds. He had a pleasant, youthful face and a prematurely receding hairline. He appeared younger and more naïve than he really was. A traveling circus fighter egged him into stepping into the ring for three rounds and a prize of ten dollars if he was standing at the end of the third round. Moose knocked him out of the ring almost before the fight started. The circus boss wanted to hire

Moose on the spot, but when Moose looked at the fallen fighter he saw what his own face might resemble in a few years. He tried to avoid fights after that, and when he was forced to take action he was usually able to throw his opponent out of a window or through a door, preferably while it was open.

Moose could see that El's abilities would be helpful as they traveled. He wasn't sure his own skills would be very useful. He was thinking about what Roz and Ruby Lee might contribute when he heard the sound of a horse stopping in front of the cantina. A saddle creaked as the rider stepped down, and leather slapped as reins were tied around the hitching pole.

The man nodded as he came through the door. He seemed pale, nervous. He removed his hat. "Ma'am", he said when he saw Ruby Lee.

"Mornin'," Henry said. "How about some coffee?"

"I'd—be obliged." He sat on a bar stool and didn't say anything until Henry poured and set up a cup in front of him. After a cautious sip, he turned and said, "I'm Jared Kirby, on my way to Amarillo, but I—I need to tell you what I saw up by Punto de Agua." He put the coffee cup down and gripped his knees with his hands. He swallowed. "Saw a burnt-out farm." He shook his head as if to dislodge memories. "A man shot and scalped. Toys and little dresses scattered around, but no kids."

“Comanches,” Roz muttered, “or maybe Kiowa. Could you tell who did it?”

“That—isn’t the worst—of it.” He took another sip of coffee, rubbed his eyes with the back of his hand. “There was a woman. She was—beg your pardon ma’am—she was…”

“Raped?” Ruby asked.

“Yes. And they hadn’t killed her. I mean, not right away. They, they just—cut behind her ankles and knees, and—left her in the sun.”

“Was she dead?” Roz asked quietly.

Kirby nodded and swallowed. “She was. The man, husband I guess, was dead beside her. The children were gone. Their house and barn, burned. She couldn’t even…,” he gulped, looked like me might become ill, before he swallowed and continued, “…crawl. I guess she just gave up. Her clothes were there, at least some of them. She didn’t even put them on.” He took a deep, ragged breath. Ruby walked over to him. She didn’t touch him, but stood close while he gained control.

“I’m sorry you had to see that,” she said.

“I’m sorry it—happened. I buried them the best I could, in the same…I need to report it to someone. The law. Is there a sheriff or marshal here?”

“No. Closest one is Tucumcari,” Moose said.

“All right,” Kirby replied. “That’s where I was going anyway,” in a voice that sounded as if he wished he was already there.

“Could you tell who did it?” Roz asked again.

“What? No. They didn’t leave much sign.” Kirby’s voice steadied. “Without arrows it’s hard to know, but I heard Mad Water’s off the reservation again.”

“Thank you for letting us know,” Ruby said, “about all of it.”

“I don’t—ever want to see something like that again.” Kirby shuddered as he stood up and put coins on the bar. Henry waved his money away. Kirby thanked him, nodded to the others, and went out to his horse.

“Mad Water’s Quanah Parker’s half-brother, ain’t he?” Henry asked after Kirby had ridden away.

“He is,” El said.

“Where’s Punto de Agua?” Ruby asked, “and who’s Quanah Parker?”

“Directly the way we’re goin’,” El answered, “and Quanah’s chief of the Comanche Nation. Does whatever he wants. We’ll have to see they don’t get our hair.”

Roz unconsciously raised a hand to his head, glanced at Moose's mostly bald pate, and put his hand down. "We'll be safe enough, long as we're prepared," he said.

Chapter Six

IMPETUS

Pablo Borrega waited by the corral until Moose and Roz came out of their quarters. The mescal jug sat in the dust by his feet. Morning sun cast long shadows. "*Buenos dias*," he said. "*Como esta*?"

"*Como*, yourself, Pablo, you little river rat," Roz replied, referring to the fact that Pablo lived in Albuquerque, by the Rio Grande. "You look like shit, and you can speak *Ingles* as well as I do. Where's the stage? And what are you doing with that dun horse? Gone and got yourself fired?"

"No, *Señor*. No." He crossed himself. "Now listen." Listen sounded like 'leesen'. "We are in *big* trouble."

"We? We, who?" Moose asked.

"You, and you, and me," Pablo replied, pointing to Moose and Roz, and then to himself. He told them what had happened. "And Juan Diego is the law. He has many cousins, many killers. They will come for you. You have no, uh…*suplicá.*"

"Prayer?"

"Si."

"You sure about that?" Roz asked, while trying to remember if Pablo had ever stretched the truth. He couldn't recall a time when he had. And he seemed sincere.

"*Certamente*!" Pablo's mouth was grim, his pupils large and black. He was genuinely frightened. "I heard Juan Diego talking to—somebody. His men would be here now, to hang you, but I killed one and the other got away."

"You could tell them we had nothing to do with it. Couldn't you?"

"No, *senõr*." He spread his arms. "I will not be here when they come. They will kill me if they find me." Pablo tilted his head and pantomimed holding a hangman's noose. He looked like he might bolt and run at any second.

"Damn it, Moose, this is a problem. Maybe we'd better get out of here."

"We were going anyway," Moose said. "Sooner might be better than later."

"Sooner, like today," Roz said. "And not later than tomorrow."

"I was hoping we'd get paid," Moose said.

Roz turned to Pablo. "Wasn't there supposed to be a silver shipment?"

"*Si, pero*—I mean yes, but," he looked away, "it was, how you say *en ingles*, a treeck?"

"A trick," Moose echoed.

"*Si.* The silver, she wasn't there."

"Why were there two armed riders?" Roz asked.

"I think—that was—the plan, the trick. They didn't know." Pablo shrugged, looked from Roz to Moose. "There was a box. I opened it. Full of heavy stones. But now we must hurry. *Pronto.*"

"You said one fellow got away, headed for Albuquerque?" Moose asked.

"*Si,*" Pablo replied. "Vicente, my cousin, evil *bastardo* that he is."

"And this happened yesterday afternoon?"

"*Si.* Yes."

Moose looked at Roz. "How long does it take to ride to Albuquerque?"

"I'd say, a day-and-a-half if he hurries, doesn't stop, and has a good horse. More likely two days if he's wounded, maybe three."

Pablo nodded. "And his leg is hurt, but I don't know how—*mal*."

"Bad?" Roz said.

"*Si.*"

"So," Moose continued, "probably two days to get to Albuquerque, a day for Juan Diego to round up a posse, and two days for them to get back here. Maybe just one if they ride hard. We don't have much time to do what we have to do. How many riders do you think there'll be?"

"I don't know," Pablo replied, "but they will be men who have killed for Juan Diego before."

"We have to be out of here in two or three days," Roz said, "or I'm going to be mighty uncomfortable. One would be better."

Moose nodded. "I doubt if we can out-run them. We'll need a head start, and then try to lose them." He turned to Pablo. "What are you going to do?" he asked.

"Why, *señor*, go with you of course."

"What?" Roz snapped. "Now listen here…"

"Hold on," Moose said. "Maybe he's right. There's strength in numbers. And he knows them. That could be an advantage."

"*They* know *him*. That could be a disadvantage," Roz snapped back.

"But I know how they think," Pablo said. "They will think we went east, or south."

"But…" Roz started to say. He didn't like to hear Pablo use the word, 'we'.

"But we go north, yes? Where there are no roads and no towns. Juan Diego will have them search all the towns when they do not find us on the roads."

"That's the direction we were going anyway," Moose said. "I think he should come along."

"Well, hell," Roz grumbled, "this whole thing is starting to feel like a circus."

"You won't be sorry, *compadres*," Pablo said, with what he hoped was an ingratiating smile. He started to lift the jug but put it back down. It was almost empty.

"Check with me in a few days," Roz muttered, "and I'll tell you how sorry I am. Moose, what do we have to do?"

"Well, first let's see to the horses and traveling gear. We'll talk with El and Ruby. See if they still want to come, under the circumstances. I hope they do. We need Henry's wagon, and El's experience."

"*Señores*, we could go faster without a wagon, *no*?"

"And starve to death while we're out-runnin' 'em." Roz replied.

"Not much of a choice," Moose said. "We're going to need some luck."

"Some?" Roz replied. "I'd say a lot. Pablo, you look like a *pampas vaquero* with that yard-wide hat and *conchos* all over your skinny pants. Why don't you go over to Pit Gardner's," he pointed to the mercantile, "and get yourself some clothes so you don't stand out like Santa Anna at a rodeo. You got any money?"

"*Si, bueno*." Pablo thought about the silver bars he'd taken. They were worth nearly a thousand dollars, but they had to be a secret, at least for a while. They had the Sandia mine stamp on them. He had enough cash in his saddle bags, and he could trade some of the guns he carried. First he'd fill the jug.

"Did you happen to see our pay?" Moose asked.

Pablo looked from Moose to Roz. Moses Avila always brought their pay in cash, on or around the fifteenth of each month. He didn't know how much they were owed. "*Si*," he said, "I almost forget. *Quantas es?* I mean, how much it is?"

"Fifteen dollars each," Roz replied, "unless they sent a bonus."

“Fat chance,” Moose muttered.

“So, that is *triente*—thirty, yes?” Pablo said, counting silver dollars and rummaging in his saddlebags to make it look like there wasn’t much more in them. “*Aqui este*,” he said, handing over the double-eagles.

“Thanks,” Roz said. “Now go get some clothes and then take a nap. Your eyes look like turds on a napkin.” Moose shook his head. “I’ll gather up some extra shoes for the horses, plus a few tools,” Roz continued, “and I’ll see if I can talk Ruby into going. Moose, why don’t you talk to El?”

“I’ll talk to both of them. I’ll be over there anyway.”

“Well, tell her I said ‘Hello’, and tell her I said she’ll be safe if she sticks real close to me.”

Moose looked at him, opened his mouth, and then walked toward the Escondido.

Chapter Seven

PACKING UP

Roz piled horse shoes, nails, a hammer, hoof rasp, and trimmer by the back door with his and Moose's bedrolls and other personal items. Spare clothing had been rolled into blankets to be tied behind their saddles or put into the wagon—assuming there was to be a wagon. Then he cleaned up the area around the barns and corrals, throwing tin cans and broken wheel spokes into a pile. It wasn't necessary, but it gave him something to do while waiting.

Roz was nervous, anxious to be gone. If someone was going to try to kill him he wanted to make it as difficult as possible. Mostly he wanted to be miles away. He looked at the place he'd thought of as home, sighed, and remembered some of the good times when he and Moose had been relaxed company for each other. Maybe too relaxed. Life had become boring beyond endurance, almost. Roz was thinking he'd prefer boring to Pablo's news, when Moose walked around the corner.

"Henry Atwater is coming with us."

"He is! How did that happen?"

"Ruby Lee called in her markers. Henry couldn't pay, and Ruby laid claim to the wagon. Seems she owns more of it than Henry does so they made a deal. The wagon goes as far as Denver where Ruby wants to stay. They'll sell it before Henry leaves for England, and split the cash according to who owes what at that point. At least that's the plan."

"Well, I'm damned. How about Elwood? He still with us?"

"He hasn't said otherwise. Besides, Ruby is going so he will, too. With you, me, Henry, Ruby, El, and Pablo we're an even half dozen. Strength in numbers."

"This whole damn thing is starting to feel like some kind of medicine show. Every time I turn around, somebody else wants to go. So far, we got a, a…Ruby Lee, a Mexican drunk, a buffalo hunter, and, and…"

"And a cook," Moose finished. "With a wagon. Which we need. You said so yourself. Plus, what with Mad Water on the loose…"

"Yeah, guess so. Well, they'll provide some interesting experiences I reckon. If we live to enjoy them. But do you trust that skinny little Pablo? I don't."

"Well, he isn't dragging a box of silver, that's for sure. It'd be too heavy. And he's as anxious to get out of here as we are."

"What if he stole it and hid it somewhere?"

"He wants to go with us and he doesn't even know where we're headed. I'd say he has a genuine problem with the *Alcalde,* silver or no silver."

"We could just tell him 'no' and leave him," Roz said.

"I'm not comfortable with that. He did warn us. He could have ridden away and left us to get caught."

"Yeah. Guess so. All right, what's next?"

"Let's get Henry's horses over here for shoeing. You can make them and I'll put them on. That Monkeybuns has big feet. You'll probably need to make them extra-large, with cleats for pulling."

"I don't suppose we could take a couple of stage horses?"

"And add horse stealing to the crime we didn't commit?"

"No, guess not. I'll grease up the wagon and see if it needs repair."

Roz was skilled at fixing mechanical things. Over time they had informally divided tasks according to their abilities. Moose usually took care of the horses and mules while Roz forged shoes and mended wheels, harness, and other equipment.

Roz was tightening rivets that held the iron rims on the wagon wheels when a small troop of cavalry rode up to the barn door.

"I'm Major Charles Braddy," the dusty, sunburned cavalryman said as he walked up to Moose, who was carefully picking rot from the frog and hard rim of Monkeybuns' hind hoof. The smell was appalling, but the temporarily lamed hoof would be sound after the area dried and hardened for a few hours.

"Afternoon, Major," Moose said. Up from Fort Sumner?" Sumner was forty miles southeast along the Pecos, toward Abilene.

"Nope. Goin' back. We've been to Fort Union and Wagon Mound. But I need to tell the fellow that runs the stage station about Comanche trouble. I guess that's you."

Moose nodded as Roz walked from the wagon, joined them, and wrinkled his nose.

"We ran into Mad Water and his band up on Ute Creek. Didn't see a sign of 'em until they were shooting into our column. Two wounded and one killed. Our men, I mean. I don't know if we hit any." The Major looked tired and discouraged.

"Got your wounded with you?" Roz asked. "I do a little doctoring from time to time. I mean splints and braces, that kind of thing."

"Had to leave one in Wagon Mound. He couldn't travel, but he'll live. The others are healing well enough. Thanks, just the same. Anyway, we don't know where they'll go next. They've been killing settlers and stealing stock. There are about a dozen of them, assuming we didn't put any out of commission. Best horsemen I ever saw. We didn't even try to follow."

The major sat on a barrel and mopped his forehead with a bandana. "We were wondering if we could leave our horses with you for an hour or so while we take a rest under your tree."

"Of course you can," Moose replied. "Turn them into that pen." He pointed to an empty enclosure. "I'll go get you a cold bucket of water. Roz, you want to finish up here?"

"I could do that, Moose, but I'd rather get the water if you don't mind."

"Thank you kindly," Major Braddy said. "We'd appreciate it."

"I don't think Mad Water's on the Albuquerque road," he continued. "Too much traffic. He likes to stay in out-of-the-way places. But I wouldn't put it past him to be anywhere between here and Raton Pass. I know your stages don't run that way, but I thought you'd want to tell travelers going north, if you see any."

Moose paused. "Do you know a Colonel Dupree? Parker Dupree?" he quietly asked, after Roz had walked toward the well.

"I don't believe so. Why? Is he in this area?"

"No, probably up north somewhere," Moose replied. "I just thought you might have heard of him."

"Can't say I have. Sorry. Oh, I meant to tell you they had fresh scalps on their lances. Couldn't see how many. They aren't just stealing this time."

Roz had come back in time to hear the last. "What were they shooting?" he asked."

"Looked like .44-40s. The new Winchesters. I expect Quanah Parker can get just about anything he wants now that he's seen President Grant."

Quanah Parker was half Caucasian. His mother, Cynthia Ann Parker, had been captured by Comanches when she was nine years old. They'd raised her, then married her to a chief. She gave birth to Quanah. Years later she was offered the chance to return to European ways, but elected to stay with the Comanches. Quanah grew up to be chief, succeeding his father, but he adopted his mother's last name. He was an able leader, fluent in English, and dedicated to Comanche independence, even if it meant killing a few whites who were equally busy killing Indians.

A treaty had required Quanah's presence in Washington, where he met the President of the United States after the signing ceremony. The treaty had lasted as long as most treaties before encroachment of Indian lands continued. But Quanah had access to resources other tribal chiefs only dreamed of, and his people were better fed and armed as a result of his influence with government officials.

"Yeah, I bet he can," Roz replied to the major. "We appreciate the information. We'll be on the lookout for him. Mad Water, I mean."

"I don't think he'll come into town," the major replied.

"No, but we're going to pass through the country you mentioned," Roz said. "We're leaving in a day or two." He explained that the last stage had been robbed by the *Alcalde's* men, according to Pablo.

"Oh!" the major said. "So now the law is robbing people they're supposed to protect? This damned place!" He shook his head. "How many of you are going?"

"There's six of us. Moose here, myself, a couple of townspeople, fellow named Pablo Borrega, and Elwood. Three or four of them can shoot. I don't know about Borrega, but he's carrying guns."

"Are you talking about Elwood Renfroe?" the major asked. "I heard he lived around here. He's worth about three good men in an Indian fight, or so they say. He was with Cap'n Burt Wright on the Big Muddy when they corralled Bear Stalking. Shot him off a running horse at three hundred yards. Wright still talks about it."

"See any other Indians?" Moose asked.

"Just a small band of Arapahoe. Way south for Arapahoe. Course, since buffalo hunters have been killing off the northern herd, you're likely to run into them anywhere. They're all hungry. They're peaceful, though. You don't have to worry about Arapahoe. Kiowa, you never know. Nor Utes. They used to be peaceful, but they killed a trader up by Denver month before last. Bleeker, Meeker, something like that.

"Well, much obliged for the water. I'd better get back to my men. We'll turn the horses in like you suggested. We all need some rest. Then we'll be on our way. Thanks again," and the major started to salute, changed his mind, and walked toward the tree.

"He seems like a nice fellow," Roz said. "Not like that puffed-up little bugger that came through here last spring."

"You mean that Captain…what was his name?"

"Armstrong. I didn't like him."

"Because he took some poker money from you over at Henry's?"

"No, Moose. I can handle losing a little now and again. It's because of the way he talked to Ruby Lee and that black-haired whore from Fort Worth. They were just watching, minding their own business. Well, mostly they were. I just didn't like the way he talked."

"I guess that's why you kicked his chair over."

"Well, I may have just stood up quick and got my foot sort of hooked under his chair leg. He upset the table as he went over backwards. Lord, what a mess. Wasn't any way to tell what he had for cards, so I got most of my stake back. Plus a—little more. Anyway, I didn't like him."

"He's not too fond of you, either, I'd guess," Moose replied. "I hope we don't need his help on the trail."

"That ain't likely," Roz said. "I heard he got transferred to Fort Morgan, up in Colorado Territory."

"I heard it was Fort Union, right here in New Mexico," Moose said, "but I hope not. If he sees you he probably won't help us."

"Yeah," Roz replied. "We've got enough trouble with a posse on our trail and Comanches out there watching for small groups. We better get some heftier guns than we've got now. Except for Elwood's, of course."

Moose nodded, not really hearing Roz's last comment. He wondered whether he was about to move closer to Suzanne, or farther away.

Chapter Eight

THE POSSE

Vicente Cordoba staggered into Juan Diego' hacienda compound. He found the *Alcalde* in the inner courtyard, drinking strong coffee laced with tequila, and smoking a thin cigar. Vicente's boots scraped gravel as he limped forward. "*Buenos dias, Patron*," he said.

The *Alcalde's* eyes opened wide, followed by his mouth. "*Que paso*? What has happened? Where is the silver? Is Pablo dead? Where is *Puerco* Jose? Are you wounded?" He asked the questions in their order of importance.

"I am hurt, *Patron*. Jose is dead, Pablo got away, and I couldn't get the silver. Yet." He took a deep breath. "But I will." Then Cordoba explained. As he talked the *Alcalde*'s eyes narrowed, his face grew red, and he fingered the razor-sharp knife at his belt.

"We didn't know that he'd, I mean Pablo—we didn't know…"

"You don't know SHIT! And you never did. Shut up. I have to think."

"But *Patron*, I'm bad hurt."

"If you don't shut up you'll be bad dead. *Comprende*?"

"*Si*." Cordoba looked down, then back up. "*Agua*? Is it, uh, all right if I go to the well?"

"Go!" he snapped. Rosalinda came out of the door. Juan Diego waved her away. *Madre de Dios*, he said to himself. *What will I tell the governor*? He had sent word by private courier to the New Mexico Territorial Governor in Sante Fe that a gift of silver would soon be presented with the *Alcalde's* compliments. Of course he, Juan Diego, would have kept most of it before presenting the remaining bars to the governor. But if he didn't get the silver back the governor would make him pay, somehow. He always found a way.

The *Alcalde* knew that in order to stay in his position he had to take care of the governor, who had even more relatives and friends on his payroll than Juan Diego did. The entire system was built on patrimony and nepotism. That was why the governor as well as district officials, like himself, had not wanted statehood. New Mexico had been proposed, along with Colorado, when both areas had sufficient population to qualify. Colorado's statehood petition had passed. New Mexico's had not.

There was only one thing to do, or maybe two; send heavily armed men to find Pablo, torture him if necessary to learn where he'd put the silver, and then kill him, "kill him, KILL HIM". Juan Diego realized he'd spoken aloud, and that he was pounding his fist on the adobe wall again and again until his knuckles bled. He turned and slowly started toward Vicente, who limped to the other side of the well.

"I—I can find him," Vicente said, "and kill him. I will."

"You have four days, or you are a dead man. *Comprende*?"

"*Si.*"

"And you will find the silver you *LOST*, or you are twice dead."

"*Si, Patron.*"

"And if you do not do these things I will cut off your *cojones*. With this knife. Very slowly."

"*S-si.*"

"I will pull you apart with horses and hang whatever is left. *Comprende*, my stupid, irresponsible, and soon to be deceased COUSIN?"

"*Si, Patron.*" Vicente turned and tried to run. His wounded leg made him slow, made him hobble.

"Stop!" He did.

"Take off your pants." Vicente looked back. Juan Diego was holding his long, sharp knife, cutting edge up. Vicente moaned.

"Off, I said."

Vicente moaned again. He fell to his knees, clasped his hands together as if praying to Juan Diego. His eyes were squeezed so tightly closed that lines radiated almost to his ears. Juan kicked him over. Vicente screamed as Juan Diego grabbed his belt, cut it with one stroke, and split his pant leg from groin to knee. He inserted the knife blade under the dirty bandage and sliced it away, taking half the crusted scab with it. Vicente began to cross himself frantically and babble *Ave Marias* as fast as he could say them.

Juan Diego slapped him. "It is a flesh wound, *estupido*!" He reached into his back pocket and withdrew a silver flask with one hand while he pried off the rest of Vicente's scab with the knife. He poured tequila into the raw wound. Vicente screamed again, and then slumped, unconscious.

He can ride tomorrow, Juan Diego thought as he took a swig from the flask, *but when he wakes he will think I did cut off his balls—as I surely would if he had any.* He almost smiled. He removed his bandana, tied it securely around Vicente's wound, and poured more tequila on the cloth. Vicente didn't stir.

Chapter Nine

THE RUBAIYAT AND SUZANNE

Roz finished blacking his boots, and then walked out on the porch and took one last look at the supplies and equipment they would take with them at dawn. All seemed in order. He glanced at stars that spread from horizon to horizon except where the barn and cottonwood tree blocked starlight like black cut-outs. It was quiet, but somewhere to the west the *Alcalde* gathered men, or they might already have started toward Mesa de Luna. Roz wished he and Moose could have left immediately, but trying to travel by starlight on rough terrain would threaten the wagon wheels. They couldn't afford a breakdown. Pablo was sleeping in the barn. The others had said they'd meet them as soon as it was light enough to see. The wagon and horses were ready to leave at first light. They'd be several miles away at sunup. Roz shook his head, shivered, and turned toward the door. He walked into the room where Moose was holding a book close to an oil lamp.

"What's that you're reading?"

"*The Rubaiyat*," Moose murmured, without looking up.

Roz picked up the empty coffee pot, looked into it, and put it back on the stove.

"Who's Ruby Ott?"

"What? Oh. *The Rubaiyat*, Roz. *The Rubaiyat* of Omar Kayam."

"Who's Omar…"

"An Arabian writer, Roz. He lived a long time ago. Now, I'd like to finish this page."

Roz stared at him for a few seconds. "What does he write about?"

"Oh, for crissake, Rozier. He writes about life. Romance, mainly. You can read it yourself when I'm done."

"I will. But I thought we might finish this bottle I been saving in honor of the trip we start tomorrow. Here," he said as he handed it to Moose.

"There's not much in it, is there?"

"No, but I figure if we each drink half of what's left as we pass it back and forth, we'll never run out. Now about that book, do you think it'd teach me some new tricks, things I don't know how to do? Though I doubt an Arab would know anything about making love the girls down in San Antone didn't know first."

"It's not like that. It talks more about feelings and such."

"Like the ache I get sometimes when I see a beautiful woman? It's right in the pit of my stomach. Hurts, I want her so bad. Did you ever have that feeling?"

"Well, I don't…I mean," Moose rubbed his jaw and waited a moment before he continued. "I can tell you this. I once heard a woman play a violin so pretty it nearly made me cry. But I can't exactly say it hurt."

"Then you're missing something good, Moose. Luella could do that to me. I wish I could have said goodbye."

"Why don't you try to find a respectable woman and settle down?"

"Oh, I tried that a long time ago. It didn't work out." Roz thought for a moment before continuing. "Y'see, I was walking out with a widow storekeeper's daughter in Fort Worth. She was fifteen, I believe. Pretty, and nice as she could be.

"Her Ma was as ugly as a spavined beaver, but her looks hadn't carried down. Anyway, her Ma caught us up in the hay mow. The old bat picked up a pitch-fork and asked, wouldn't I like to get dressed and come on over to the preacher's house to be hitched?

"'Yes ma'am,' I said. 'I'd like that. Just let me run home and get the ring I was gonna' bring over tonight when I asked for little, uh, can't quite remember her name. Little somebody's hand. Just let me go get that pretty ring. I know you're going to love it.' Well, I went home, all right. I got my horse saddled, and I ain't been back since."

"Hell, Roz. One problem shouldn't change your whole life. I . . ."

"And in Amarillo, I was digging a cistern for a near-sighted dentist who was also a barber. Come to think of it, those are pretty good occupations for a near-sighted fella'. Anyway, I was digging this cistern between their house and the stable. I'd dug down about waist deep. It was mighty hot. I was sweating' and had my shirt off. I was only about nineteen, I guess. My muscles showed more then, you know.

"So the dentist's wife, Emma, her name was, she walked out and asked me if I wanted to come in the house for a cool drink. She walked like she was stepping on stones in a river, and she smiled at me in a way that made it hotter than it already was.

"She was pulling the top of her dress out and blowing down the neck of it. Her cheeks were damp, and her hair had begun to come down a little. She looked right at me and lifted her skirt and began to fan it to cool herself off. I knew there was something on her mind.

"Moose, I could no more have kept digging that hole than I could've jumped over the house. I went inside with her. We only got to the back porch, where there was a little cot.

"'When does your husband come home?' I asked. 'Not for hours,' she said. Well, sir, she was wrong. The next thing I know, a door slams, and this fella is squinting and waving a shotgun at me.

"I jumped up and said, 'Don't shoot, mister,' just as he did. You know those big iron bowls on top of a cream separator? Well, he hit that. It rang like the bells at heaven's gates. A big yella' cat was sleeping in the bowl. It came out of there like a Fourth-of-July rocket, screaming and scratching. Emma began to scream, too. The dentist was cussing and trying to reload.

"Me and the cat ran out of there, and I believe I beat the cat to the alley. I cut my own hair after that and hoped I'd never get a toothache.

"I saw Emma once more. She asked if I wanted to come back and finish what I'd started. 'Ma'am,' I said, 'I'd just as soon let somebody else dig that ditch.' Seemed like that confused her. Then she got mad. I left town.

"Y'see, that serious stuff hasn't worked out for me any too well," Roz concluded.

"I don't believe you were picking the right ladies," Moose said. "Now let me ask you something. Just suppose you were with a single young lady of marrying age. Let's say you're out in a garden in the late afternoon with the smell of roses in the air. You're having tea and little cakes so sweet you want to lick your fingers, but maybe you lick hers, instead. Maybe you kiss her, and you read to her from this book. You have plenty of time. You kiss her again. And you make love as night falls and the stars come out. Now wouldn't that be satisfying?"

"It would, sure enough, Moose. All except for the little cakes and roses and the like. Y'see, I like to get right at a thing."

"Well, I think *you're* missing something, Roz."

"It seems to me that we're going to the same place. I just get there faster."

Moose sighed. "I guess we're all different. Men, anyway."

"I don't see as women are much different from men. Not in my experience. I think they just don't have the same opportunities. Maybe I'll dedicate myself to making opportunities for 'em," Roz said with a grin, after draining the bottle and wiping his mouth on his sleeve. "Besides, I don't see you setting out in the moonlight with anybody. What I'd like to know is, have you? Or is it just book-talk you're giving me? Now, I realize there isn't anybody in this dried-up town to be courting, but . . ."

"Roz, for crissake, I'm trying to read."

"All right, I'm going to take a short nap. Anyway, I'll bet you never have. Done it that way, with poems and cakes and stuff. Maybe I'll go dream about it. You know, give it fair consideration."

Moose settled himself in the chair and stared at the book. He didn't see it. He saw another place and time. He *had* loved that way, with memories he'd tried to forget, but knew he never would. His mind took him back, as it had so many times before.

After Moose had finished studying with the Jesuit Brothers of Loyola Preparatory School, he'd found a job as a night clerk in a New Orleans hotel. Most of his time was free, and he'd used it to continue his education by reading books from the public library. He read the limited supply of English classics, but preferred books about the westward expansion, such as Zebulon Pike's journals, accounts of the Lewis and Clark expedition, and the very popular book written by John C. Fremont after his return from the trip that acquired California from Mexico without a shot being fired. He read at his desk after he'd finished his tasks of cleaning and organizing the lobby.

Then the hotel manager asked Moose to maintain room rental records and post receipts. He enjoyed the work and did it swiftly and well. That was followed by a request for an inventory of sheets, blankets, supplies, and food.

He was asked to make up lists of items needed for purchase. All these things he did skillfully, in addition to being able to relate well to the paying clientele. Gradually, he gained a systematic knowledge of running a hotel.

After winning the confidence of the hotel owner and manager, Moose was asked to transfer to day work and become the assistant manager. His pay was increased, and he was pleased to be able to have better clothing made, and to visit a barber when he felt the need.

He didn't go to the library for several weeks after the promotion because of the increased workload, and because he was able to borrow books from the hotel owner. However, when he tired of the owner's collection of translated works from Homer and Virgil, he returned to the library, expecting to encounter Miss Hattie Pockle, the usual librarian. Moose had managed to start a precarious friendship with the thin, gray-haired, and apparently disdainful Miss Pockle. He'd discovered she protected an extremely shy personality with an air of brusque authority announced by pursed lips, a suspicious eye, and a finger raised to suggest quiet. She usually greeted him with a hissed inquiry about where he had been and why it had taken so long to return the last borrowed volumes. He steeled himself for the encounter.

He was stopped in the doorway by the sight of a buxom, dark-haired young woman making notations in a ledger as she inspected returned books.

Sunlight from the high windows made her hair sparkle. She tucked a curl over her ear with one pale hand while writing with the other. As he quietly approached, he noticed full lips below a freckled nose. She was concentrating, and two small lines separated eyebrows that curved above dark blue eyes. She looked up and smiled.

"May I help you?"

"I—I don't know. If you can. I mean, I'm sure you can. If, if—"

"If what, sir?"

"If you have what I need. NO! I didn't mean that. What I, uh-"

"Why don't we start with your name?" she asked, her smile widening.

Moose caught his breath and said, "It's Moose Banner, miss. Morris, I mean. Banner," he said again, immediately aware that once would have been enough.

"Ah, you must be the M. Banner whose name I find on all these cards.

"Yes, I've read many of the volumes. But not nearly all."

"Of course not." She smiled again, and Moose couldn't tell if she liked him, if she was just being friendly, or was having fun at his expense.

"I merely meant that I found your name on several of the cards in books I've read about exploration of the West. Have you read about Fremont's travels?"

"Yes, I did, and I really enjoyed it. I'd love to see that country someday."

"So would I. In particular, I'd like to see the Rocky Mountains. I'd like to follow Fremont's course all the way to California. I could do it, too, if I was allowed. But not by myself."

Moose searched for a response to the emphatic statement. There seemed to be several meanings mixed up in what the young woman had said. He was delighted that they shared an interest in the West and hoped he could draw her into a discussion. He appreciated the way she lifted her chin when she said that she "…could do it."

The "but not by myself" comment seemed almost like an invitation, at least to continue the line of conversation.

"Yes? You were going to ask me something?" She smiled mischievously. Small dimples appeared. "Why, Mister Banner, I do believe you are flushed. Is it too warm in here?"

"No. No, ma'am. I—"

"You must call me Suzanne. Suzanne Marie Pelletier. I don't want to be a 'ma'am' for some time still. Now, what were you going to ask me?"

"I believe I was going to ask your name. Now I have to think of another question." The young lady was very direct and engaging. Moose found himself smiling and beginning to relax.

"I can tell by what you read that you have an inquisitive mind. I've no doubt that you'll find it possible to ask many questions, sir." She placed her hands on the desk top.

Pretty hands, Moose thought. He looked at them for a moment and then raised his eyes to her face, carefully avoiding the bodice of her dress. She had the deepest blue eyes he'd ever seen. He'd thought her hair was black, but realized that it was a very dark shade of red. Her milk-white skin looked as though it had never been exposed to direct sun. Her dimples were still there. Her head was tilted as she waited for him to speak. He cleared his throat but didn't manage to say anything.

"Perhaps you have come for a book, and I'm delaying you. If so, I'm..."

"No. Certainly not. It's just..."

"Then what have you come for?"

"A picnic." Moose couldn't believe he'd said something he hadn't consciously considered, something that came from a part of his personality that was unfamiliar. For a moment he seemed as much a stranger to himself as she was.

"Pardon me?"

"A picnic. I want to go on a picnic. With you. I mean, maybe that's too forward. I shouldn't have…"

"I'd love to."

"You would?"

"Yes. Saturday. Of course, Clarissa would have to come, too. She is my companion. Since you and I don't know each other very well, it would be advisable." Moose had a mental image of picnicking with two young women when he wanted to be with just one, but he thought he could be happy in her presence with a regiment of cavalry if she'd continue to look at him as she was doing now.

"But, don't worry," she added. "Clarissa has been with me since I was an infant. She is older than the river and won't be any bother unless you misbehave. You wouldn't misbehave, would you, Mister Banner?"

Moose returned her smile and said, "Certainly not. I'd—I'll be a complete gentleman." Moose was, in fact, a gentleman and always had been. For the first time in his life, he'd pledged to be what he already was, while wishing he didn't have to be.

"So, shall it be Saturday?"

"Yes," Moose replied. "How will we meet?"

"Do you have a carriage?"

"No, but I'll hire one."

"Come to twenty-one Saint Charles Place after ten in the morning and we'll go in search of a lovely spot to spread a picnic lunch. We'll have to be back by three. Will that be suitable?"

"Yes. Very. After ten. Twenty-one Saint Charles Place. I'll be there."

"Good. Remember, not before ten. Now, I'm sure you didn't come here just to ask me to a picnic. Are you looking for a book? Something new to think about?"

"I believe not, thank you. I have something to think about. I'll, uh, appreciate that thought, instead."

"Until Saturday, Mister Banner?"

"Yes. Until Saturday."

Chapter Ten

WAITING

Moose had been in a daze during the rest of the week. He'd smiled when he didn't have to. He'd greeted hotel guests with genuine joy. He'd gone to a more expensive barber and had a clothier alter a new, lightweight suit. He'd had conversations with his mother that didn't include mention of Suzanne, but that left the older woman looking thoughtful after he'd left the room.

On Saturday, he walked to a livery company where he had arranged to rent a shay. He drove to Saint Charles Place, a shady street lined with magnolias. Number 21 was an imposing, two-story brick townhouse with a broad veranda and white columns that supported a balcony with wrought iron railings. He drove up a circular drive and stopped before the portico, hoping the horse wouldn't decide to do something unpleasant. At one minute after ten, he turned the doorbell with his right hand while holding his hat and a small bouquet of daisies with the other. He heard footsteps and Suzanne telling someone, "No, I'll get it."

Moose caught his breath when she opened the door. Suzanne was dressed in white with a pale blue sash that matched the band around the crown of a wide-brimmed white hat made with a material Moose couldn't identify. She wore white cotton gloves, and her skirt touched the ground. She looked up at him, smiled, and extended her hand. Moose's first, brief thought was that she looked delicious, like an exotic, pale dessert. He put the thought away as being inappropriate.

"Have you brought me those?" she asked.

"What? Oh, these! Yes." Moose handed the flowers to her with a slight bow.

"Why, Mister Banner, how thoughtful. I love the color. I could put them in water, but I think I'd like to take them with us. This is Clarissa." She indicated a slight, worried-looking woman who peered at Moose and said, "Mistuh Banner, suh. Welcome. I'll jus' go get the picnic basket," and she bustled away into the dim recesses of the house.

"Clarissa is a free-person now, of course, but she always was. She's been with me since my mother died. I don't know what I'd do without her. She'll be no trouble. She'll read while we talk."

They drove to a park by the river and found a shaded spot in which to hitch the horse. Suzanne picked another sun-sheltered place to spread a blanket while Clarissa moved away with a book. Suzanne asked him about his family, his life, his interests, and his plans. She asked what he really thought about the Civil War, about the pain and confusion of the aftermath—the period of "reconstruction"—and about the westward expansion and the burgeoning railroad systems that were mapping and building across the West.

She explained that her mother had died in childbirth when Suzanne was five years old. The infant, a girl, had died with her mother, and she had no other brothers or sisters. Her father never remarried, but had "an arrangement" in downtown New Orleans where he spent many entire nights. "I've never seen her," Suzanne said, "and probably never will. But let's not discuss the matter."

Moose and Suzanne talked until she said, "Look at the sun! What time is it? We'd better be getting back." On the drive home, she asked if he'd be coming again the following Saturday. As he drove away to return the horse and buggy, Moose thought it had been the most glorious day of his life.

He was there the next Saturday, and the one after. His employer and his mother asked him about the change in attitude and schedule. He told them about Suzanne with a mixture of pride and happiness, but still felt he wanted to savor the best and most private thoughts.

He'd asked about her father, and she'd told him he was a partner in the cotton export business. They were agents for large growers in the area, and their clients were in England and France as well as in the rapidly developing textile industry in New England. "I believe the business does well and used to do even better," she said. "We once had several servants. Now, just two. You'll see 'Old Dave' around the place. He lives above the carriage house. He takes care of the gardens and the horses and stable. He won't come inside the house unless he must. He's been around since before I was born. Father freed him as the war ended. He left for a month, but then came back. I guess he'll always be here, like Clarissa."

"Do you see your father often, talk with him or spend time with him?" Moose asked.

"Not very much," she replied.

"And what kind of person is his partner? Do you see him?"

"No more than I'm compelled to," she replied, looking away. "He's Parker DuPree. He was Colonel DuPree during the war."

Moose had heard of him. DuPree had the reputation of being fearless as well as reckless. He had commanded a company of Confederate cavalry that harried Union troops who were busy destroying railroad bridges in Southern states so neither equipment nor supplies could reach Confederate forces. His efforts had been effective, even against vastly superior numbers, until his forces fell victim to the problem he was trying to prevent. In the end, his riders had neither food nor ammunition. He'd surrendered along with Lee's other officers at Appomattox.

"He was well regarded by Union forces," she continued. "They've asked him to go west and take a post in the Indian territories. I wish he'd do that."

"Why doesn't he?" Moose asked.

"Let's just say—he thinks he has reason not to," she replied, and didn't seem to want to discuss the matter further.

As they walked one warm afternoon Suzanne stopped in the deep shade of a live oak tree from which Spanish moss trailed almost to the ground. The river murmured nearby. She looked up at him and waited. Moose kissed her. As he did, the brim of her hat pushed across his eyebrows. She removed the hat with one hand, and Moose saw that her eyes were closed. She came into his arms and he kissed her again. Her lips parted. Moose caught his breath. He could feel the pounding of his heart, and he kissed her until he heard the rush of his pulse. When he released her, she looked down but stayed in his arms. "Oh," she said, breathlessly. "Oh, Morris." She raised her chin and stood on tiptoe. Moose kissed her again and found he could actually breathe at the same time. After a long kiss during which Moose felt he was growing taller, lighter, and impossibly blessed, she said against his chest, "I think we'd best be getting back."

One August morning, when Moose came to the door, Suzanne held his hand tightly and said, "Clarissa won't be going with us today. I think she's done quite enough for us, don't you?" When Moose smiled and nodded, she continued, "I'd like to have a special day, and I have a surprise for you." She smiled. "A gift," and she pointed to the hamper over her arm. "I know a place where we can watch fireflies when it grows dark. Would you like that?" Moose said he couldn't think of anything he'd like better. "Then let's be off," she said. "We've several miles to go."

As they rode along the sun-dappled avenues and out into the countryside, Suzanne told him they were going to a private garden, owned by her father's partner. "He and my father are on business in Memphis and won't be back until day-after-tomorrow. He rarely comes here, anyway. He says it's too lonely. This is where he lived when his wife died. It's a lovely place. I've been here a few times."

They moved along a winding drive and past a shuttered two-story mansion. Shadowed figures moved quietly among the small buildings that had been the slaves' quarters. "Most of those people have nowhere to go," she told him, "or, at least, they think they haven't."

They continued through expansive gardens and down toward the river. They stopped and hitched the horse by a large, ornate gazebo. Suzanne led them inside, and Moose saw the gazebo was screened to keep mosquitoes out. There was a wicker table and chairs. The chairs weren't comfortable, but Moose went to the buggy and brought back blankets the livery company had provided, shook them out, and folded them to make serviceable seat cushions.

Suzanne suggested a walk along the river before their picnic and, once again, they found a shaded spot to be together. This time the kissing was longer, sweeter, and more urgent and uncomfortable in a wanting, wishing way. As the sun began to set, they hurried back, glad to be away from the insects that rose as the afternoon breeze subsided. They ran up the steps and closed the screen door.

"This is the gift I wanted to give to you," she said as she caught her breath. She handed Moose a copy of *The Rubaiyat*. "I'd like you to read it to me if it isn't too dark. Parts of it, at least. Start with the first page."

Moose turned the cover and saw that on the overleaf she had written, "To My Dearest Morris, My affection, forever. Suzanne." Moose savored the inscription, kissed her again, and began to read aloud with the book turned toward the setting sun. After a few pages, Suzanne opened the hamper and brought out a small lemon cake, which she cut into small pieces. "Here," she said and popped one into his mouth. "I know you can't read and eat at the same time, but you are handy with your mouth, I must say." She laughed, kissed him, and gave him another small bite. Moose swallowed and licked his lips and his fingers where bits of lemon frosting clung. Suzanne moved her fingers to his mouth. "Mine, too," she said, huskily.

Moose kissed her and felt his hands moving as if of their own accord along her body and toward her breasts. Suzanne pushed the wicker table to one side. They looked at each other without saying a word and then spread the blankets that had been seat covers on the floor. Their clothing was discarded in the rush of time that becomes no time. The unused picnic cloth became a cover. The sun went down, the sky turned red, and a mist along the river colored the trees until the evening glowed, crimson and wet as a broken watermelon. Moose knew he had never lived, or if he had, it was for this moment. He was certain he could remember everything he had ever heard or known, and none of it was important. He knew what he wanted to know—that the future promised a world more precious than any he'd dreamed, and the lines drawn by evening shadows marked his future from the past as surely as the river moved on, never to return in the same form.

"Turn your back, Dear," Suzanne said. It was the first time she'd used the term "Dear," and it seemed to Moose she could say only that one word and make him happy forever.

They drove back with carbide lanterns casting a dim, orange light on the sides and back of the horse, serving more to warn other buggies of their presence than to illuminate the road. The horse seemed to remember which way they had come and was eager to return. Sooner than seemed possible, they were at Suzanne's door.

The following Saturday was similar except they didn't walk, and they waited anxiously until sundown. Their lovemaking was longer and sweeter than before. "My father will be gone from Thursday until Sunday," she told him. "Perhaps if you came to the side door after dark Thursday night?" He did, and was just in time for work the following day. He was at the side door that night as well, as soon as it was dark enough to not be noticed.

Moose had the notion that if he was to ask her hand in marriage, he should first speak with her father. He felt it was the proper way to begin. He also thought she might not be ready for that kind of commitment, and he was apprehensive about the answer she might give. It seemed, in a way, easier to face her father than to hear her response. He asked if he could meet her father. "Yes," she said, "but not yet."

They agreed to meet again and spend a day along the river. When they returned at dusk, anxious to spend another night together, they saw lights in several windows. "That's strange," she said. "Clarissa must be up still. She usually goes to bed with the birds and leaves one lamp for me. Perhaps Father returned early. I'd better hurry in. Good night, Darling." She kissed him. "Until next Saturday. I'll send word."

On Wednesday Moose was posting accounts while dreaming about their next meeting and wondering if he might risk making a mid-week visit, when the hotel's stable hand came to him and said, "There's a colored woman at the back door, suh. Says she needs to see you." He touched his cap and left. Moose walked to the back and found Clarissa on the step. She was crying.

"Oh, Mistuh Banner. What we goin' to do? She's gone. Suzanne's gone," she sobbed.

"But, but how did…?" Moose began, and then Clarissa reached into a pocket and gave him a note. It was folded and sealed. He tore it open and read:

My Dearest Morris,

I must hurry to write this. I cannot leave you without some word of what has happened. It was arranged two years ago that I would marry Mister DuPree, my father's partner. I wasn't informed until later, and I postponed and postponed as I have no feelings for him. I wanted to wait until October, when I would have been a legal adult and able to do as I wished, but that is of no consequence now. My father learned of our courtship. He informed me that Mr. DuPree owns everything we have, including the business and this house, due to gambling debts of which I was not aware. If I do not marry as he wishes my father will have no home. Clarissa and Old Dave would have nowhere to go. Father will force me to leave on a packet boat tomorrow morning for St. Louis where I must marry Mr. DuPree. We will travel to his assignment on some frontier post in the Dakotas where he will accept an appointment in The Army of the United States. Clarissa is not allowed to come with me and that, too, breaks my heart. Father knows she aided us and believes she should have told him.

Please do not follow. I couldn't bear that. It will be very difficult to do what I must, and much more difficult if you are near. I can only tell you this. I have loved you, and I do love you, most sincerely. I must hurry and pass this to Clarissa. I will tell her to take it to you after I am gone.

Unending love,

Suzanne

P.S. You can never know what you have given me.

Moose slowly came back to the present, the dim lamp light, the sparsely furnished room. He folded the note and put it back into *The Rubiyat*. Soon he'd move many more miles away from New Orleans and the only real passion he'd ever known. Maybe it was just as well. She was no longer there, and wherever she'd gone Moose's heart had followed, or maybe it was lost, maybe forever. But if he could just see her, talk to her. She was up north somewhere. They were going that way. Perhaps a miracle…he put the book down and closed his eyes. The memory of her smile, her voice, her touch, faded and faded until it was almost gone.

Chapter Eleven

LOBO ALTO

Vicente had returned after four days, limping and saying he and the others could find no trace of Pablo. Juan Diego doubted if he had tried very hard. Now he was out of patience. He needed to think.

Rosalinda giggled as she walked up behind him, reached around, and began to unbutton his fly.

"This is not the time, Rosalinda. There are things I must do. Run and get Carlos Mejia for me."

"But then I will have to dress," she pouted. She turned him toward her, looked up at him with cinnamon eyes under long lashes, and slowly lifted her breasts with her hands.

"Of course you will have to dress. What do you think? I would have you running around *con nada*? Now hurry! *Andale*! I cannot waste time."

When Rosalinda brought aging Carlos Mejia, barefoot, bowing, and dropping his sombrero on the parlor floor, she tossed her long, raven hair and flounced up the stairs, shapely white ankles flashing under her ruffled skirts. For just a heartbeat Juan Diego thought how much pleasure it was going to be to find her and re-kindle her passion. The thought might have started an erection if he'd had time to think about it.

"Carlos, my friend, I have a mission for you of some importance."

"*Si, patron*." He dropped his hat again and bent to pick it up. Lamplight reflected off of his bald pate.

"Put that damned thing on your head. You are blinding me." Carlos did. It hid his eyes and most of his nose.

Juan Diego shook his head. "Carlos," he said, "I want you to go down to the river and find Lobo Alto. Bring him here, to me."

"Lobo Al…he frightens me, that one." Carlos stepped back, nearly losing his hat in the process.

"You would rather get the Padilla brothers?"

"No, no gracias." Carlos crossed himself.

"I didn't think so. Lobo won't hurt you if you tell him I sent you. Tell him to come as soon as he can. Tell him there is—money for him. *Comprende*?"

"*Si, patron.*"

"Now go! And throw that hat somewhere you can't find it. I will buy you a new one if you hurry." He thought for a moment, "But only if Lobo comes." *And if he doesn't I will have to use the Padillas, but they are loco, those two.*

Lobo Alto, half Chiricahua Apache and half something else that not even he knew, was over six-and-one-half-feet tall, rail thin, ugly as a drowned possum, and quick as a cornered diamondback. He wouldn't say how many men he'd killed, but rumor put the number in the dozens. Lobo did nothing to dissuade the reports for he rarely spoke. He stood, silently looking down at Juan Diego. His yellow eyes seemed to smolder like hot coals burning holes in a dark blanket.

"Can you do that?" Juan Diego asked while trying to get over the fact that Lobo had come into the room without a knock, without a sound. He had simply—appeared. "Can you find Pablo, make him show you the silver, and kill him?"

"Of course." Lobo's voice seemed to come from a deep well.

"You will have to hurry. He was near Mesa de Luna and he is probably at the stage station, or somewhere nearby. He is armed, and I didn't think he was dangerous, but he killed *Puerco* Barranca and wounded my cousin, Vicente Cordoba, that worthless piece of *ching*. I will pay you two hundred dollars, American gold, if you…"

"Five," Lobo said. The word seemed to echo somewhere deep inside his elongated body.

"Five hundred? Are you buying a ranch? My men don't…"

`"I am not one of your men. Five."

"No. *Imposiblè*. I cannot pay that much."

Lobo flamed a glance at Juan Diego. He turned and started to leave.

"Wait," Juan Diego said. Lobo stopped, but didn't turn around. "We have always been friends, and I…"

"You would cut my throat for ten pesos."

"No, I would not." *I'd get someone to do it for me.* "All right. Five then, but you will have to take Vicente with you."

"Why?"

"Because he can save you time. And because I might kill him if he stays here." *And because I don't trust you*, the Alcalde thought.

Lobo stared for a long moment. Then he rumbled, "He's hurt. He could die."

"But not right away. He can show you where the stage stopped, and he knows what Pablo looks like. You might find the silver nearby, but don't spend much time looking. Finding Pablo will be more certain."

Lobo started to leave, then slowly turned toward Juan Diego. A crooked smile cracked across his dark face. "Two hundred now."

"One." There was silence. "All right. Two."

"I will be back. With the silver. And Pablo's ears."

"How, uh—soon?" Juan Diego asked. Lobo stared at him. He didn't speak, and he didn't blink.

"Well," said Juan Diego, looking away, "hurry, *por favor*." When he looked back Lobo was gone.

Chapter Twelve

STARTING

Moose swung the door open. He'd just come from a pre-dawn check of the horses and equipment. "Ready?"

Roz got up from the chair he'd been dozing in, looked at it, patted the back, and slid the seat under the table. "I am," he said, adjusting the collar of his shirt. "Do you think Ruby Lee will make her bed in the wagon, or sleep out on the sweet-grass plains under a blanket of stars with only a handsome fella' like me to keep her company?"

Moose snorted. "I think she'll be complaining about trail dust, horse flies, and blisters. You'd best plan to bed down alone if you want to get any rest."

"I'm considering broader possibilities. She may need me to keep her warm."

"It's more likely we'll get shot in the back or scalped before you get your fantasies satisfied," Moose replied. "Anyway, it's time to go. Henry has his gear in the wagon and he's walking Paco around in circles. Ruby Lee is boarding up her place, and I've got all my stuff ready to load."

"Boarding up! Why would Ruby Lee be boarding up that little adobe?" Roz asked as he tilted his hat forward. "It was empty when she found it. All she did was sweep it out and trade favors with some handsome young fella' to make her a door."

"Hell, Roz, how should I know? I saw her with her lamp on the porch, nailing boards over the door and window. She had nails in her mouth and didn't tell me. Maybe she plans to come back if we don't make it."

"Well, I thought she had more faith. We'll get her to Denver City. And I don't think she'll want to come back. Do you?"

"Rozier, I don't know what she'll want to do. And I don't particularly care. It's almost dawn. We have to get out of here. Are you ready?"

"I put my stuff on the wagon early this morning when I tied the little canvas cover over the wagon for Ruby Lee. Plus, I brought her a little wood stool she can put by the fire on cool evenings. All I have to do is saddle old Buster."

"Then let's get going. Why don't you bring my bay when you come back with Buster? It'll save me a minute or two."

Roz's eyebrows went up. "I'll be glad to do that, Moose. But, you know, the last time he bit my hat and almost kicked me in the side. Might have stove me up pretty bad."

Moose sighed. "Alright. Bring my things to the wagon. I'll get the bay. And Buster. Seems your lot is to build awnings and fix seats for fancy ladies to be comfortable while I take all the danger with hammer-headed animals."

"What makes you think a horse is more dangerous than a—woman of pleasure?"

Moose looked at him for a long moment and said, "You have a point. You'll likely die from one's company before a horse or mule kills me." He turned on his heel and went to the corrals.

Roz stamped his boots on the wood floor and touched off a fresh round of pigeon protests from the loft. "Go to it, girls," he said with a glance at the ceiling. "It's all yours. I'm off to the land of cool days and quiet nights." *Assuming we get that far.*

Ruby Lee was glad to be leaving Mesa de Luna. She'd only meant to stay one year and had ended up staying five. She had thought she'd get to Denver City or San Francisco sooner, but she couldn't afford stage fare for a long trip and no other opportunity had been presented. It felt good to be going somewhere. She'd felt safe in Mesa de Luna—bored but secure. She'd earned as much as she needed until people began to move away. She made friends easily, although mostly male. She liked to talk, and men liked to talk with her. One day Roz had asked her how she'd come to be in her line of business.

"Well," she said, seriously, "I used to be a Franciscan nun, back in Fayetteville."

"Really?" Roz replied.

"No, not really, you knot-head. If I told you I'd have to make up an entertaining story, and the truth is something I don't like to talk about. Or even think about."

But she did remember. She remembered a drunken stepfather who watched her grow into puberty on the Arkansas farm. For years she had tried to avoid his hands, but the cabin was small. Her mother tried to intervene and was ridiculed. One hot evening, he threw her mother out of bed and threw Ruby in. Her mother attempted to stop him and was knocked senseless. After that, her mother cowered in a corner or went outside until his passions subsided.

On a winter afternoon, Ruby quietly tied her clothing in a bundle, added her mother's best dress, and took five of the family's ten dollars. Her mother anxiously watched. Ruby feared she'd cry out, but she didn't. Ruby looked at her impassively for a moment. She'd felt betrayed in spite of her mother's early efforts to help. She couldn't summon compassion. Fear and humiliation had hollowed her. She felt her mother should have done something, should have taken them both away, but doubted her mother would ever leave the poor bargain she'd made.

Ruby sighed, opened the door, and closed it quietly behind her. She tied her bundle on the mule and rode all night and most of the next day. She sold the mule at the first stage stop to a horse trader, who frowned until he saw that the animal wasn't branded. Ruby bought a ticket to Fort Worth, rode the coach across the Red River ferry to Texas, and never looked back.

She'd worked for a madam in Fort Worth and another in Amarillo. She'd lost count of the number of prostitutes who'd told of sexual abuse and a mother who could not or would not prevent it. At the bordellos, Ruby had been cooperative and had developed social skills, but had never trusted women, never knew quite how to relate to them. She was careful of men, but found them easier to understand and control. She'd defended herself when necessary, and eventually regained her sense of dignity.

She'd longed to be financially independent and had headed toward Santa Fe, thinking she might earn enough to get to California, but had run out of resources in Mesa de Luna. She'd carefully hidden a small amount of money for the day when she could continue toward California. That day had never come. But at least she would be moving and it felt good. There was risk, but there were six of them, well-armed and able to fight if it came to that.

A broad smile stayed on El's face as he packed his gear. He'd be on the trail with the best friends he'd ever known. It would be good to get out of New Mexico's heat, good to see a green hillside and clear water. He'd learned to form friendships after coming to Mesa de Luna. For the first time he felt he fit in, that he was like them in some ways at least. The thought of leaving made him regretful, but he would have had a difficult time putting it into words.

When he'd learned Henry and Ruby Lee were going he was flooded with a warm, satisfied feeling he didn't mention to anyone. It seemed he'd have just about everything he'd ever wanted. He'd travel with his friends and see new country almost every day. He could show Ruby Lee what he knew and loved. Maybe she'd learn to like it. There was danger, but he'd known danger before. It wouldn't be worse than the war. Buck was already saddled, and Mingus was tethered and ready to be led. El waited, smiling, showing more patience than he felt.

When the sun rose above the eastern horizon, Mesa de Luna had faded into the background. Not even the tallest branches of the cottonwood showed on the sun-brightened horizon. After several miles on the east road to Tucumcari they turned north onto a ridge of sandstone and hard pan a few miles short of the Pecos River, hoping to fool the pursuers for at least a few hours.

El had suggested that he should ride ahead while staying within sight, and that Moose should ride on one side, even with the wagon while Roz rode on the other. Pablo and Henry would bring up the rear.

"They're not likely to just ride up behind us," El had said, to Henry's relief. "They'll try to get in front, but we'll probably be able to see them as soon as they see us. All the same, be careful and fire a warning shot if you see them coming."

They moved all day under a hot sun until they found the Pecos River, sluggishly trending northwest to southeast. At dark they camped well away from the trail by the Pecos. El doubled back to see if anyone had followed; apparently no one had. They decided against a fire, had a simple meal, and went to sleep early. Ruby slept in the wagon by herself, and no one asked to join her. The second full day showed them how stiff and sore muscles can be if they aren't accustomed to long days in the saddle or a hard wagon seat. The third day was a little better.

They were on the trail again after breakfast on the fourth day, still with no sign of a posse. They began to relax but remained cautious, watchful. Ruby clucked to Monkey Buns although he didn't need prompting. He steadily pulled the buckboard up the faint game trail behind El. Moose had ridden forward to talk with El while Roz and Pablo were off somewhere, looking for fresh water for their canteens. El had told them to go easy on the water, to save it and get used to doing with less, but so far they hadn't. Henry brought up the rear on Paco, and let Ruby drive the wagon.

Ruby noticed that each person seemed to take various responsibilities without much discussion. Henry cooked breakfast and the evening meal without being asked. Roz gathered chips, sticks, brush, or whatever he could find to make the fire. He brought water when it was available, washed out pots, and assisted Henry when he could. Ruby cleaned the enamelware and cups and put them away. Pablo and Moose looked after the horses. They unsaddled, hobbled, and rubbed them down. El assumed responsibility for their security. He was awake sooner, and stayed in the saddle longer, than anyone. He ranged far ahead but was rarely out of sight. Regular duties as well as risk and discomfort seemed to make each person more essential, a more important part of the group.

The days passed uneventfully. The travelers and animals settled into the routine with slow but steady progress through the daylight hours. The country hadn't changed. The Pecos River meandered back and forth to their right. They found relatively level ground and old game and Indian trails a few hundred yards from the river. Sagebrush plains stretched away to the horizon. Mingus roamed free but stayed close to the group. El didn't think it was necessary to tie him.

On the morning of the fifth day they approached a low hill. El was ranging ahead as usual. He stopped on the crest and stood in the stirrups, staring at something ahead. Heat waves made the hill seem to dance. His buckskin appeared to rise above the ground and, at other times, disappear.

Ruby Lee couldn't tell whether El was moving or standing still. She shaded her eyes with her hand and squinted, but sweat ran into the corners and made them burn. She wiped them and tried again. She felt better when she knew what El was doing. She looked again to see if El was in view. She saw him more clearly now. He wasn't moving. He sat on his horse and watched something on the other side of the hill. When Moose and Roz reached him he motioned for them to stop. Then he pointed.

As Monkey Buns pulled the buckboard to the crest of the hill, Ruby Lee saw, a quarter of a mile ahead, three black spots jumping up and then falling or fluttering back to earth. They looked like bits of black paper lifted by a whirlwind, only larger. They went up, fluttered, and came back down in the same place. Ruby stopped the buckboard near El. Henry and Pablo joined them.

"That's mighty strange," Moose said. "What is it?"

"Birds, I think," El answered. "Vultures, or maybe crows. But I can't see what they're doin'. It ain't natural."

The black specks jumped and fluttered. "I'm going down," El said. "I'll motion to follow if it's safe."

"If it's birds, why wouldn't it be safe?" Henry asked.

"Well, because I don't know what it is."

"I guess birds ain't goin' to hurt us," Henry said.

"It might be a Comanche trick," Roz answered. "I'm going, too. If we start running back, take cover."

Ruby Lee remembered what El had told her. If they were attacked by Indians she was to back Monkey Buns around as tight as she could to make it easier to upset the wagon. They could take cover behind it and shoot over it. They were to hobble the horses if they had time. "No sense getting the horses shot if we have anything else to hide behind," he'd said.

Pablo, who had no Indian experience, had asked, "Couldn't we just outrun them? We have good horses."

"Nope," El replied. "Not Comanches. Maybe with mountain Indians. They don't ride as good. But you may as well be afoot in Comanche country. Horse's only good to hide behind if you're attacked. And then only if it's dead." Pablo looked thoughtful and kept quiet.

El walked the buckskin down the trail and kept the Sharps rifle across the pommel. Roz rode beside him, gun drawn. Those who remained behind saw the spots grow more active as Roz and El neared them. They stopped and studied the fluttering spots, and seemed to be looking at the ground around them. They motioned the others to follow.

When they were closer, Henry said, "Looks like buzzards." Now Ruby could see the red heads above coal-black feathers. She didn't like buzzards. They looked like birds God hadn't finished. They seemed partly undressed, and that made them unattractive. The irony of the thought didn't occur to her.

El said, as they rode up and stopped, "Looks like they're tied with some kind of string or thong. There's been Indian ponies here, and over there's a moccasin print."

Roz got down to look at the print. "Here's another," he said. "Bigger."

El rode in a wide circle around them. When he returned, he said, "Five or six Indians. Tracks go northeast. Probably plan to come back this evenin' or tomorrow morning."

"How fresh are they?" Roz asked.

"I'd say they were made about dawn."

"Why did they do this?" Ruby asked.

"They're gatherin' feathers, I think." El answered. "They use 'em for headdress and the like. Decorations for their lances or shields. Gives them big medicine. They probably meant to get eagle or hawk feathers, but buzzards got here first."

The buzzards tried again and again to escape, until they drooped at the end of their tethers, fluttering occasionally when they regained strength.

"What they've done is, they've kilt that rabbit," El said, pointing to a patch of gray-brown fur. "They laid out a bunch of snares in the grass. Strips of leather with slip knots. The eagles or buzzards, whatever, land and hop toward the rabbit. They get their toes caught. They can't get loose."

Roz walked to the nearest bird, grasped it by the neck, and carefully cut the line from it while it struggled and tried to bite his hand. It hopped away when released and, with clumsy effort, took to the air. Roz pulled up the stake that had been driven into the dry soil. "Clever," he said. "These little knots get tighter but they won't come loose," and he showed the others how the noose was drawn over knots in the line that were easy for the slip-knot to cross in one direction but not the other.

Ruby Lee took the line and stake, and thought how different it was to handle something that had last been touched by Indians. It seemed more real than artifacts she had seen in Mesa de Luna. It almost seemed alive, or like the Indians might appear beside them. She shuddered and handed it back to Roz.

"Where are they?" Moose asked El, who was studying the horizon.

"Not far, I'm thinkin'. Probably hunting up the Pecos, within a half-day's ride. They'll be back to see what they caught before coyotes or bobcats ruin it. We'll skirt the river, give 'em some room."

"We'd best get going," Roz said as he tossed the leather noose and stake close to where he'd pulled it up. He began to free the other birds.

"Don't you think we should leave them alone?" Ruby asked. "The Indians will know we were here."

"They'll know, anyway," El responded. "They can read our tracks like a book."

Each had a drink from their canteens, which Pablo seemed to enjoy more than anyone. Henry handed out pieces of cornbread he'd made in a cast-iron kettle the night before. El took up the left point and Roz the right as they turned west, away from the river.

Moose, Pablo, and Henry rode together beside the wagon and talked quietly. Ruby watched Monkey Buns' broad back and saw his hips and head move up and down as he walked. She listened to the sandy swish of the wagon wheels and the occasional crunch of a small pebble. She wished someone would drive Monkey Buns so she could rest inside the canvas cover. But she didn't ask. She wanted to do her part. She wanted to be as capable as any of them. And she didn't want any requests to bed down in the wagon with her. She wasn't in the mood, and she knew the trouble it could cause among a small group of men. It could add difficulty to a long trip that might not end the way they all wished. Even if they didn't get killed.

She might not like Denver City, if she got that far. The Denver people might not like her. She could go back to Mesa de Luna if she had to, and live in the little adobe, but she hoped it wouldn't be necessary.

Roz and Moose might not live to see the Columbia River Valley and the salmon-filled rivers of the Northwest. Henry might not go east from Denver City to New York, and England, like he wanted. Pablo might not find whatever it was he was looking for, especially if he was looking in the bottom of a mescal-filled canteen.

It was going to be a difficult journey at best. She meant to make it easier if she could. The rhythmic whisper of the wagon wheels on the sandy soil, and the heat reflecting from the canvas, made her nod off so that she dreamed of lofty, snow-covered mountains and clear streams where trout darted through the shallows, while far overhead a bald eagle soared as an Indian boy set snares in the sharp rocks below.

Chapter Thirteen

INTERSECTION

Granny Schneider threw stale bread to the old, one-eyed fighting rooster. "Here, Adler," she said. "This afternoon we'll have beans, my pretty." The rooster cocked his head to peer at her. He didn't understand the words, but he knew where bread and beans came from, good supplements to the crickets and mealy worms he scratched out of the refuse piles after the woman's pigs had rooted through them.

Lobo Alto and Vicente Cordoba walked their horses down the nearly-deserted street. Lobo pointed toward the old woman feeding the scrawny chicken. "Ask her," he ordered.

Vicente Cordoba glanced at Lobo, then reined his horse to where the woman stood by her door, shading her eyes. "Where are the stage station men?" he asked, with what he hoped was a sincere smile. The rooster crowed as if a string choked its neck.

"What?"

"I said where are…"

"Gone," Granny Schneider replied, "you come to replace them?"

"No, *Señora*, we just want to talk. Where did they go, if I may ask?"

"You can ask—but I don't know. They was gone before old Adler, here, woke me up. Left in the night. Several days ago. Mighty strange, I'd say. Who are you, anyway?"

"Just a friend," Vicente said, showing more of his black teeth. "Just passing through. *Quién*…I mean, who—would know?"

"Eh?'

"Where they went?"

"Oh. Sorry, don't hear too well. Try Pit Gardner over there at the mercantile. That adobe with wagon wheels leaning on it." She pointed. Vicente tipped his hat and rode back to where Lobo impatiently sat on his horse.

"Well?"

"She doesn't know. Said to try the mercantile. There."

They walked their horses and tied them to the hitch rack in front of Gardner's building. Strings of dry, red chilies hung by the plank door. Blue paint peeled from the shutters. Wagon wheels of all sizes and states of repair leaned against the walls as if they hoped to lift and roll the adobe away.

"What can I do for you?" Pit said as they entered. Pit noticed they didn't remove their hats.

"You can tell us where everybody is," Vicente said with a grimace, wishing his leg didn't ache whenever he walked.

"Everybody? Like who?"

"Like the fellows that run the stage station. And the saloon, or restaurant, or whatever. Seems like the whole place is deserted."

"Damned if I know," Pit said, although he had a pretty good idea. He glanced at Vicente, then at the tall skinny fellow who looked like an upright snake. Both were heavily armed, dust covered, and mean-eyed. "But maybe I can help you. Anything you need? Clothing? Food? Ammunition?" He wished he hadn't said the last word. Their cartridge belts were stuffed and he didn't want to remind them. They appeared as if they might draw and fire at any moment.

"We'll help ourselves," the tall, ugly one said.

"Lobo, look," Vicente said. He pointed to a pair of black leather pants with conchos on the outside seams. "Pablo's."

The tall man stared at the pants and slowly turned his head toward Pit, his golden-yellow eyes, glinting. He pulled a long knife from the beaded scabbard at his belt. Pit reached for the pistol he kept under the counter. Lobo's hand streaked out and gripped Pit's wrist almost before it had started to move. "Where," he said gripping Pit's wrist until it hurt, "are," he tightened the grip, "they?" He placed the point of the skinning knife at Pit's throat. "Tell me. Now."

"I, I don't know." The knife moved. Pit felt blood trickle from his throat and down into his collar. The yellow eyes bored into him.

"One—last—chance," Lobo said, pressing the knife point a little deeper.

Pit looked at the eyes, the scars, the expression that hadn't changed. The knife began to rotate, hurting. Then he knew. The fellow would probably kill him no matter what he answered. Pit waited, thought of a childhood prayer, and then said, "Go straight to hell!"

Lobo paused, looked into the merchant's eyes. A warm feeling crept up the back of his long neck, a feeling he rarely experienced, a feeling that came only when he met someone who wasn't afraid to stand their ground. Slowly he removed the knife and then wiped it on Gardner's shirt sleeve. He smiled briefly. Gardner stepped back.

"You," Lobo said, turning to Vicente, "take what you need."

"Clothing?"

"And food."

"What food…?"

"Jerky. Beans. Corn meal. Dry food. If there isn't enough we'll kill the old woman's chicken. Now hurry."

Vicente piled a several-day supply of foodstuffs on the counter. Lobo stayed close to Gardner who hadn't moved. Vicente carried the items out and put them into their saddlebags. Then he came back in. "I think that's enough," he said. "For a few days."

Lobo reached into his pocket and put three gold pieces on the counter in front of Gardner. He extended a long, bony forefinger, pointed at Gardner, made the sealed lips gesture, and then drew his finger across his throat. Gardner didn't blink. Lobo almost smiled again.

"Too bad," Lobo said to Vicente, as they were walking out of the building.

"About what?"

"About adobes. They don't burn."

"*Si*," Vicente said, wondering if Lobo had tried to be humorous. *No*, he thought, *he wouldn't.*

“Now, Lobo said, “we ride in wide circles until we find their tracks.” They left the village and rode into sand and sagebrush, circling in an ever widening spiral until the sun sank through layered evening clouds like a sliced eyeball dropping into a pail of dried blood.

Here,” Lobo Alto said, a day later, “and here,” pointing to tracks on the ground. “They stopped. No fire.”

“They are afraid,” Vicente Cordoba replied, a thin smile stretching his lips over black teeth. “They know we are coming. We can get down now. Rest for an hour.”

“No,” Lobo said. “No rest.”

“But our horses need…”

“Tomorrow we will take their horses and eat ours.”

“They will have food,” Vicente said, not relishing the thought of horse meat.

“Maybe,” Lobo replied, “but I like horse.”

Vicente shook his head. Lobo had eaten most of Vicente’s jerky after he had eaten all of his own. *I may have to kill him*, Vicente thought, *and then I’ll go to Texas.*

Chapter Fourteen

PLAGUE

The morning sun was well up in the sky when Roz exclaimed, "Damn, Moose. There's a lot of hoppers around here." He swatted one off of his shirt front as they continued to ride west.

They'd come several miles after breakfast at another dry camp. Moose batted two grasshoppers from his sleeve. They flew away on yellow and brown wings that whirred with a noise midway between a rattle and a buzz. They soared higher than the bay's head before curving to land twenty or more feet way.

"Wind's coming up," Moose said. "Hoppers can't fly into it. Fact is, they must be locusts of some kind. I don't think grasshoppers can fly at all."

"Whatever they are, they have little sticky feet," Roz replied.

As they continued, the hoppers began to jump and fly at almost every step. Some of them lit on the horses, which didn't seem to mind. Some lit on the men, who brushed them off.

"They are starting to make me nervous," Pablo said as more and more of them took to the air.

They heard a shriek from the wagon. They turned and saw that the light-colored canvas seemed to attract the insects. They were flying and landing on it by the thousands. A few bare areas of canvas could still be seen, but they were rapidly being covered. They began to land on Monkey Buns, and he pitched and snorted. Ruby held the reins with one hand as she swiped at her head with the other. Several had flown into her hair and were tangled. They were kicking and buzzing all over her head. She shrieked again as she tried to pull them out.

Roz turned his horse to help as El raced past, slid to a stop at the wagon, and jumped to the seat where he took the harness reins and wrapped them around the whoa-stick at Ruby's side. He reached into the covered wagon bed and pulled out a jacket that he put over her head. He pushed her into the enclosure, and then turned to see Roz spurring his horse to the wagon in time to catch El's horse that had turned to bolt. Moose and Henry were close behind. Pablo was coming up the trail at a lope, swatting and trying to control his horse.

"Get in the wagon," Moose shouted.

"Hobble 'em quick as you can," El added, as he jumped down to take his horse from Roz. They pulled hobbles from saddle bags and tied them around the front legs so the horses could hop but not run or walk normally. Mingus shied away and El let him go. The men climbed into the buckboard's bed under the sagging canvas cover. Ruby Lee was swearing, picking grasshoppers out of her hair, and shoving them under the edge of the canvas.

They tried to adjust to the small, crowded space. Moose pushed the water cask and cornmeal sack over the end-gate to make room. Roz picked up Pablo's jug and dropped it on a large rock he'd noticed. The buzzing hoppers and creaking wagon springs masked the shattering sound. They tucked the canvas around themselves as well as they could.

"Jesus!" Roz exclaimed, as the canvas sagged further and one of the supporting wood strips cracked. He struck the weighted cloth with his hand and many of the insects flew or fell off. Soon all of them were hitting the canvas, knocking off layers of scratching, buzzing insects.

"Listen," El said. At first, no one could hear anything more than the hoppers hitting the canvas where they'd cleared it as well as the periodic snort of one of the horses.

Then they heard a deeper hum, a drone that became louder and louder. "*Jesus y Maria,*" Pablo said. "I need—*mescal,*" and he started to raise the canvas. Moose put a hand on his arm. "I just, I'm, I need—" He didn't say he needed a drink, but they knew, and he knew they did. He struggled to get free of Moose's grip, but he might as well have tried to lift his horse.

"Sit on the edge of the canvas," Moose said. "Hold it down with anything you can." They busied themselves as Moose held Pablo, who began to sob.

"You'll be all right," Moose said. "You'll be all right." The drone became a rackety roar, and the dim light all but vanished. They could neither hear nor see each other clearly.

Monkey Buns couldn't go forward because of the way the reins were tied. He tried to break them but couldn't. He began to thrash and back up until the wagon tongue had nearly reversed the front wheels. He shivered and stamped alongside the wagon that rocked and threatened to overturn at any moment.

"Hold on," Henry yelled, but no one heard him.

Ruby put her mouth to El's ear and shouted, "What about the horses?"

"They'll…be—", and she couldn't hear the rest. Ruby caught El's meaning more than the words. She gestured at the canvas, which they continued to swat. El patted her hand and then pressed the canvas edges down so that only a few insects found their way inside.

How many can there be? Ruby wondered.

Moose leaned toward Roz and bellowed, "I read about this happening in China. They ate the farmer's crops."

Roz heard only a few words, "I…about…China. They…ate…farmers."

Minutes seemed like hours. Finally, the sound began to diminish. It faded until there was only an occasional pop as another flying insect hit the canvas and careened away, buzzing as it went. Then it was quiet, but almost dark.

"What the hell," Moose said as he released Pablo. "It can't be night already." Then he saw light coming from a crack in the bed of the wagon.

They moved the canvas back and peered out at a landscape as bare as the moon. It might as well have been a desert or a vast, dry lake bed; there wasn't a leaf or a blade of grass as far as the eye could see. There were only a few crooked branches where sage brush had stood, and none of them were smaller than a man's little finger. The ends of the branches were frayed, chewed off by the ravenous insects. The branch stubs and the canvas cover were dark brown, stained by the tobacco-like substance in the hopper's jaws. The canvas seemed intact, except for the stain. The air had a dry, metallic taste, like copper coins in one's mouth.

The horses twitched and plunged. Moose's big bay had lain down and tried to roll with the saddle on. Hoppers were mashed on the saddle and matted in his hair where he had thrashed among them. Moose hurried to help him up.

El straightened Monkey Buns, who was white-eyed and throwing his head up and down as far as the reins allowed. Froth and blood flecked his chest, but the blood came from the snaffle-bit, and El saw that the cut was minor. El's buckskin stood motionless. Mingus was nowhere in sight.

Roz and Pablo gathered the hobbled horses and brought them to the buckboard.

"Goddamn it," Henry said as he held up the empty corn sack. The insects had chewed through the burlap. The meal had spilled out and all of it had been eaten.

They looked south across the stark landscape and saw a dark cloud of locusts swarming just above the horizon. In a few minutes, it was gone.

"God-a-mighty," Roz exclaimed. "I never saw such a thing."

"Me, neither," Pablo said, crossing himself. He had regained his composure, had even waited for a few minutes before swallowing from the canteen. Then Pablo saw the broken jug and slowly picked up the largest piece. He dropped it and turned away.

"Well, this is a hell of a place to be traveling," Henry said as he threw down the empty sack. "Guess we'd better go to the river."

"I don't think so," El replied. "You can see they came from the north, same as the river. Doubt if there'd be anything over there except a river full of drowned hoppers. I say we go west, out of their path. We might find some grass for the horses. Some water we can drink. And go easy on the water. We may not find any for a while. Shame about Mingus. I've had him a long time. Maybe he'll come back, but I doubt it. He probably ran halfway to Mesaluna. We'd better get movin'."

No one said anything. It was one of the longest speeches they had heard El make. And it seemed he was right. A river full of dead locusts, or grasshoppers, or whatever they were, wouldn't help them. And moving away from the river might improve their chances of losing the Indians and whatever pursuers had been sent to find them.

"Let's get to it," Roz said as he checked the cinch and mounted. "We've got a long way to go."

They continued west, toward the setting sun, making a trail toward mountains that only El had seen. They left tracks on a dusty plain that seemed as if no living thing had ever walked upon it. The wagon rolled out a continuous ribbon impression across the red-brown earth, but a fitful wind rose and with it clouds of dust that erased all signs of their passing.

El pulled his hat down and turned up the collar of his coat, breathing through his nose to keep dust out of his mouth. The buckskin walked as if on an invisible line. El relaxed, knowing that while the wind blew they were safe. He'd been in danger most of his life, except while in Mesa de Luna where in-door living and boredom were even worse. He hadn't realized how much worse until he'd started traveling open country with the only people he cared about. In spite of the danger El thought life couldn't get much better. He turned his mind back, and memories began to flow like wind-fanned pages of a discarded book.

Chapter Fifteen

BUFFALO HUNTING

El had been unsure what to do with himself after the Civil War. He knew he'd need more space than the family farm and two-room cabin in the Kentucky hills afforded. After Lee surrendered the Confederate flag and troops had been mustered out, El walked across-country to Council Bluffs, on the banks of the Missouri. There he met three hard-drinking, hard-fighting buffalo hunters looking for a replacement "skinning hand." He asked what had happened to the last one. The hunters changed the subject.

"It's easy work," the leader told El. "You just need a couple of good knives, a whetstone, a horse, and a blanket. We'll supply everything else."

The lead hunter was a large, dirty fellow named Emil Zetlov. He wore rough clothes made of buffalo hides with the hair turned outward. With his own stringy hair and beard of roughly the same color, he looked like an ill-tempered grizzly. El thought he must smell worse than the buffaloes the skins had come from.

One of the other hunters was called Mingus. El never knew whether it was his first name or last, or if it was his only one. He seemed to be closer to Zetlov than the third hunter, whose name El didn't learn before it was too late to matter.

"You'll be paid by the hide," Zetlov said through long, yellow teeth. He mentioned a figure that seemed reasonable enough, but he grinned in an evil way when he said it.

When they sat for their first meal, El learned they meant to deduct from his earnings for the food he ate. He figured that unless he starved himself, he'd end the hunt with nothing to show. Plus, he'd borrowed against income for an emaciated horse owned by Zetlov. The horse was almost as old as El, himself. He regretted going with them from the start, but thought he could stick it out through the summer. He planned to give back the horse and leave them when they went downriver in the fall.

El learned, as they started toward Sioux country on a poled barge, that the hunters were more dangerous than either the Sioux he'd heard about, or the Union soldiers he'd fought against for nearly three years.

After two days on the barge, and not even as far upriver as Sioux City, the hunter whose name he didn't know drank too much. He threatened Zetlov and got his throat cut with Zetlov's skinning knife. He was dumped into the river. He never came up, but the coffee-and-cream-colored water boiled red for a few seconds as the barge was poled by. That bothered El more than the deaths he'd witnessed in the war, partly because he thought he had escaped such sights, and because it seemed so unnecessary. The barge crew didn't seem to care one way or the other.

Above old Fort Pierre, in Dakota Territory, they left the Missouri and rode their horses west. One night at the campfire, Mingus told El about a bet they'd had the previous season. Zetlov had gotten drunk and wagered that he could walk right into a buffalo herd wearing his skins, and not be noticed.

"What happened?"

"Oh, he was noticed, all right!" Mingus said while Zetlov glowered. "He was walking bent over. About the size of a young heifer. The cows didn't pay him much heed, but then this big, old, hairy bull got a look at him. Figured Zet was a cow he'd missed. Came running with his tail in the air and his lip curled up, romantic like." Mingus paused to relish the memory.

"Well?"

"Old Zet, he had himself a problem. If he stood up, the bull would likely charge him and stomp him to butter. But if he didn't, he was about to get himself screwed. I thought I was goin' to have to shoot him."

"Which?" El asked.

"Why, Zetlov, of course. We'd lost our skinner and I can't abide ruinin' good buffalo hide, prices high as they are." Mingus doubled over with laughter. Zetlov threw hot coffee at him, which made Mingus draw his knife while Zetlov grabbed a rifle and cocked it. They stared at each other for a long minute.

When El judged it was safe, he said to Mingus, "You never told me what happened. What the old bull did, I mean."

"I'm assumin' you mean the buffalo bull. Well, sir, that big hairy fellow run right up behind Zet. He got a whiff of him and stopped so fast he set down and skidded on his tail. Never smelt anything that bad, I reckon. He turned and ran one way while Zet ran the other. I like to bust a gut laughing'."

"I think I'll cut your guts out," Zetlov said, and the threats and fighting started over again.

After two weeks of Zetlov and Mingus drinking and arguing they found the edge of the great northern herd. That was when El learned how a successful "stand" was made.

Buffalo poured across the plains like miles of molasses while they migrated from summer to winter pasture, or back. After arriving they separated into smaller grazing groups, and it was common to encounter scattered bunches of ten to a hundred in the rolling sand hills of Nebraska Territory.

Zetlov and Mingus approached the small groups from downwind. They set up their long guns and shot from as much concealment as possible, although there sometimes was very little. But the beasts were near-sighted, and if they didn't detect motion, they didn't seem to know where the noise was coming from. If the shots were well placed, and the buffalo dropped without commotion, the others would "stand" in confusion until the last one had been killed.

Then the skinner's job began.

El skinned the dead animals by making cuts with a sharp, pointed knife around the legs just above the hocks, and up each leg to the belly where he connected the four leg cuts with a cut from neck to tail. He circled the anus and tail, and circled the head with a cut just below the ears. Then the skin was ready to be removed.

He pulled the hide with his left hand while freeing it from the carcass with paring motions of a round-ended knife in his right. At the same time, he "flensed" the hide, removing fat deposits, which otherwise slowed the curing process and made the hide too heavy to handle.

Calves were the easiest. He could handle them without the horse. Yearlings and small cows were comparatively easy, also. The hides pulled free without much cutting, and they weighed less than mature hides. But the older cows and bulls were heavy, and they always carried fat deposits that had to be scraped away.

He couldn't roll a large carcass off the hide without the help of his horse. When he had skinned as much as he could reach, he bunched the hide against the backbone. He secured a lariat loop around a front leg and used the horse to pull the animal over to lie on its other side. He finished freeing the hide and "pegged" it by cutting small slits around the outside edges and driving ten to twelve pegs through the holes and into the ground to prevent curling as it dried, skin-side up and hair down.

After pegging, he went to the next animal and started over. With several weeks of practice, he was able to skin and peg up to thirty animals per day. He knife marked each skin to show ownership. Several times he noticed Indians watching from a distance as he worked. He kept a wary eye on them, but they didn't come close.

After the pegged hides had dried for two or three days El rode back to retrieve the pegs and stack the hides for pickup by a freight hauling company that followed the hunters. To help the haulers find the hides he tied a piece of colored cloth to the top of a long stick and planted the stick vertically. If it blew down or was removed by Indians the collectors usually could find the hides simply by looking for buzzards and crows in the sky above the rotting carcasses. Collectors kept track of who owned the skins and paid the hunters when they saw them.

Freight wagons carried loads of hides to the Missouri River barges, and then returned for another load. The hides were barged to Omaha, Saint Louis, or Chicago, where they were turned into buffalo robes for use in sleighs or buggies. A few of the lighter ones were made into coats, mostly worn by men on the frontier.

Skinning was difficult, dirty work. Zetlov and Mingus would have none of it, and they expressed no gratitude when El struggled into camp to eat a few bites, and then collapse on his blanket to sleep until morning. Sometimes they woke him, shouting and fighting, but he usually dropped back into sleep until the sun woke him to start the day's routine over again.

If the shooters made large kills, they rested until El caught up. They complained, but they needed him and they left him alone, except for insults which El struggled to ignore the same way he'd ignored junior officers he hadn't liked. One evening when they were complaining about the number of dead animals still to be skinned, El asked why they didn't have two skinners.

"Most outfits do," Mingus told him. "We used to, but we had trouble hiring people 'til you came along. Why don't you let 'em bloat in the sun for a day? That's what I used to do." El tried it once. The cuts were easier to make, but the smell was more than he could stand.

El became used to working by himself and coming to camp only at night. He could tell where it was by sporadic shots during the day, or by smoke from the evening campfire. They cooked with buffalo chips, which produced very little smoke, but Mingus threw on clumps of green grass or, when available, sage brush or soapweed for a smudge of smoke that El could follow. The threat of Indians didn't seem to bother Mingus or Zetlov.

Sometimes El had to find the camp after dark. He'd look for the wink of their camp fire, which he could see for several miles if it wasn't behind a hill. If he couldn't see the fire, he roasted hump or tongue, and slept under the buckboard by his hobbled horse until dawn, when he'd hunt the camp again.

One early morning he was following horse tracks toward the camp when he heard the firing of lighter guns interspersed with the dull boom of the buffalo rifles. He rode in the direction of the sound as fast as the old horse could move the buckboard. When he topped a rise he saw that Indians had surrounded the hunters. The camp horses had been driven off, but were still hobbled from the night before. The hunters had taken cover among the carcasses killed the previous afternoon. The Indians were closing in.

El fired the carbine he carried in the wagon, although the Indians were out of range. When they heard him and saw him clattering down the hill, they picked up a wounded companion and withdrew across an arroyo. They left two dead warriors on the blood-stained grass. El watched them ride to the top of the far hill where they waited without dismounting.

Emil Zetlov lay dying with a belly wound and a bullet-shattered hand. He had been loading and firing with the other hand, and would soon have been overwhelmed and killed. Mingus was already dead.

"Where the hell have you been?" he asked. El didn't reply. "Get me a drink," he demanded. El brought a canteen, and Zetlov drank noisily before leaning back with a groan of pain. The fingers of his good hand clutched at the seeping wound in his belly.

"I'm gut-shot," he groaned, and El nodded. "I won't make it through the night, god-damn-it-to-hell." He tried to stand up but couldn't.

"Listen, you skinny bastard, I want you to go get me that handgun." He pointed at his saddlebags. El didn't move.

"Now," he yelled and doubled in agony. El didn't answer.

The hunter coughed and cursed. He tried to load the buffalo rifle while staring at El with red eyes and open mouth. When he had almost finished loading, El kicked the rifle away. This sent Zetlov into fresh gusts of profanity. Then he began to cry and asked El to shoot him. El extended the canteen, which he ignored. By mid-morning, he had raved, convulsed, and died.

El had decided what to do as Zetlov's life-blood drained into the soil. First, he retrieved the hobbled horses the hunters had ridden. They had hopped almost a half-mile away. He left his old horse hitched to the buckboard.

He decided to ride Zetlov's big buckskin and use Mingus's bay for a pack horse. He'd let the old-timer go free. It could stay on the prairie or follow El and the other horses if it wanted to. He saddled and bridled the buckskin, made a quick bundle of food, clothing, and equipment, which he secured on the pack horse. He left both of them hobbled.

He drove the old-timer around the area and gathered all the dried buffalo chips he could find. He pitched them into the buckboard as he picked them up. When he had a full load, he lifted the two dead Indians, who appeared to be only boys, atop the chips. He placed their meager belongings beside them.

He unhitched his old bay and let it go. It stood uncertainly as El set the wagonload of chips on fire. He walked to the hobbled horses and watched the white-hot chips incinerate the wagon and its contents.

He left the hunters where they lay after taking their guns and ammunition, a watch, a few coins, and other useful items.

He didn't know if he could elude the Indians, but he meant to try. He'd noticed that his every move had been watched. He'd treated their dead with honor, and he was well armed and organized. He was preparing to leave the area. El hoped they couldn't afford to lose more warriors.

Long rolling hills led south toward the Platte River. The old horse followed for a few miles, and then stopped to graze. El knew he wouldn't see him again.

Following the north bank of the winding Platte, he kept to himself and he had no trouble. At Fort Kearney he traded one of the buffalo guns and the watch for supplies. He continued west and began to see a country he liked better and better while he experienced a respite from four years of killing. When he reached the point where the North Platte and South Platte Rivers forked, he traveled several miles upstream and then forded both. He continued along the South Platte toward the mountains.

He became an exceptional hunter and kept himself supplied with venison and antelope, some of which he dried and carried in his pack. He became adept at tracking game and men, Indians and whites alike. He made buckskin clothing when his shirt and pants wore out. He grew more satisfied as the months and miles passed, more at peace with the broad, open country, more a part of it.

He needed income for ammunition, salt, flour, and sundries, and he agreed to hunt for Jules Beni, general-store owner and the founder of Julesburg, in Colorado Territory. Then El worked for the large cattle ranch owned by John Iliff, the acknowledged "Cattle King" of Colorado, and for Jared Brush, who later became governor of the state and for whom the town of Brush was named. He also found and fixed problems such as stock depredation or sheep-herder encroachment, and his presence and growing reputation were usually enough to solve the difficulty. He was never comfortable in town or at ranch headquarters, and became restless when town or ranch duties involved anything other than hunting or 'line riding'.

For a short period he hunted meat for groups of emigrant wagons traveling the Overland Trail from Fort Morgan to old Fort Saint Vrain. He often stopped at the cottonwood grove called Fremont's Orchard, where he saw the charcoal of old campfires and rings of loaf-sized stones used to anchor teepees. Indians had used the grove for many years, but there had been no recent signs of them.

He returned to Nebraska and was hired to be a U.S. Army Scout out of Fort Kearney. He was involved in a few skirmishes with Pawnee and Sioux, and one time led a group that rescued white hostages taken by the Sioux from a small group of Oregon-bound travelers. The tension and conflict didn't suit him and he resigned.

El worked when he had to, but if the job didn't allow the use of his outdoor skills, he wasn't satisfied and didn't do well. Routine reminded him of buffalo skinning or the back-breaking farm work on the poor-earth patch in Kentucky. As he hunted along the Platte River, he watched increasing numbers of settlers coming west. The railroads built fuel and water stations each few miles along the line, and rail-section maintenance crews were brought in to start small towns. There were general stores, lumberyards, and saloons within a day's ride, all along the hundreds of miles of rail route. El moved west to find areas less settled.

He went back to Colorado Territory, rode along the South Platte, and followed the trail south of Denver, past the Manitou Springs revered by the

Arapaho. He rode along the Arkansas River to Bent's Fort where he was employed for a few months, bringing fresh game to the fort's cooks. He traveled back toward the mountains and Pueblo, and south over Raton Pass. He thought he might go to Texas or even turn west for California. He hadn't decided where to go when he entered New Mexico Territory, and he didn't feel a need to rush the decision.

He found himself in Mesa de Luna. He formed a friendship with Henry Atwater, as well as an edgy appreciation for the charms of Ruby Lee Ahearn, who had red hair like himself, but who was different in every other way. He'd stayed, the first time he hadn't moved since leaving his family's Kentucky farm.

"This is better," he'd said to himself. "For a while."

Chapter Sixteen

BIRTHDAY

The day dawned bright and hot with a yellow sky above parched earth. There was no morning dew, and no plant life to receive it if there had been. The hobbled horses waited motionless; there was no graze in sight and the horses didn't seem inclined to forage.

Henry turned from the small, crackling fire of sagebrush stems, looked toward El who sat on his horse at a distance, put two fingers in his mouth, and loosed an ear-splitting whistle.

"Good God, Henry! I wish you wouldn't do that before I wake up," Roz exclaimed from his blanket under the buckboard.

"Doubt you'd ever wake up if he didn't," Moose said. He and Ruby Lee were sitting on the wagon tongue with steaming cups of coffee in their hands.

"He could at least say something first. Turns a man sour, being woke like that."

"He called you twice," Ruby said. "You never even stopped snoring."

"That's right," Henry said.

"It is," Pablo agreed, sounding as if he'd said eet ees. He lowered his canteen and wiped his mouth with his sleeve. "*Ching!*" he muttered as he shook the canteen. "*Nada.*" He turned it over and one drop of moisture fell to the dust at his feet.

"I don't think I snore," Roz said as he sat up. "Moose never mentioned it."

Moose smiled at Ruby Lee and shook his head. "I mentioned it, oh, maybe a thousand times. I was raised right by the Mississippi River. Used to hear steamboats all night long. A steamboat's the only thing I know can make more noise than Roz."

"Roz," Ruby said, "I know exactly what it's like to sleep over a sawmill. You make the damnedest racket I ever heard. If Moose didn't mention it, it was probably because he had a headache."

"This is a fine thing to be hearing from friends soon as I wake up," Roz grumbled. "Besides, I thought you might want to wish me a 'Happy Birthday' instead of insulting the way I rest."

"Is this really your birthday?" Henry asked.

"It's August twenty-sixth, ain't it?"

"I believe it is," Moose said, after counting the days they had been on the trail.

"Well, this is the day that Missus Well's little boy was born. Early on a Sunday morning. Twenty-eight years ago. Eighteen and forty-seven. Annie Domino."

"Who's Annie Domino?" Henry asked. "That your ma's name?"

"No, Henry. It's what they say after a date. Annie Domino." Roz rolled out of his bedroll and stood, shaking his arms to start circulation.

"For crissake, Rozier," Moose exclaimed, "It's anno domini. A.D. It means when we started counting the Christian calendar."

"Sounds about the same to me. Anyway, they say I never cried. I just smiled all the time, is what they told me."

"Might have snored a little," Ruby said.

"And started talkin' before learnin' to roll over," Henry added.

"How about singing 'Happy Birthday' to me? Anyone? Pablo? Moose?"

"I don't want to scare the horses," Moose said.

"Ruby Lee, how about it?"

"Roz, if you ever hear me singing, we'll both be in heaven."

"Well, that's a song I'm not anxious to hear. Henry, I ain't even going to ask you. Doubt if you could carry a tune in that coffee pot."

"Well, that's too bad. Cause I was the only one was goin' to do it. But since you talk to me that way."

"Oh, go ahead if you want to. Reckon I can listen to just about anyone if they're singing 'Happy Birthday.' Because it's short."

"Nope. Not now. Not after the way you referred to my singing voice."

"Moose said I sounded like a steamboat, so I think I'll just whistle 'Happy Birthday' to my own self."

"While you're up, Ol' Steamboat," Henry said, "You might as well have some coffee. Can't get Pablo there to drink it."

"Maybe you can later," Roz replied. He was looking at Pablo who regarded his canteen with genuine sorrow.

"We got to find water today," Henry said. "How far did El say he thought Mora River is?"

"He said he thought we'd cross it this afternoon. Hope he's right," Moose said. "He's coming in. We'll ask him."

When El came to the wagon, Henry handed him an enameled iron plate of pancakes and a small jug of molasses. "Didn't see anything," he said when asked. They knew he meant he hadn't seen a posse, Indian tracks, smoke from other campfires, the Mora River, significant wildlife, or anything else worth reporting.

"You still think we'll cross the river this afternoon?" Roz asked.

"Best I can estimate," El answered, "But I was some west of here when I come this way two years ago." El took a long look across the barren hills to the western horizon. "We got to save water today, folks," he added, looking at Roz and Pablo. "We may not find any 'til tomorrow."

"I sure hope we do," Pablo said. "I can't stand being out of mescal and water, too."

The sun beat down from a sky like molten brass. Once in a while they came to small depressions holding rapidly evaporating water covered with dead grasshoppers. Not even the horses would drink it.

They grimaced and moved on through still air. Perspiration soaked riders and horses. Distant hillsides danced and wavered in the sun. Wind would have been welcome; even a hot wind that raised dust from the denuded landscape.

"Let's not stop for lunch," Moose said to the others as they rode in the withering heat. "Let's keep going as long as the horses are up to it." Henry and Roz nodded. No one answered.

At mid-afternoon, Ruby Lee became aware of Pablo drooping in the saddle. "Pablo, come here," she said through parched lips. He straightened and reined his horse closer to the buckboard where Ruby sat in partial shade.

"Do you want to tie your horse behind the wagon? Come up here to rest a while?"

"*Gracias*, Miss Ahearn. I'll be fine. I'm just waiting for a cool drink and…we'll find the Mora, *no*?"

"El says we'll find it. So, we'll find it. But if you get to feeling light-headed you come up here in the shade."

"*Bueno. Gracias*." Pablo let his horse follow Moose's big bay which had assumed the role of lead horse among those that stayed close to the wagon. Pablo's horse followed the bay so close his nose bumped the bay's tail with every other step. Once in a while it closed its eyes for a few seconds. Then it stumbled and woke up.

It occurred to Ruby that people's horses seemed to take on some of their owner's characteristics. El's buckskin was constantly vigilant. It watched the ground and sky with ears switching forward and back. It never appeared to tire. It didn't interact with the other horses when it was hobbled and turned loose at night.

Paco carried Henry quietly but alertly. He was a sorrel with light colored mane and tail. He was consistently gentle, but determined. He came when Henry called. The other horses usually had to be caught in the morning.

Roz's black gelding, Buster, sometimes stood patiently until Roz opened his eyes, but at other times he hopped away faster than the men could run. Someone would have to retrieve him with another horse that had been saddled and bridled.

"Goddamn horse," Roz had said one morning. "One day I can't catch it. The next it wants to sleep with me."

Moose's bay was big and strong. It had to be. But it was quicker and more agile than one would expect of a horse its size. Moose had never named it as far as Ruby could recall.

She began to wonder if the horses changed to become more like their owners, or if the owners picked out and bought horses that were most like themselves.

Monkey Buns didn't particularly resemble her, she thought. He was muscular and tireless, steady and quiet. But, he wasn't her horse. He'd have to have red hair and cuss like a trooper. The thought made her wonder if the heat was going to her head.

El rode up to the buckboard and said, "Doin' all right, Ruby Lee?"

"Fine, El. Where's that damned river?"

"Not sure. Shouldn't be too far ahead. Let me know if you need anything."

Ruby didn't answer. *What the hell does he think I might need?* Then she felt guilty. He was only trying to help, and he'd have done as much for any of them.

Roz had heard part of the exchange between Pablo and Ruby. He began to glance at Pablo to see that he didn't become too red in the face, or too pale. He'd seen travelers become ill from sunstroke and heat exhaustion.

The sun seemed as hot as ever while it dropped toward the western horizon. Late afternoon hadn't brought relief. The men pushed their hat brims lower and lower as the sun sank. Blisters formed on their lips.

They rode past the time they normally stopped for the night. They didn't want to eat, and they didn't want to face waking up the next morning without water for themselves or for the horses.

El ranged far ahead. He returned every hour or so to check on them. Their misery was evident, but they pushed on and so did he. No one spoke. It required too much effort, and there was nothing worthwhile to say. The horses began to slow and carry their heads lower.

Henry found some smooth pebbles and suggested they put them in their mouths. It helped for a while. Then they brought no more saliva.

Ruby's face felt hot, but when she touched it, it seemed cool to her fingers. She realized it was because her dry hands were so much warmer from being in the sun, holding the reins hour after hour. She noticed her fingernails had begun to split.

They rode on as the sun fell and the western sky turned red, then gold. Night stretched across the sky from the east like a dark blue shadow, and the evening star pinned the thin, last light above the horizon.

El appeared in front of them. "It's there," he said. "About three miles ahead. Let's stop for an hour and let the moon come up. We don't want the horses to run when they can't see."

It was the longest hour Ruby could remember. Pablo didn't remember it at all. He was asleep in the wagon.

Finally the moon rose like orange fire, hardening and diminishing as it climbed. The harsh landscape turned silver and black, and it seemed they could see almost as well as in daylight. Lightning flickered miles away to the west. It was too far to hear thunder.

A cool breeze sprang up from the direction of the river. The horses smelled it and strained at their bits.

"Let's stay together," El said. "There may be Indians. They need water, too."

Roz and El rode ahead at a quick walk. The others followed with Ruby and the wagon in the middle. After a few minutes they saw a dark line of tree trunks and branches with moonlight reflected from the water which seemed to be on all sides of the bare trees.

"She's out of her banks. Flooded," Roz said.

"That's more good than bad," Moose replied. "Should have washed the locusts downstream."

Then they were splashing, laughing, and drinking. This should be boiled, Henry thought, but to hell with it. I'll worry about that tomorrow. He held the reins while Ruby jumped off the wagon and walked in the water that swirled her skirts. Her first thought after drinking her fill was that she had to figure out a way to wash her hair. It seemed more important than anything else.

They found a hill where they could watch the stars and hear the river as they made preparations to spend the night. El hobbled Buck and unrolled his blanket near the wagon. Bats dove and swooped above, visible only as shadows.

"Best drink I ever had," Roz exclaimed. "How about you, Pablo?"

"Almost," Pablo answered with a grin. He held his canteen with shaking hands. "Almost. I wish that jug hadn't of broke."

"Me, too," Roz said. "I'd help you drink it if it was here. But it isn't. So pretend it's a river of whiskey. It's the right color, anyhow, near as I can tell in the dark."

Henry had a fire going, and, in spite of the depleted state of their stores, he'd managed to cook something that smelled good. They gathered around the small flame - all except Pablo, who was standing in the moonlight beyond the horses, bent over at the waist.

Vicente Cordoba slowly lifted his head. The cloud of buzzing locusts diminished toward the southern horizon. He looked at his hands, the sleeves of his new shirt. They were an even, tobacco-colored brown, like the reins of his hobbled horse that he'd gripped with all his strength while the horse tried to pull away from him during the hopper storm. He had tried to not breathe while the insects crawled all over his face and clothing. The air smelled like cold ashes and vinegar. His wounded leg throbbed.

He turned toward where he'd last seen Lobo, half expecting him to be gone. Lobo's horse stood disconsolately in the dry stream bed, his reins lowered to the sand below, and *into* the sand. Vicente rubbed his eyes. Had Lobo somehow been buried? Vicente felt momentary relief—until the earth began to move. Lobo sat up with sand streaming from his clothing. He removed the extra shirt he had tied around his head. He got to his feet and shook himself like a dog. "*Madre de Dios*," he swore, "today we would have caught them. Now…?"

"Where will they go," Vicente asked, while carefully massaging his leg above the wound that had begun to seep and smell like ripe carrion.

"To water, *estupido*. That way." Lobo pointed north, the way the locusts had come. "Let's go." Lobo untied the hobbles and put them in his saddle bags. "*Andale*."

"*Pero…*" Vicente started to say.

"No 'but's. Get on that horse and follow me."

"I—don't know if I can stand up. My leg…"

Lobo mounted and rode away.

Someday I will bury you in sand, Vicente thought, *and you will never get up.*

Chapter Seventeen

FIGHT AT THE MORA RIVER

The rising sun warmed the backs of their necks as they looked at the serrated line of mountains stretching west beyond the rolling plains. The peaks were many miles away, but it was a relief to see them.

"Three long days to the mountains, if all goes well," El said. He looked behind them, the way they had come.

Moose nodded. "How are you feeling this morning, Pablo?" he asked.

"I am some better, I think," Pablo answered with a pained smile.

"Ready for breakfast?" Henry added. "Got side-meat and fried mush here. Wouldn't want it to get cold."

"I'll try a little," Pablo replied. He seemed to like it, but finished in less than a minute.

Henry shook his head. *No wonder he's so damned skinny*, he thought.

Roz looked at the rocky ridge beneath them. He saw that it continued on the other side of the river. The river had cut through long ago, and now flood waters rushed through the narrow part between the two hillsides. Below the narrow channel, the river quieted and could have been easily forded by horses, but the banks were too steep for the wagon. Farther upstream, the land flattened and the banks were more gradual. The water was wide and slow. It looked like a good place to cross.

"How deep do you think it is?" Roz asked El, who was looking at the wide, smooth area.

"Don't know. Probably not too deep. May have trouble gettin' the wagon across, though."

"Think we ought to wait 'til the water goes down some?"

"No. I don't think we'd run as much risk crossin' as we might if we stay put. There's somethin' about the feel of this place I don't like. We should leave soon as we can."

"You're the trail boss," Roz said, surprising both of them. "Long as you don't get us killed," he added with a grin.

"Ruby Lee, you up to driving that wagon across, or do you want Henry to do it?" El asked.

"I drove it here. I'll drive it over there."

She and El stared at each other for a few seconds. El said, “All right. I'm going' up to that flat spot. See if we can cross there. If not, I'll keep lookin’. When I find a good crossing, I'll motion you to come on over. Stay up here so you can see me when I find it.”

When they were packed and ready, El rode several hundred yards to the low bank and urged the buckskin into the water. It walked a few feet and then had to swim. El held the Sharps rifle across the pommel as he slipped off and let the buckskin tow him until it found footing on the other side.

He looked back at them and shook his head. He pointed upstream, where he intended to try to find a better place for the wagon.

He turned the buckskin upriver. An Indian rose from behind a rock on the far hillside, earth-colored, almost invisible but for the motion. El was looking the other way. The Indian started toward him. Then another popped up. Moose, Roz, and the others yelled and waved, and Henry whistled, but the water made too much noise.

The first Indian began to run from rock to rock, closing the distance to where El was judging the river's depth. Soon he’d be close enough to use the rifle he carried. Several more Indians appeared among the rocks, moving toward El.

Moose reached over, pulled the long-barrel Colt from Roz's holster, and triggered two quick shots that echoed to the far hillside and back. El snapped his head up. He saw where Roz and the others were pointing. He began to run the buckskin along the river bank. The Indians aimed and fired, but El was out of range. Several more appeared.

The Indians spread out. They took advantage of scant cover, but the rocks ended at the bottom of the hill. They had to cross the level area between themselves and El. They ran a few yards, dropped behind sage or creosote bushes, and ran again. Only one or two were in sight at any time, and they made bobbing, inconsistent targets.

El dismounted, leveled the Sharps across the saddle and waited. The Indians jumped and ran, jumped and ran.

"Why doesn't he shoot?" Ruby asked while clutching Moose's arm.

"He will, Ruby Lee, about—now," Roz said.

They saw the spurt of smoke from the muzzle and watched the nearest Indian throw up his arms and somersault backward before they heard the dull boom over the river's restless muttering.

El reloaded. The Indians stayed hidden. Roz saw one move. Another. They were resuming the attack.

El waited. Once again there was a puff from the Sharps; an Indian folded like a broken doll before the sound of the shot reached them. The others dropped out of sight. El mounted the plunging buckskin and ran further upstream before stopping to dismount and take his station behind the horse.

"He's keeping them out of range," Roz said. "They can't get close enough to do him any harm."

El motioned frantically to come upriver. He pointed to a spot on the bank opposite where he stood.

"Look," Ruby said. She pointed away from El to the far hillside across from them. Several mounted warriors had crossed the high ground and were galloping along the opposite bank toward the quiet water below the rapids.

"They mean to outflank us," Roz shouted. "We got to get to El. He can't cross back over. They'd pick him off in the water."

It was apparent that if they stayed where they were, the Indians would surround them. If they hurried upstream, they had a chance of crossing where the superior range of the buffalo gun would keep the warriors at bay.

"Come on," Henry said, and urged Paco down the hill. Roz followed.

Ruby snapped the reins on Monkey Buns' back and drove straight down toward the river with Moose and Pablo close behind. They hit the level part on a dead run and soon were opposite El. He had fired two more shots as they came.

El's gun boomed again. Roz looked back and saw mounted braves riding up the hill where the travelers had been only moments before. Buster pranced and spun at the water's edge. "Get up here, Ruby," Roz yelled and slapped the saddle skirt behind him.

"No, by God," Ruby shouted. She drove Monkey Buns into the water. He pulled mightily but lost his footing just as the wagon began to float. The current turned him so that he was swimming almost straight against the flow instead of toward the opposite bank. They floated toward the narrows.

Monkey Buns floundered, began to sink. "Come on, damn it, come on," Ruby urged, willing him to swim. He struggled. His head went under and then came up again. It was clear that he couldn't swim with the wagon and harness dragging him down.

Then Moose was there, on the upstream side. He reached and put a lariat loop around both hames on Monkey Buns' collar, and the bay began to pull. Still the wagon drifted downstream toward swift water and into range of the Indians' guns.

Pablo appeared on the other side. He threw a loop over the brake handle and added his horse's swimming ability. Slowly the buckboard began to move across the current. Monkey Buns floundered and gasped until his feet touched bottom.

The horses plunged forward when they felt the river's bed. The wagon surged and began to rise as its wheels touched. There was a lurch as the right front wheel fell into a hole behind a submerged tree limb. Water pushed against the bottom of the wagon box. It poured in and was trapped against the side of the canvas cover.

Monkey Buns and Moose's bay yanked forward. The pivot pin broke, dropping the front of the wagon into waist-deep water. The horses kept going with Monkey Buns pulling only the traces and front wheels. Ruby had wrapped the reins around her hands. She was jerked off the seat and pulled through the water to the bank before she could let go. She looked back to see the wagon roll over on its side. Clothing, food bags, and boxes swirled in the eddy behind the wagon.

Pablo's lariat, still caught on the brake handle, was snubbed to the saddle horn, pinning him to the seat. His horse went over backward and screamed as the wagon rolled onto one of its legs. Pablo fell into the current by the wagon as it began to roll. A hand came up, then sank beneath the capsizing wagon box. The horse floundered, pitched, and pulled free. Pablo's saddle bags dropped into the current and vanished. The horse struggled to up the bank on three legs, the fourth dangling grotesquely. Pablo's hat surfaced and slowly floated down stream.

Ruby ran back toward the wagon. Moose reined his horse around and caught up with her. She reached the wagon side as the current slowly rolled the buckboard once more until it stopped with its right-side wheel slowly spinning.

An arm came up, a shoulder. Moose leaned over and picked Pablo out of the water. His head had been crushed. Blood ran from his ears and nose.

Ruby gasped and looked away. She couldn't catch her breath. Her vision clouded and her ears roared.

Moose dropped Pablo's body and picked Ruby up by the shoulders. He held her waist with one hand as he guided the bay out of the river to where El had taken cover behind a mud bank. "We lost Pablo," he said.

"I saw," El replied. "We'll come back for him. Right now we got to get to higher ground. Take Ruby to that tangle of drift logs. We can hold them off from there."

Former floods had piled sun-bleached cottonwood trunks along a gravel ridge beside the river. The trees afforded good cover for Ruby and the men, and some protection for the horses. Roz had already tied Buster behind one of the broken trunks. He ran back with his carbine. Henry took Paco's reins, while El and Roz walked backwards, covering for the others as they gained shelter among the old trunks.

"I should've known better. I almost got us all killed," El said. "How's Ruby Lee?"

"I'm all right," she answered. "But, God, to see Pablo like that…I just, I just feel so bad."

Roz started to reach for her, saw El's face, and moved aside as El touched her hand. She withdrew it and turned away from them. They waited behind the pile of drift logs, looking in all directions. As evening shadows lengthened, they saw the Indian band move out of hiding. Those on the near bank gathered their dead, swam across, and rode to the top of the rocky hill. The Indians looked back with defiant gestures before moving slowly out of sight.

"Do you think that's all of them?" Henry asked.

"I expect it is, or they'd not have taken the spare ponies," El replied. "I'll go get Pablo's body. We can bury him here. I'll have to shoot his horse. See what you can save of the wagon and supplies."

They left after Pablo was buried in the sand by the log pile. They traveled toward a sinking quarter moon and, just before dawn, found a place to stop in a small ravine by the river bank. At daybreak Henry cooked some of their scant supplies rescued from the overturned wagon, supplemented by fish that El found floundering in the shallows where flood waters had abated. They ate quietly, apprehensive about their safety and the fact that supplies were now very limited. They felt the loss of a companion. They wondered who might be next while trying to suppress the thought.

The trip had become even more difficult than they had anticipated. Each dealt with their feelings in his or her own way, but they watched their companions to see how stress affected each of them, noticing changes in the behavior of others before they saw it in themselves. It affected the way they related to each other and that, like the terrain, was unfamiliar.

Vicente Cordoba felt as if he had been riding for hours, maybe days, maybe forever. His leg flamed with pain that seemed to vibrate with each agonizing movement. His head spun. His mouth was dry. He was beginning to see things that weren't there.

"Your leg stinks," Lobo said. "Ride behind me."

"I think it is infected," Vicente replied. "It burns like fire."

"Let me see," Lobo said. "Ah," he added after Vicente had carefully lowered the edge of the bandage and revealed fiery, corrupted flesh, "you will not live long."

"What!"

"The red line. Blood poisoning. When it reaches your heart…" Lobo snapped his fingers.

"Shit!" Vicente shouted. He felt anger; he felt hot and cold at the same time. He thought he might try to kill Lobo now; or he might cry instead. He didn't know what to do, or think. His vision blurred. He took a deep breath. "I will outlive you," he muttered.

"Shut up," Lobo replied. "The horses need water, and I will need the horses."

Chapter Eighteen

IT'S HOW YOU SAY IT

Ruby sat on a patch of dried grass, scratching at the sand with a twig. "You should eat something, Ruby," Henry said. She had taken no food since breakfast the day before.

"I can't. Not yet. I can't get Pablo out of my mind. The way he looked. If only I hadn't driven that damned wagon into the river he'd be here now."

"Henry's right. And it ain't your fault," El said for at least the tenth time.

"Thanks, El, but that just doesn't help."

"Ruby Lee," Roz said. "I got a question.

"What?"

"Are you blaming El for crossing the river?"

"Of course not. I wouldn't, and you know it."

"Well, are you blaming me for leading us down the hill, hell bent for leather?"

"You know I'm not. I wouldn't do that."

"Or Moose for tying onto Monkey Buns' harness that way?"

"No."

"How 'bout Henry for having a wagon in the first place?"

Ruby bit her lower lip and shook her head.

"Well, if any of us hadn't done what we did, Pablo might still be here. But we did, and he isn't. Blaming yourself isn't going to change it."

Ruby looked down and didn't answer.

"So, what I want to say is, you made him welcome. We all did. And aside from getting his mescal jug broke, he was settlin' down some. I think he'd have been all right after a while. And he died tryin' to help somebody he cared about. That ain't so bad, the way I see it."

Ruby began to cry. El looked at Roz with a nod and a small smile.

Moose cleared his throat and said, "I agree. Completely."

"Alright," Henry said, "I'll clean up. I wish we'd been able to save more supplies. I'll do the best I can with what we've got, but it's goin' to be a little thin until we get to a trading post. Ruby, drink this coffee. It's weak, but it'll do you good.

“I’ll go huntin’ tomorrow,” El said. “We’ll get along.”

Moose looked at the wagon. Roz had managed to make a temporary swivel pin from an iron brace that had supported the back of the box. It would hold for a while. But the canvas cover was ripped, and the wooden braces that held it up were splintered beyond use. Ruby would have no shade until they found a willow thicket or other source of wood strips. The water cask was unharmed. It had been full, and Moose guessed that had helped it to survive the roll-over.

Roz and Henry had felt with their bare feet in the muddy water. They’d found the heavy cast-iron cooking pot and one of the frying pans, which they dried over the fire so the iron wouldn’t rust. The coffee pot had stayed tied to the rear axle, and the bag of pinto beans that Henry stored in it hadn’t fallen out. The other cooking equipment was lost. It was a sorry looking kit, but it would have to do.

“You goin’ to be able to travel, Ruby Lee?” El asked.

“I can. In a minute.” She walked to where Roz was straightening the springs under the buckboard’s seat.

“I want to thank you,” she said. “You are a true friend.” She gave him a hug and turned away.

Roz was pleased and disappointed at the same time. Something in the way she said it made him realize she'd never look at him the way she had before the trip. In fact, he didn't see her the same way, either. He'd learned how capable she was. She could do many things and do them well. She could take care of herself. He felt like he'd lost something, but didn't know what.

Ruby had hugged him like his aunts used to before he left San Antonio. It wasn't the kind of hug Roz most appreciated. Nice, but that was about all he could say for it. Roz felt hollow somewhere in the region of his stomach and he knew it wasn't hunger. Not for food, anyway. *Damn*, he thought, *things are changing too fast*.

Roz had always been comfortable with women. He'd grown up without male influence. When he was five his mother died and his father disappeared. Roz grieved and eventually gave his affection to his aunts. He met women customers in his aunt's tea room. He ran errands for them and sometimes served tea to them. He rarely needed discipline or correction and, on the rare occasions when he did, each aunt promised that the other would "deal with him."

Women began to look at him differently in his mid-teens. He grew to medium height, but his lean frame made him seem taller. He tanned easily in the Texas sun. He had sun-bleached hair, dark blue eyes, and a wide, white smile. His hands were large and strong, and he walked with an easy, graceful step. He genuinely liked and understood women, and he turned his attention to each one as if she had something precious to give him. Many did.

He related well enough to men, and although he nearly always felt a competitive edge, most of them weren't aware of it. He spent time drinking and playing poker with them, and he courted their daughters, sisters, and, on occasion, their wives. Competition and apprehension made him cordial, but cautious. He smiled and bantered, but remained alert. Roz had felt he could always count on his charm. But now Ruby was changing, or maybe he was. It was disconcerting.

He became aware of Henry's swearing. Monkey Buns didn't want to go back into the traces. The trauma was too fresh in his memory. He balked for Henry, and Henry asked Moose to help push him back.

"I don't think we'll have to push him," Moose said. "Let me talk to him."

"Talk to him!" Henry replied. "He won't understand a word you say."

"Just watch," Moose replied. He walked over to Monkey Buns, looked into his eyes, and stroked his neck gently. He said, in the calmest, most soothing voice he could muster, "Listen, you jug-headed, lop-eared son-of-a-bitch. Either you back into those traces," he continued sweetly, "or I'm going to break all four of your legs, one at a time."

Monkey Buns gazed back for a moment, relaxed and half-closed his eyes, and backed carefully to where he could be hitched.

"Well, you just proved a thing to me, Moose."

"What's that?"

"It ain't what you say. It's how you say it."

"That's a fact, Henry. And it's about the only thing I ever learned from Roz. Not that he does it right all the time. But sometimes he does."

"Let's go," Roz said. "I'd like to get to those mountains as soon as we can."

El looked thoughtful. He'd heard the entire exchange. He'd never known how to say what he felt most strongly, and when he tried people didn't seem to understand what he meant. Maybe he could learn something from Roz. It wouldn't be easy; Roz could be difficult. Like the time El had told a group at Henry's that up north he'd seen mountains too tall to climb.

"That's ridiculous," Roz had exclaimed. "I've seen damn near every mountain in New Mexico, and I could climb every one of them. So could you if you wanted to."

"Some of those mountains are so high the snow never melts," El had said. "Like Pikes Peak at the head of the Arkansas. And you couldn't climb 'em, neither, Roz."

"Well, I think I could," Roz replied, but something in El's conviction had made him say it less emphatically than usual. He'd added with a grin, "But it'd be more like Henry to tell me a tall tale, don't you think?"

"I ain't even been there," Henry had said, "so how would I know? Though they do sound like mighty tall mountains."

"If you ever go, you'll see I'm right," El had replied. And now they really would have a chance to see them, and El could point out the ones he wanted them to look at.

Lobo saw the wagon tracks leading to the river. *One, maybe two days old,* he thought. *First I need water. Then I will decide what to do.*

After he and his horse had drunk their fill, Lobo noticed Vicente's horse drinking, but Vicente was twenty yards from the bank, trying to crawl.

"Help me," Vicente croaked. "I can't..."

"You fall off?"

Vicente nodded. "Help," he croaked again.

"Well, well," Lobo said. "Now we will see how bad you are." He squatted down in the shadow of his horse and waited, yellow eyes glinting, picking up the color of the blow sand.

"P-please," Vicente moaned. His good leg pushed sand while the other, swollen to almost twice normal size, dragged behind him, looking like it might split open. He pushed with his elbows, with the good leg, and made a few more inches through the drift. His eyes were red, his face, fevered and dry. Blood flecked his cracked lips. He opened his mouth, closed it, opened it again.

"I am going to help you," Lobo said, a guttural snarl. He stood up, grasped Vicente by the collar, and dragged him to the river, dropping him in the mud near the river's edge. Vicente tried to elbow his way to the water, but couldn't get purchase in the mud. He moaned and tried again and again, and then lowered his head and drank from Lobo's boot print that had filled up with muddy water.

"We will see how long you last," Lobo said as he tied his horse to a driftwood snag. "Not long, I think." Then he began to read the tracks he'd found.

The group with Pablo had come directly to the river. The edges of the wagon tracks in the mud had dried halfway to the bottom, so Lobo could tell the group was no more than a day ahead. He found the unshod prints of Indian ponies. He began to walk wide half-circles around Vicente and their horses. He found a place where blood had pooled, and where Indians had placed a badly wounded or dead comrade on one of their horses. Then another. Slowly he worked out the facts. The group he was after had surprised the Indians, or the Indians had surprised them. The horse that pulled the wagon had been running when it crossed the river. At least three other shod horses had also run into the water.

Lobo shaded his eyes and looked across. He saw a mound of sand by a crude driftwood cross. "Excellent," he muttered. "One less." He had moment of concern: it could be Pablo buried over there. A dead man couldn't tell him where he'd hidden the silver. He untied his horse, reined it toward the water, and swam it across. Crows rose and complained from the carcass of a horse, too ripe to butcher.

Lobo got down and began to dig with his hands until he found the crushed skull. He'd never seen Pablo, but it looked like it might be him. Vicente would know. He'd have to get Vicente across the river, and based on how Vicente's leg looked, Lobo thought he'd better hurry. Vicente would not survive the night.

Chapter Nineteen

STONE HOUSE BATTLE

At day's end they seemed a little closer to the mountains, and they began to encounter grass and other plants the locusts hadn't eaten. They traveled slowly, letting the horses graze. The horses were ready to eat anything except cactus. Moose said he'd read they could burn the spines off of cactus plants and that horses would eat it before they starved. It hadn't come to that.

"I read once how to find plants people can eat," Moose said, after they'd stopped to make evening camp. "Wish I could remember more about it."

"Wish you could, too," Roz replied.

"I think I'd know wild onion. Or horseradish," El said.

"At least we'll have sage soon," Henry said. "And maybe anise."

"What's anise?" Roz asked.

"It tastes like licorice. In fact, I think that's what they make licorice with."

"Wouldn't that be good," Ruby murmured.

They talked a while about what they'd like to eat if they could have anything they wanted.

"Well, the best thing we can do is let the horses graze and get to those mountains as fast as we can," Roz said. "I just can't enjoy talking about something we don't even have."

"I think it helps for a little while," Moose said. "But you're right. We need to get there."

"Then we can bake trout with wild onions and anise," Roz said.

Moose just looked at him, and then spread the slicker he'd carried on the big bay's saddle to make a pillow.

Ruby lay on part of the canvas they'd salvaged and covered herself with the rest. Roz and Henry made comfortable places by the fire. El wandered out into the night and waited for his eyes to adjust. He checked the stars and made sure he knew which direction he was looking.

A wolf howled a tremulous cry, far out on the prairie. Another answered from a distance. El felt alone, felt he needed something he'd never had. Not even with his present friends. He wondered what it was, wondered what he was looking for.

The night breeze brought the faint smell of dried grass and creosote. A thinning moon rose hard and yellow. El began to walk a wide circle around the embers of the campfire.

At dawn he circled back two miles, looking for sign of pursuers. He shook his head when he came back to the breakfast fire. "Nothing," he said, but Moose could tell that El wasn't comfortable.

"How come those mountains don't get any closer?" Roz asked. Two days and nights had passed since they had left the bloody crossing of the Mora River.

May have been further than I thought," El responded. "They're so high it's hard to tell how far they are." The mountains were various shades of blue in the morning sun. The tips of the peaks showed white.

"Snowed up there last night," Moose said. "It looks cold, and it's already hot down here, although the sun just came up."

"Goin' to be a scorcher," Henry said as he poured coffee. "Wish we were already there. There's bound to be food we can gather. And game."

Ruby noticed Henry didn't look at her when he said, "game." She thought it was because of Pablo's horse. They'd had to shoot it due to the badly broken leg caused by the overturning wagon. Henry had said that they might as well cut some shoulder steaks. Ruby said she didn't want to eat Pablo's horse. Moose agreed. El hadn't said anything, which wasn't surprising, but Roz hadn't either. In the end, they rode away, leaving the horse for the buzzards.

They'd weighed the risk of alerting Indians, but decided to shoot game if possible. El hadn't found anything the previous day. Roz had hunted in a different direction. He, too, came back empty-handed. Ruby had begun to think Henry was right about the horse.

"Don't worry," El said. "We've got plenty of water, and we'll get to the mountains before we starve to death, I reckon." El had a way of saying things that weren't comforting, even if true.

"I read people can last two or three weeks without food," Moose said, "but only two or three days without water."

"I know they aren't that far away now," El said. "At least, the foothills aren't. Maybe today I kin' find some prairie chickens or a rabbit."

"I'll clean the coffee pot," Moose said to Henry. "We'd better go before it gets too hot."

El nodded. He and Roz went to deal with the horses that looked better after cropping grass most of the night. Buster hopped away. Roz swore at him for being a hammer-headed jackass, and El caught him with the buckskin after saddling up.

"Much obliged, El," Roz said. "But, you know, I think I'll just shoot this flighty bastard when we get to Or-e-gone. He sure does exasperate me at times."

When Roz threw the saddle on him and tightened the cinch, Buster drew in a deep breath and held it. Roz waited until he had to exhale and then finished tightening. "Up to your old tricks, aren't you? Must be feeling better."

They followed a small stream that flowed into the Mora from the northwest. The water was clear and cool. It ran through reeds and over a sandy bottom. Grass grew in small meadows, some not larger than a corral.

Blue sage bordered the meadows, and Moose was interested to see lush grasses growing by the creek within a few feet of dry, high-plains plants. The country was changing. Here and there a shelf of tan-colored shale protruded. Flint ridges appeared at the edge of some of them.

The land began to fold, to show the effects of water erosion in a wetter time. The creek they followed was hidden by willows. It had cut back and forth into the tableland. Travel was easier on the relatively level hilltop beside the creek. El stayed on the ridges and Roz could usually be seen riding on the other side of the small valley, parallel with El. Either would raise an alarm if Indians were encountered, and then race down to the others.The wagon was starting to come apart. Roz's repairs had held for many miles, but it needed more help than they could give it without better tools and a forge. One of the rear wheels wobbled. Instead of a straight track, it created a ribbon impression that wove back and forth over the smooth track of the wheel in front of it.

A spring under the buckboard's seat had broken where it had been bent in the river. It was replaced by the fireside seat that Roz had made for Ruby Lee in Mesa de Luna. It provided a stiff, hard ride. Ruby folded the canvas top and sat on it.

Grass was starting to look good to Ruby. *Why can't I eat what a damned horse eats*? she thought. *Why do we have to have all kinds of food, when a horse just eats grass and grows to the size of that buckskin. And why stop there? Elephants eat grass and other plants, and they're a damned sight bigger than horses. So the biggest animals eat the stuff we're riding through, and I feel like I'm about to starve to death, even if I know I'm not.*

El kept turning and watching their back trail.

"What's bothering you?" Roz asked. "You think the Indians are following us?"

"No, I don't think so," El replied. "We'd see 'em if they were. It's just—I don't know. Seems like…I'll have a look see after dark."

"Sounds spooky," Roz said with a grin. "I'll be glad to help you."

El looked at him, wondering if he'd heard right. "You?"

"Yeah, I'll guard the campfire until you come back," Roz said. He settled his hat and smiled.

El shook his head and urged his horse forward. He smiled too, away from Roz so Roz couldn't see.

Evening dropped like a blue blanket. Coals from the fire whipped sparks into the evening breeze until the fire died and the travelers slept.

Once again the new day promised heat. They hurried to get started in the relative cool of the morning. An hour later Ruby realized both El and Moose were stopped. They held up their hands and appeared to be listening. "Whoa, Buns," she said.

The faint sound of shots came from upstream, the way they were going. Roz and El hurried to the wagon. "Don't know what it is," El said, "but we better find out." He put the Sharps across the pommel and checked to be sure it was loaded. Then moved forward and then saw that the banks on either side opened into a valley. Cottonwoods framed a small, stone house beyond a corn field. Low hills surrounded the house, corral, and out-buildings.

Three Indians were firing at the stone house from the cover of a watering trough. Two others, partially screened from the house by a tall, wooden-wheeled ox cart, drove their long lances into a sagging figure that was tied to a corral post. The figure wore white, red-stained by many lance thrusts. Ruby faintly heard the lance wielders laughing and shouting between the sounds of shots. They didn't seem to notice or care about the rifle fire from the house.

Roz glanced at El and Moose. Roz drew the long Colt revolver as Moose unbuckled a saddlebag and reached for his Smith and Wesson .32 pocket gun. El dismounted. He steadied the buckskin and placed the Sharps across the saddle seat. Henry stayed on Paco, his Winchester carbine in his right hand. El looked at them and nodded.

Roz spurred Buster down the hill with Moose and Henry close behind. As they passed the end of the cornfield, they heard a shot from the house. Splinters flew from the corner of the ox cart, and one of the lance-wielding Indians spun, holding his arm. The other ducked behind the cart. He looked up when he heard running horses.

The Indian saw Roz bearing down on him. He raised his lance as Roz shot him in the chest. Buster leapt over the cart tongue, and Roz reined him hard right toward the Indians with rifles. He rode directly through them, shooting one as Buster hit and sent another sprawling.

Roz felt a burn between his ribs and right arm. He watched in surprise as his hand released the revolver. It went spinning into the dust. He turned Buster with the other hand and saw the Indian who had shot him. He had been hidden behind a corner of the barn. The Indian was levering another shell into the chamber when his head exploded. Then Roz heard the boom of El's Sharps. He watched Moose fire into the face of the Indian Buster had knocked down.

The last brave held his injured arm and ran for his pony. Henry fired a moment before a shot came from the stone house. The Indian's body jerked one way, then the other, as two rifle slugs tore through it.

There was a moment of silence. The door of the house burst open. A dark-haired woman dropped a smoking carbine and ran to the corral, shouting. "Juan. Juan. *Madre de Dios, Juan*." She clutched the still figure and rocked back and forth, crying.

A boy stumbled through the door, followed by an older girl in a long skirt. They stopped short of the crying woman. The girl sank to her knees in the gravel of the yard. The boy pulled the bloody lance from the shaking hands of the first Indian Roz had shot and drove it into the Indian's body again and again until it stopped moving. He whirled and broke the shaft against a corral gate. Then he sank to the ground and sobbed.

Ruby sprang from the wagon even before Monkey Buns stopped. She ran to the sobbing woman and tried to pull her from the body. The woman held on for several minutes as Ruby attempted to talk to her. The man didn't move. He was dressed in the homespun cotton clothing and leather sandals of a Mexican farmer. The woman straightened his pants legs and pulled his sleeves down to cover more of his arms. She patted his hand, slowly let go. Ruby began to guide her back toward the house. Both were smeared with bright blood. The girl rose and followed.

Henry dismounted and muttered, "*Mestizos*", as he cut the thongs that bound the dead man to the post. The body slumped, and Henry eased it to the ground. The boy ran to help. He was wild-eyed. "Papa," he said over and over as he wiped at his father's shirt front and tried to smooth the dead man's hair. Henry started to reach for him to move him away.

"No," the boy shouted furiously, and he resumed wiping, smoothing, trying to do something, anything. He folded the dead man's arms across his chest, but they flopped free. He rubbed his hands in the dirt and rubbed dirt into the seeping wounds. Then he ran to the corral and was sick.

"Poor little bastard," Roz said to Moose, who was staring first at the boy, then at the pocket gun in his hand.

"I believe that was all of 'em," El panted as he rode up. He had counted ponies and saw that they matched the number of dead Indians in the yard. "If there was more out there, they'd have shown themselves by now."

The Indian's horses, small, wiry mustangs, were tied to the far side of the corral with one long leather rein looped around the lower jaw and back to a loop around the neck. As they pulled back, the loop around their necks shut off their wind.

One was down, shot during the exchange of fire with the house. The others strained, ears back and white showing around their eyes. One of the tethers parted with a snap, and the little horse wheeled and ran up the hill. It stopped.

"He'll stay around," El said. "Let's secure the others. We may need 'em." He and Henry moved toward them slowly.

Moose looked at Roz. At first, he thought Buster had been hit. Blood was running from his withers to his foreleg. Then he saw that it came from Roz's fingers. "Roz! You're shot," Moose exclaimed.

"I believe so," Roz said, looking at his arm. "I'd forgot." He began to dismount but his right hand wouldn't grip the cantle. He hung, half on and half off of Buster, with his left foot still in the stirrup.

Moose jumped down to help. “Crissake, Roz, you're losing a lot of blood. Ruby,” he shouted. “It's Roz. I need help.”

“By damn, I *am* shot,” Roz said, as though he hadn't believed what he saw the first time. “My hand won't work.” Moose helped him to the ground. Roz heard his own voice as if it came from a tunnel. His knees buckled, and he fell forward before Moose could catch him.

“Quick, Ruby,” Moose shouted. “Let’s get his shirt off.” Roz felt the shirt being torn from the cuff to the shoulder.

“I can’t see,” Moose added. “I’m going to cut it away. There. Ruby, I need some clean cloth. Can you find some? Hurry! This is bad.”

Roz dimly heard a girl’s voice speak in rapid Spanish. He saw Ruby and another woman run toward the house in what appeared to be slow-motion. The girl in the long skirt knelt beside him.

“Miss, can you press down here? Moose said. “Both hands. That’s it. Hold tight. I’m going to take off his belt. Roz, can you hear me?” Roz nodded while trying to focus on Moose’s face.

“Good. Roz, listen. You’re wounded in the shoulder, under the arm. I don’t think the arm’s broken, but the bullet hit an artery. I’m going to try to make a compress with your belt.” Roz started to get up.

"No, Roz. Stay there. Try to relax. Here's Ruby. Thanks Ruby, and . . ."

"Mrs. Romero," Ruby said.

Moose glanced up and nodded. "Now, Miss, roll that up good and tight. Yes, like that. Press it on the wound. We need a few strips to bind his arm to his side. Tie them together. The belt isn't long enough. Good. Those will keep the compress in, I think."

"Is it stopping? The bleeding?" Ruby asked after a minute or two.

"I think so. Miss, if you could slowly let go. Now, let's watch. I think it's better. When it stops, we'll get him into the house."

Figures seemed to weave as they moved above him. Roz tried to focus. He looked up and smiled at Ruby Lee. She didn't smile back. He smiled at a Mexican woman with dark hair and kind, red-rimmed eyes. He smiled at one of the most beautiful girls he had ever seen. She was crying. He wondered why.

"This is Mrs. Romero, "Ruby said, as if speaking from the top of a tall ladder, "and her daughter, Lilia."

Roz looked at the two new faces. As they blurred, there seemed to be four. "*Señor*," one or more of them said from a great distance, "*Como esta*?"

"*Nunca mas bueno*," Roz replied. "Never better." The faces spun, the sun went out like a blown candle, and a cool, smooth hand lowered his head onto something soft.

Lobo Alto sat on a white drift log, staring at the body he'd dug out of the sand while Vicente had watched and blubbered. Vicente had confirmed that it was Pablo. Then he'd crossed himself, said half of an Ave Maria, and died.

Lobo wondered how Pablo's head had become crushed. It didn't matter. Pablo wasn't going to tell him anything. Pablo wore almost new clothes he must have obtained from the trader in Mesa de Luna. They weren't fancy; he hadn't bought fine clothing with silver. But the trader hadn't had fine clothing to sell, so that didn't mean anything. Pablo's pockets were empty. His saddle and saddle bags were gone. Probably the others had taken them.

The group Pablo had traveled with didn't have many horses or a fine wagon. Of course they wouldn't have had time to buy a new one even if they did have the silver. It could be hidden in the wagon. It would be too heavy to carry on a horse. Did they have it? He couldn't be sure. If they didn't, maybe they had something else valuable? Probably not. Certainly not the wagon, which Lobo didn't need, unless for carrying the silver box. Not their horses either; horses were easy to steal.

Maybe Pablo had hidden it? If he had, it was somewhere between Point of Rocks and Mesa de Luna. Would he have carried the heavy box to Mesa de Luna, maybe on one of the stage horses? No. He wouldn't have wanted others to see it. The abandoned coach had been at Point of Rocks where Lobo and that idiot Vicente had stopped and made a cursory search. Juan Diego had been right. It had made more sense to catch Pablo and make him tell, but now he wasn't going to tell anyone anything.

Lobo pondered. If the silver was in their wagon he could kill them and take it. If it wasn't, he could make a more thorough search at Point of Rocks, which was five or maybe six days ride back the way he had come. But with luck he could catch the group and look into their wagon in just one or two days. If the box wasn't there maybe he wouldn't even have to kill them. He didn't mind doing so, but if he didn't need to he'd save himself the trouble. And now he could travel faster alone. It was convenient that Vicente had lived just long enough to identify Pablo, and now they lay together on the sand. Buzzards waited on bare cottonwood branches like undertakers, hunched old men in shabby black coats.

Chapter Twenty

MENDING

A small fire burned in the stone fireplace at the end of the room. Shadows moved across the ceiling as someone worked near the fire. Roz's first thought was, *Damn, that smells good.*

"Glad to hear you're awake," Moose said. "And it is good."

"Did I say that? I thought I just thought it."

"You've been saying a lot of things. You've been talking about roses and little cakes."

"That doesn't sound like something I'd say." Then he remembered the girl's face. "Normally."

"*Señor* Ross," the woman said, "you are awake. I will bring you something to eat."

"Thank you. That's really, I mean, I appreciate…I," and then he was sleeping again.

"Ma'am, he doesn't know what he's missing," Moose said, nodding toward the kettle of vegetable stew. "Though I do wish we could get some food into him."

"You may call me Manuela, *Señor*. I am not old enough and perhaps not wise enough to be called *Señora*. Manuela, or Mrs. Romero, if you prefer."

Moose smiled.

"I wish you to thank Mr. Henree for me. I cannot say his last name. Mr. At–Atwad?"

"Atwater," Henry said grumpily from the bench outside the door where he and Ruby were sitting with cups of coffee. Henry turned and looked through the door, elbows on knees.

"Manuela to you, too, Mr. Henree. And you, Miss—"

"Ruby will do," Ruby said.

"So, I will thank you, Mr. Henree, for—burying Juan." Manuela's quick smile faded and she choked.

Henry's frown softened. "It's all right. Miguel did most of the work, anyway."

It was true. The boy had dug with a fury until exhausted. Then he'd handed the spade to Henry, who'd finished the job. They'd buried Juan at the top of a hill overlooking the house and barn.

El and Moose had dragged the dead Indians far down the creek and made a mass grave for them in sandy soil in the bottom of a coulee that emptied rain water into the creek. There was an undercut bank, and it was a simple matter to cave the bank in over the bodies and add a few more shovels of dirt. They came back and saw Miguel sitting by his father's grave. The house was quiet.

The next evening Mrs. Romero made *posole* and flour tortillas. Henry thought it was one of the best meals he had ever eaten, and he said as much to Mrs. Romero.

"It is in the spices, Mister Henree. Some I grow. Some I find, out there," and she indicated the hills with a sweep of her arm. "Also, *medicina*, how you say—?"

"Medicine, Mama."

"*Si. Es bueno por*…is good for Mister Ross."

Ruby had watched Lilia and Mrs. Romero wash and bind Roz's wound after applying an astringent made from crushed yucca leaves. It appeared Roz would be fine if the wound didn't become infected, but he'd lost a lot of blood from the severed artery. The bullet had glanced off of the upper-arm bone, and shock had numbed the nerves in his hand.

"He'll likely be fine. But he ain't goin' to be ridin' for a few days," El said. "Not even in the wagon."

"So. We will—care for him until he is—well," Mrs. Romero said. "Miguelito," she called, holding a large iron spoon above the stew kettle. "Miguelito!"

Henry saw him on the hill, sitting by his father's grave. Miguel shook his head when his mother called.

"I'd go get him for you," Henry said, "but it looks like he wants to be left alone."

Mrs. Romero came to the door and looked at the boy sitting in the moonlight. She turned to Henry. Tears coursed down her cheeks. She dropped her gaze and went back inside.

"It's a black time, Ruby," Henry said. "A black time."

"God, Henry," she said. "I never knew it would be so tiring." She leaned her head against the stone wall. Seconds later she was sleeping. Henry motioned to El, who picked Ruby up carefully and carried her to the wagon where he placed her on the folded canvas and put his rain slicker over her.

When El returned to the house, Henry was dozing on the bench with his hat over his eyes and his knees drawn up. El saw Roz in the firelight, sleeping in the rope mattress bed. The girl was curled up on another. Moose and Mrs. Romero conversed quietly.

Coyotes yipped and yodeled far out in the night. El walked up the hill beyond the corral. Drying cottonwood leaves rattled in the breeze. He circled around the fresh grave and the boy who watched him, being careful to stay far enough away to allow privacy. He counted several shooting stars. He remembered he'd seen many about this time in previous years. *End of August*, he thought, *and time is getting away from us*.

In the clearing below, the faint flicker of light from a window showed where people were helping each other cope with living and with death, which El knew was just one more part of life's system, the end of one journey bringing the beginning of another.

A coyote howled again, faintly answered by another. A cool breeze flowed over the drying prairie grass. Slowly El's knotted neck muscles began to relax. He could hear and see better. The stars danced and sparkled, sharp as flint chips. A nighthawk dipped and soared above the creek which wound its silver way across the meadow and past the corn field. A field mouse rustled for seeds in a weed patch nearby. The Milky Way glowed unbroken, like a flowing river of stars.

A closer coyote, or maybe two or three, warbled their night music, tentative and haunting, and then abruptly stopped. The stars seemed to grow closer and the house, farther away. El became a receiver, a receptacle of night messages. The hair on the back of his neck rose. Something was out there, watching.

"We will not stay here, Mister Henree. Not now. When Mister Ross is ready, we will go with you," Mrs. Romero said to Henry at breakfast on the third day. "Juan and I, we build this place of rocks so it would be, be—*muy huerte.* How you say?"

"Very strong, ma'am," Henry said as he looked at her closely.

"*Si*, and the roof of grass, so it will not burn but a little. And now, *no es importante*. Juan is dead. So." Her shoulders dropped. "We will not stay. We will go with you."

Henry nodded, surprised at his relief. "We'll, uh, be glad to have you," Henry said. He looked at her and then looked down. Miguel rose from the table. Moments later Henry saw him climbing the hill behind the cottonwoods.

Henry told Moose and El the Romeros wanted to travel with them.

"Makes a bigger party," El said. "And they shouldn't stay here. It's only goin' to get worse for a while." Moose nodded.

"What do you mean, worse?" Henry asked.

"It's because of what I seen up north, and down here, too. The buffalo's all being kilt. You'd think there's too many to kill 'em all, but there ain't. I skinned near two thousand myself. In one summer. And there's hundreds, maybe thousands of hunters. Plus, some just kills for tongue or for sport."

"And makes the Indians fightin' mad."

"It isn't just that," Moose interjected. "The buffalo gives them nearly everything they need. Food. Leather for clothing and tepees. Robes to sleep on. Probably more I don't know about."

"They're hungry," El added. "And desperate. They got no way to live after the buff's is gone."

"So they try to stop us," Henry mused. "Can't blame 'em, in a way."

"Some's just mad, specially the young bucks. Others is starvin'," El said. "It's a sad thing. I feel bad when we have to kill 'em."

"Sometimes they don't give us a choice," Moose said, looking at his hands.

"That's true enough. All the same, I feel sorry for 'em."

"Me, too," Henry said. "Fact is, I feel sorry for all of us."

"I'm turning in," Moose said. He liked to spread his bedroll in the straw under the oxen's shelter. There was a warm, dry space between the wooden feed bunks and the shed's wall, and Moose enjoyed the contented sighs and small noises the great beasts made when they were resting.

Henry got his blanket and returned to the bench by the door. El had begun to sleep beside the wagon, whereas Roz was still using the bed that normally belonged to Miguel.

"How are you today, *Señor*?" Lilia asked, after Roz had healed for more than a week.

"Fine, but you got to call me Roz. *Señor* makes me think I'm somebody I don't know." Roz looked at her remarkable face, and, again, the rest of the world seemed to disappear. "I'd like to go outside if you'll help me." Lilia smiled and took his good arm.

"Whoa, not so fast," Roz said. "I got to see if I can get my legs under me." Lilia helped him stand, and then walk slowly through the door and into bright sunlight. Roz leaned on her with his good arm as they walked around the corner of the house.

"Here is the garden," Lilia said. "And over there, that field where we had wheat. It is inside now, for making bread." They turned the corner. "Up there is the well. Father says—said it is the best for many miles."

Roz stumbled, and she caught his arm with surprising strength. The nearness of her, smelling like soap and sunlight, and the warmth of her hand as she steadied him made him wish they could walk on forever.

"I think this is far enough," she said as they came around the last corner. Roz just made it back to the bench before falling. He sat, letting the sun bathe his face.

"Now you must have something to eat," Lilia said. She returned with a bowl of cornmeal gruel flavored with honey and sliced apple. She brought a cup of hot, strong tea.

"Where do you get honey?" he asked.

"My father, he…" She took a deep breath. "We have bees. When you are strong again I will show you."

"And the tea?"

"My mother, she gathers plants. This is what, Mama?" she called through the open door.

"We call it *jalisca, señor*. Do you like it?" Manuela asked as she came to the doorway.

"I don't know, ma'am. Could be it takes a little getting used to." When Manuela failed to suppress a small smile, Roz thought, *Why didn't I just say I like it? That's what I normally would have done.*

"It does, *Señor* Ross. But it is good to—heal you. And if you have more, you may begin to—like it."

"I expect I may. And, uh, I want to thank you, all of you. For taking care of me. I was a handful there for a while. I really appreciate it."

Manuela smiled at Ruby. "I think you'd do the same for us, *Señor*."

"Yes, ma'am."

"Well," she replied. "It is good. We help each other," and she turned back to the cornbread she was making.

"It is good," Lilia echoed.

It really is, Ruby thought. She had begun to appreciate the Mexican woman who hadn't judged her or even questioned her, and she realized she was beginning to feel protective of Manuela and her daughter. It felt good to draw close to women. She hadn't been able to enjoy Miguel in the same way as Manuela and Lilia because he was so tense and withdrawn. She had no experience with boys of his age, and she assumed Miguel would return to normal in his own time.

Alcalde Juan Diego paced the length of the hacienda's covered porch, lighting cigarillos, puffing and making them glow red until his fingers scorched, throwing the butts into the courtyard, and lighting another. His eyes burned like embers. His neck itched. Lobo and Vicente hadn't returned. More important, the silver hadn't returned. Juan Diego didn't like losing valuable things, or money that would buy valuable things. Most of all he didn't like not being able to make good on a promise such as the one given the governor. Perhaps he should have waited, but the silver shipment had been almost in his hands, and now it was lost, at least for a while.

Juan Diego decided, snapped the cigarillo away, and walked to the corral and *granero*, where he would find Carlos Mejia sleeping in the barn-like structure. Carlos would round up Juan Diego's male relatives. They would work for free, unlike the Padilla brothers. Nine of them would be deputized: teams of three to go east, south, and north. He knew his quarry would not have gone west, toward Albuquerque where he waited.

The most capable trio would be sent north where that ass, Pablito, probably went with the silver and whomever he'd found and persuaded to go with him. One man of the east-bound team would report back and tell him what had happened after Pablo went to Mesa de Luna, if that is where he'd gone. The last three would go south, and Juan Diego didn't care if they ever came back—unless they were successful. Time was sifting away like a fistful of sand. Time was money, and Juan Diego hated to waste money, not to mention his hard-earned reputation. If he was to be governor someday he had to act quickly.

Chapter Twenty One

ACQUAINTANCES WELL MET

Homemade beeswax candles cast a warm glow. Lilia was removing seeds from *poblanos*, large chilis that would be used for *rellenos* the following day. Manuela, Moose, and Ruby were carefully sorting small stones from a pile of dried pinto beans in the center of the table while Roz and Henry watched. When they had finished Manuela gathered the cleaned beans and put them into a burlap bag.

"We have no money, *señores*," Manuela said. "We—have much food. Beans, cornmeal, flour, salt. We have honey and sugar, a little."

"That'll be fine," Henry answered. "Fact is, we was out of food when we found you."

"It is good we have something to, to—trade."

"Yes," Moose said. "And we appreciate it. How far do you plan to go?" Then he was embarrassed. He thought that Manuela might think he was only interested in the food. "You are welcome to go as far as you like. To Oregon if you want to."

"Oh, no, *señor*. Perhaps to Pueblo. In Colorado. I have a sister there. If that is, is *agredable*, how you say…?"

"Agreeable, Mama," Lilia said.

"The children, they have better English," Manuela said. "Juan, he teach them what he learns in mission school in Taos. I was from Lapadero. There, we have no school; Juan, he teach me, too."

"You speak it real well, ma'am," Henry said.

Manuela smiled at him. Henry colored and looked at his shoes. Roz recalled that Henry had disdained the Mexican farmers and families that had passed through Mesa de Luna. *This should be interesting*, he thought. *Maybe old Henry will soften up.*

"We'd like to use some of your tools and the forge," Roz said. "We need to fix our wagon before the wheels fall off."

"Of course," she replied. "*Certamente*."

"Moose, you're goin' to have to do the work. I can go out to the corral, and I can tell you what I think is best, but I can't do much."

"Good idea," Moose replied. "Let's go look at it."

Moose rose while Lilia gripped Roz's good arm to pull him up, her firm breast brushing Roz's forearm. *I may never stand up by myself again*, Roz thought. *Wonder how hard it would be to shoot myself, once this heals.*

As Moose and Henry walked across the yard, with Roz and Lilia trailing behind, Moose asked, "Henry, did you cut your beard?"

"Well, yes, Moose. I did. After I took my bath in the creek this mornin'. I thought it was gettin' a bit tangled."

Moose suppressed a laugh. He couldn't remember when Henry had taken a bath, much less trimmed his beard.

"Looks good," he said while fingering his own. "What did you cut it with?"

"Manuela's got some sheep shears. They're hangin' on a nail inside that shed. I sharpened 'em on a black rock that's right by the gate. Manuela told me where it was."

"Uh-huh," Moose grunted. "Guess I'll do the same this evening." He was thinking about the fact that Henry had said Manuela twice within one minute.

"Say, Moose, Manuela gave me a full twist of Juan's chewing tobacco. Would you like some?"

"Thanks. I'd like to keep a little, though I don't generally use it."

“Roz don't either, much,” Henry replied. “Says it stains his teeth. But El will be glad to see it, I reckon. He was about out.”

“I expect he will, at that. Did you go up and talk to the boy last night?”

“Went up, but he wouldn't talk to me. I tried. Wouldn't say anything. Comes down to eat a little and goes back. Think he's scared of us?”

Moose thought a moment. “I don't know. I don’t think so. But so much is changing for him. He probably feels his life is coming apart.”

The following morning Moose went to Miguel sitting by the grave. Moose smiled and sat down on the grass. The boy didn’t move.

“I think it's time you had your own horse,” Moose said.

Miguel looked up, surprised. “*Señor*?” he said.

“How old are you?” although he knew. He had asked Manuela.

“I am fourteen. In seven weeks.”

“It’s time,” Moose said. “You know the black-and-white paint horse?”

“No,” Miguel stated. “I will ride no Indian horse.”

“He's a good horse, Miguel. And he doesn't know he belonged to an Indian.”

"*Señor*," Miguel said, lip quivering, "I will ride no—no Indian horse," and he started to rise.

"Wait," Moose said. "Let me tell you something. Then you decide."

Miguel stood, fists clenched. Moose thought he might run, but Moose was sitting near the grave, which was the place that Miguel came when he wasn't taking care of the oxen or the chickens.

"Horses belonged to the Spanish first, not to Indians. A Spaniard, Coronado, lost many horses when he and his army came through here."

"I know about Coronado, *señor*. That was a long time ago."

"And," Moose continued, "that horse may have been stolen from a family like yours. I thought I saw saddle marks on his back. Indians, at least these Indians, don't use saddles." Miguel was silent.

"One last thing. Even if the horse did belong to Indians, it isn't his fault. Sometimes things happen that aren't good. Even to horses."

"I hate Indians," Miguel said as he turned away. But just before dark Moose saw him at the corral, peering closely at the back of the paint.

"It will be hard—to leave this place," Manuela said as she washed supper dishes. While Lilia dried and put them into a small cupboard on the wall. "It is the only home the children have had."

"How long have you lived here?" Roz asked, carefully raising his right arm. It felt better after nearly two weeks of healing.

"Since before Miguelito was born. Lilita was a baby," and she looked at her daughter as if she were a small child still.

"Miguel, Mama," Miguel said. "Papa—called me Miguel."

"So he did, Miguelit—I will try."

"Lilita!" her daughter said, while smiling and rolling her eyes.

Manuela looked at her children. She felt hurried. Moose had told her about the flood water they had crossed and how it was calm, but then moved faster and faster as it approached the narrow part where it tumbled and roared over boulders that had fallen into the swift current. She imagined how they had nearly lost control, nearly lost all that was important to them. Now she had two fatherless children who needed her. And they would leave their home. She hoped she could keep them safe, somewhere.

Manuela took a deep breath. "I will try," she said again. Shaking her head, she turned to Moose and Roz. "Thank you for fixing the cart."

"Welcome," Roz said. "And I believe the yoke will work better now." He had spent hours improving the heavy, white-oak yoke and hickory bows. The bows were too narrow. After Moose had shown him how the oxen had difficulty fitting into them, Roz carefully enlarged the holes in the yoke so that the bows could be spread a little more. It was something he could manage while sitting, using one arm. It felt good to work and stretch sore muscles.

When he was satisfied that the bows could be spread wide enough and still fit into the enlarged holes in the yoke, he showed Henry how to brace them apart with pieces of tree branch. Then they were soaked in the stream for two days. After that they were put into the yoke and dried in the sun. When the braces were removed the bows stayed open. It had taken Roz nearly a week, but there was little else he could do. He wasn't ready for long days of travel.

"Now they won't rub sores on their necks," he'd told Lilia. "I like animals to be as comfortable as they can be." She'd smiled approval and patted his hand.

"What do you think of the wagon?" Moose asked.

"I think you and Henry did a good job. Looks like it'll go a few more miles if old Monkey Buns doesn't decide to lay down on the job."

"He's up to it," Ruby said, "And so am I. With canvas over me and a springy seat, I'm ready to get to Denver. Manuela, are you going to ride with me and Roz?"

"Yes. Some of the time. And I will walk. I miss walking." Manuela hadn't felt like walking since the attack unless there was at least one person with her who carried a gun. Then she felt she was imposing, even though Henry offered at least once each day.

"We'll have plenty of chance to do that," El said. "Are you sure you don't want to ride one of those Indian ponies?"

"Thank you, *señor*. I think, no. I can walk or ride the wagon." No one suggested that she climb up on the tall ox cart, although the oxen could have pulled her with ease.

"All right," El replied. "We'll take the ponies, anyhow. No tellin' what may happen to our stock on the way. We could need 'em before we get where we're going. Miguel, you can help me and Henry with the horses. Roz'll be better directly, and he can spell you now and again."

Miguel looked at El curiously. He sometimes had difficulty understanding what El meant. He decided to keep quiet and learn as he went along.

Manuela had told them what she wanted to transport, and what she was willing to leave behind. Most of the kitchen goods were to go, but no furniture. All of their extra clothing was packed. Most of the food would be taken. The plow would stay.

"What will you do with the chickens?" Henry had asked one morning after they had been there for more than a week.

"We will eat them while we are here. We will not take the rest."

"What about those hand tools?" Roz asked.

"I don't want them," Manuela responded. "Can they help you?"

"I believe we should take the shovels, hammers, axe, and saw and the like. If that's all right with you? We have an axe, but it isn't much good."

"Of course. As you wish, *señor*. You are welcome."

Finally, the time to leave had come. Tools had been loaded on the ox cart along with bulk grain, flour, sugar, and salt. Juan Romero had owned a fine Mexican saddle although he didn't have a horse. It was much too large for Miguel's pony. Manuela could sell it for cash in one of the larger towns, and the saddle became part of the load. A canvas tarpaulin was tied tightly over the cart's box to keep out rain.

Manuela wouldn't allow Miguel to carry a rifle as he wished, but she had let him keep a skinning knife with a curved, six-inch blade. Miguel had spent hours sharpening it, testing it by shaving the hairs on the back of his forearm. As they sat talking in the house on the last evening, Roz made him a scabbard out of scrap leather. Manuela reached into a box and pulled out one of his father's belts. Roz showed him how to drill a hole in the belt so that it fit.

"Now, don't be cuttin' too much off the tail-end of that belt," Roz told him. "You don't want to make it too small, as you'll likely grow as big as your pa."

That brought the first smile they had seen since the day they arrived. It didn't last long, but in that instant Roz thought the boy looked more like Manuela than he had at any other time. Miguel was quiet while the others conversed. He slipped out of the room when no one was watching.

They talked and planned until a crescent moon rose, tinting the tops of the cottonwoods with silver. It had been nearly full when they first came to the farm.

"I believe we'll be ready to leave right after breakfast," Moose said, as he rose and stretched. "I guess it's about time we got some rest."

"Sleep well," Manuela said. "And be careful. Send Miguelito in if you see him."

Moose, Henry, El, and Ruby left the house and walked toward the wagon where Ruby had continued to make her bed.

"Must be hard to leave," Ruby said. "They had about everything they needed."

"Yes, but it's easy to see why they want to go now," Moose replied. "Too many memories."

"Wait," El said as they walked past the ox cart. "The corner of the tarp is loose. I know I tied it, just before we went in to eat."

"Anything missing?" Moose asked.

"I packed the tools in that corner," Henry said. "Are they there?"

"I'm not sure," El said as he raised the canvas and peered in.

"Let me look," Henry said. "I know where I put 'em. There's the axe, the hoes, the…one of the shovels is missin'."

Moose involuntarily glanced up toward Juan's grave. "Where do you think Miguel is?" he asked.

"Can't see him," Henry said. "Why?"

"Not sure," Moose replied. "I was just wondering."

"Might be up at that grave," El said. "That's where he usually goes. But what would he…we better get up there!"

"Miguel! Miguel," Ruby called as they hurried up the hill, but when they arrived, there was no sign of him.

"Well, that's a relief," Henry said. "He's probably just out walkin' somewhere."

Moose remembered Miguel asking where he and El had buried the Indians. Moose had explained, and Miguel asked for detail, as if he wanted to fix the spot in his mind. Moose thought he had asked so he could focus his hatred on a known place.

"I don't like it," Moose said, mostly to El. "He was talking about where we buried the Comanches. I think we'd better see if his horse is gone."

"Where'd he go with just a shovel, a knife, and…Shit! That pony'd better be here." The corral held the other horses. Miguel's paint was nowhere in sight.

"We got to go after him," El said. "Now." They were saddling their horses when El noticed a white spot bobbing, moving quietly toward them.

"Let's wait a minute," he said, pointing at the movement. Then they could see Miguel riding the paint. He held the reins in one hand and the shovel over his shoulder with the other. He was smiling.

"Where the hell have you been?" Henry asked.

"You ought to know better than, than—to be runnin' around in the night," El said. Ruby pursed her lips and kept quiet. She and Moose were looking at the dark stains on his hands.

"I want to know what you been doin'," Henry said.

Miguel looked at him and handed him the shovel. He dismounted and turned the paint into the corral before going to the watering trough, where he carefully washed his hands and rinsed his knife. He looked closely at it before putting it back in the scabbard.

"It is done," he said. He turned and walked to the house.

Several days had passed. Lobo had found no opportunity to inspect the wagon. It seemed that someone was always loading or unloading it, or sleeping in it. He'd almost stumbled onto the stone house and the small farm with the group's wagon sitting near the barn. He'd quickly retreated and staked his horses two miles back. Then he walked to where he could watch them from the hills above the farm.

Lobo was patient, staying miles back during the day, and coming near at dusk; leaving again at dawn. He'd watched the boy dig up dead Indians and take scalps. He knew that one of the men was injured, that they had ponies taken from the Indians, and that a farmer was buried on the hill. The tall red-headed one acted like a scout, always watching, always armed, sometimes moving at night. These are strange people, he thought. Maybe even dangerous. I will be more careful than usual.

Chapter Twenty Two

NO RETURN

The next morning Roz pulled on his boots with his good arm. Then he walked out to Moose's bedroll. Moose propped himself on one elbow and told him what had happened when Miguel returned with the shovel.

"But he wouldn't talk about it?"

"No."

"Did he come from his Pa's grave?"

"No, from the other direction. Maybe from where we buried the Indians. Do you think we should go look?" Moose asked.

"Hell, Moose. What good would that do?"

"I think Manuela would want to know, except we don't know what to tell her. I guess we could tell her what we suspect."

"Which is what? That her thirteen-year-old son dug up some Indians and scalped 'em or cut 'em up or what?"

"Roz, think. Wouldn't you want to know if you had a kid that went somewhere in the middle of the night and came back with bloody hands?"

"Yeah, I guess."

"Well, I think we'd better tell her before we get started. I don't know what she can do about it, but that's her business."

"Think we could have breakfast first? I saw some biscuits, and Manuela is making chicken gravy."

"I suppose so. But," Moose leaned closer, "I'm going to tell you something and I don't want you to repeat it to anyone. Specially Manuela. Understand? Promise me."

"Good God, Moose. It must be mighty important. You never asked me to do a thing like that before. Not in the three or four years I've known you. So, what is it?"

"Five."

"Five what?"

"For crissake, Rozier. You've known me five years."

"Okay. Five. Now, what's so important that I'm not supposed to tell Manuela?"

"Shhh. It isn't Manuela, exactly. It's—well, I've always liked fried chicken, as I think you know. But I'm so sick of eating fried chicken I'm afraid I'll choke on the next bite."

"I'm about to lay eggs, myself. But I guess we can stand it one more time. This is the end of it, you know. We ain't taking the rest of them with us, thank God."

"Amen," Moose replied.

"However," Roz added, "you don't seem to be getting any smaller, so fried chicken don't seem to disagree with you."

"Small comfort."

"Anyway, let's go to the house. I want to watch you and see if you really do choke, which I doubt on account of you seem able to eat just about anything."

"You're just a fountain of compliments this morning, aren't you."

Roz opened, and then closed his mouth. Moose looked at him for a moment, then started toward the kitchen without saying more.

Miguel bolted his breakfast and went to his father's grave. Lilia excused herself and followed him. When the dishes had been cleaned and packed away, Moose asked Manuela if he could speak with her. He told her what he'd seen the night before.

"*Madre de Dios*," she said as she crossed herself.

"What do you want to do? Can we help in some way?"

"I don't know. I will talk with him, if I can. He is so much like his father. I mean, he will do a thing if his mind is made up. But that? *No comprendo*," and her eyes filled with tears.

"Do you want to talk with him alone, or would you like for me to be there?"

"I—I will go up to him." She turned and walked slowly up the hill as Lilia came down.

"That boy worries me," El said. "He don't act right, the way he moves around and doesn't say anythin'."

"Worries me, too," Henry replied, "to say nothing of his ma."

When Lilia came to them she was pale. She shaded her eyes with her hand. Her lips were a thin line. She looked at the western horizon as if to wish they were already gone.

"There are scalps on Papa's grave," she said. "Mama's crying, and Miguelito won't talk to her."

They packed before noon. Horses were saddled. Wagons were loaded and ready. There was nothing left to do. A warm breeze rustled the cottonwoods and brought the aroma of drying sage from the surrounding prairie as they slowly moved toward the top of the hill. Manuela looked back once. The house and corrals seemed empty to her, dead. Crows had already gathered in the cornfield as if they had been waiting for an invitation. She crossed herself as they passed the fresh grave with its sinister decoration. Her eyes filled as she walked away. She held her head high, clasped her arms together, and shivered.

El looked toward the west. High, marbled clouds seemed motionless. The mid-day sun was bright, but the breeze felt cool and refreshing. He took the point, ahead and to the right of the procession. Moose rode to the left, Roz to the right, closer to the wagon. Henry urged the oxen with gentle prods until they decided to follow. Then he brought up the rear.

All except Lilia, Miguel, and Manuela were armed. Ruby kept a hand-gun under the wagon seat. Moose had consented to carry a rifle in a saddle scabbard, although he hoped he wouldn't have to use it. Miguel and his knife rode wherever he was inclined to go. They warned him of the danger of straying too far from the main body. If he heard, he didn't acknowledge.

Lilia rode one of the Indian ponies. Like her brother, she rode well from the beginning. She'd picked out a dark bay with a long mane and a tail that brushed the ground. She named it Bluebell and, after daily rides while Roz was recovering his health, it did whatever she wanted it to do.

The horses from Mesa de Luna were filled out from the hay and grain they'd been fed at the farm. However, they hadn't been exercised much and were reluctant to go forward, except for El's buckskin which acted as if he'd been let out of jail.

The traveler's pace had been slow before they found the Romero family. It was even slower with oxen plodding along behind them. El looked back at the odd entourage and thought about the additional time required to get to Colorado. He'd have to pick their course carefully. It wouldn't do to get lost. They'd be lucky to beat the snow in any case.

Buster was tied to the end-gate of the buckboard where Roz could keep an eye on him. He walked peacefully for a while, watching Roz recline on his saddle in the back of the wagon. He snorted. Roz saw his ears go back as he flashed white around his eyes. He jerked his head up and snapped the tether. He whirled and ran past Henry, toward the corral and the hay he'd been enjoying. Henry chased him for nearly a mile, caught him, and brought him back.

"What can we tie him with?" he asked Roz.

"There's a braided lariat in the ox cart. He ain't gonna' break that, I reckon."

"What do you think spooked him?"

"Hell, Henry. He wasn't spooked. He's done that trick a thousand times. Used to jump clear out from under me. He thinks and thinks on it. Then he acts as if he's afraid of a little weed or a bird or something. I think I'll shoot him. Yes, sir, I think I just will."

Henry chuckled to himself as he tied Buster securely. He didn't believe Roz would trade the horse for any other, much less shoot him. "He is an ornery bastard, isn't he? I think maybe you *should* shoot him. Never does what you want."

"Want me to do it," Ruby said with a laugh. "I could use some practice."

Roz grinned and said, "You hear that, old Buster? These folks agree with me. One of us is likely to shoot you. What do you think?"

Buster wasn't paying attention. He was busy chewing on the braided rope.

Lobo watched as the travelers started north-west. Now, he thought, I know where they will go, to Fort Union, Raton Pass and probably Colorado.

They are slow. I can cut them off at Raton. First, I'll go down and see if they left anything I can use. There are chickens in the corral. They may have left something in the garden. Maybe food for the horses. Then a good meal and a bed. There is plenty of time.

Chapter Twenty Three

THE QUESTION

"I don't think we'll make it to Fort Union today," El said. "It's up in those foothills."

Henry and Pablo squinted to see where El was looking. A dark line of blue-gray showed above the rolling, olive-green prairie. Beyond the line, mountain peaks were capped with faint bluish-white snow which had been clearer in the morning sun. The snow seemed to disappear in afternoon shadows.

"Wish we were in the mountains," Henry replied.

"Might not be too comfortable. Y'see the lightning under them clouds up north? It'll probably bring more snow in the high country, "El said. "I think we waited too long. Fall's almost here."

“Guess so,” Henry said. “We don’t have time to spare, anyhow. We need to be gettin’ on to Pueblo and Denver. Startin’ to look like we might have to winter in Denver or Cheyenne or someplace thereabouts.”

El couldn’t think of anything he’d rather not do than spend an entire winter in a city, or even a town.

“We’ll have to see,” he replied. “I’d best get back up on point. Just came back to see how you’re doin’.”

“You going to pick a stopping place?” Henry asked.

“Unless you want to.”

“No. I was just wondering’.”

Let’s go to the top of that second hill. That’s about an hour, I reckon. No need to hurry. We should be at Fort Union tomorrow afternoon.”

“Sounds good to me,” Henry replied. Roz nodded.

After the evening meal Moose and Roz walked away from the fire and stood near the horses, listening to the wind. They heard notes from El’s harmonica, distant and sad. Miguel was gone, roaming the night as he had done at home.

Moose watched the flickering pinpoint of light from the campfire. When one of the women moved in front of it, it seemed to go out for a moment, then reappear.

"I guess Fort Union's just a few miles away," Moose said. "El says we'll be there sometime tomorrow."

"Well, I'd like to see the place. But I don't want to run into that Armstrong fellow."

"Maybe he'll be out on patrol."

"It'd be my luck that he's been promoted and don't even go on patrol."

"Now, Roz, that's just asking for trouble. Besides, he's probably forgotten about you."

"Maybe. But I doubt if he'd forget about twenty dollars."

"Twenty dollars! You never told me you took twenty dollars."

"Well, Moose, I won most of it. Fair and square. I didn't know it was that much 'til the next day. Some of those bills were stuck together."

"With what? Your right and left hand?"

"No. With Armstrong's drink. That he spilled on the table. When his chair tipped over."

"Uh-huh. Just tipped right over, didn't it. Those chairs were mighty unstable. Especially when you started losing pots, the way I heard it."

"I can't help what people say."

"I hope he doesn't want to put you in the stockade."

"He can't do that, can he?"

"I don't know what he can do. This is still Federal territory. It isn't like it was a state yet."

"I'll be glad when it is," Roz replied. They were quiet for a few minutes. "I want to ask you something'."

"What's that?"

"I wonder if you think Lilia and Manuela are comforted by their praying and crossing and the like?"

"I don't really know. I hope so. Why?"

"I was thinking that people of a certain religion like to stick together. Seems they can understand each other better. And maybe they don't want to—to mix with people of other religions."

"That may be, but I don't get what you're driving at."

"Well. I was just thinking that it might be hard to be with somebody that don't believe what you believe. Long-term, I mean."

"For crissake, Rozier. If you got something to say, just say it?"

"All right. Now just suppose, for the sake of argument, that you and Manuela got sweet on each other. But you believed one thing and she believed another. Why, I wonder…"

"Roz, you aren't going to get me wrapped up in your own question. Are you trying to figure out if your not going to church would be a problem if you and Lilia…?"

"Something like that, I guess."

"Has she given you any reason to think she might be serious about you?"

"No, but…"

"Well, I don't see the problem."

"I don't want there to *be* a problem. I was just trying to think ahead. You know, in case something did happen. Now—or later. What would I do?"

Moose shook his head. "Are you afraid she wouldn't like how you think? Or are you afraid you couldn't live with what she believes?"

"Never thought of it that way."

"Well?"

"Uh, I'm going to try to say a thing that isn't easy to say." He scraped the toe of his boot over a clump of grass. "You know how I like animals and plants and pretty sights."

“Yes,” Moose said, wondering where the conversation was going.

“Well, I do. And I think that’s what we’re all made of. I mean, we’re made of what we eat. And breathe. We grow from nothing except what we eat and drink and what our mothers ate. Don’t you think?”

Moose just looked at him.

“And when we die, we become part of the soil and the dust. And plants grow. And cows or goats or whatever eats ‘em. People eat the cows, and around we go again. Isn’t that so?”

Moose, who was raised in a Catholic home, in a predominantly Catholic neighborhood, was growing uncomfortable even though he hadn’t been inside a church since he was a child.

“So, what are you driving at?”

“I’m pretty happy, just being a part of that circle, Moose. I don’t want to go into a church and start singing and kneeling and—and doing all the things they do. I don’t feel a need to. Do you know what I mean?”

“I don’t know if they need to, either. They may just like it.”

“No, Moose, if you get to doing a thing it becomes a habit. Pretty soon you *need* to. I don’t want to be like that.”

“You want to stay out of churches?”

“That’s right.”

"Are you saying you *need* to stay out of churches?"

"Well, maybe I do. I don't know. But I don't want to spend my time there."

Both thought for a few minutes. Moose said, "I don't feel the same way you do about religion. But I respect your right to believe what you believe. I even admire that you figured out what you think."

"Don't you know what you believe?" Roz asked.

"Not entirely. But I'm comfortable with that, at least most of the time. Oh, sometimes when I see someone die and I don't think he believed in a kind of heaven, it makes me a little sad. Like that Indian I shot. I doubt if he was religious, and I don't know what's in store for him. But mostly I'm happy not knowing the answers, not thinking a lot about it."

"Hmm," Roz said.

"I guess I'm not satisfied with being in line to become a rock, a toad, or a daisy, Roz. But I can accept you for your beliefs and respect the fact that you've got some."

"Well, maybe she could, too," Roz said quietly.

"Question is, could you accept hers?"

"I don't know. I think so." Roz was quiet, but he studied his boots in a way Moose had learned meant he wasn't through talking about something.

"Do you think their praying helps 'em get through losing a mate? And a father?"

"You'd have to ask them, Roz."

"I'm afraid they wouldn't understand why I wanted to know."

"Why do you?"

"Well," Roz sighed, "It's on account of my father. My mother was a good woman, Moose. She died when I was five years old. My pa about went crazy. He wouldn't talk to me or anybody. He didn't eat much and didn't clean himself up. After a few months he left.

"I've promised myself I'll never be that way, no matter what. I'll never let losing someone hurt me that much."

"What happened to him?"

"I don't know. He never came back I waited and I hoped, but he never did. My aunts raised me. My mother's sisters."

"You never told me any of this. I mean, you didn't have to, of course, but . . ."

"I don't like to talk about it much. But lately I've been wondering if my Pa had religion, would it have helped him get through? Would he have stayed with—me?"

"I think I see."

"See what?"

"You missed him." Roz nodded. "And you probably believe as your pa did. I mean, that you don't need church or a minister's help. Is that right?"

"Maybe, far as I know."

"And you don't mean to suffer the way he did."

"No. Not if I can help it."

"Let's assume for a minute that religion does help. But you don't hold with it."

"All right."

"But you fall in love with a good woman, who could die and leave you. Are you following me?"

"Uh-huh."

"Well?"

"I guess I'd have two choices. Get married and get religion. Or stay like I am, avoiding both. Like I've been doing."

"I think there's a middle road, Roz. Love somebody and risk being alone if something happens to them. Really alone. I think the question's deeper than can you accept her with her church-going ways? It's more like, what are you going to need for yourself? So you won't be too afraid to take a chance."

"Thank you. I believe that helps."

"You're welcome. I'd be glad to talk about it anytime."

Roz extended his uninjured hand and put it on Moose's shoulder.

"I figured you would." He turned and walked toward the fire.

Chapter Twenty Four

LATE SUMMER STORM

They awoke to a cold wind that swept clouds down from the mountains. Early sun touched the cover of the buckboard, but brought no warmth. The wind lifted and snapped the canvas corners until Henry tied them more securely.

As the clouds raced above, the distant mountains vanished. A gray curtain seemed to fall in front of the dark line of hills they were trying to reach in order to find Fort Union. Closer hills became blurred outlines. The weak sun was obscured. All color seemed to drain from the landscape.

The wind increased. El pulled hobbles from the wagon, motioned to the others with one hand as he held his hat with the other, and hurried toward the buckskin.

Dust and tumbleweeds rolled toward them. A flock of small brown birds rushed by. Lightning began to strike the ground. At first it was several miles away, but it marched across the dusty hills like a demented giant. Thunder grew louder and was almost continuous.

Manuela and Lilia took cover in the buckboard with Ruby and Roz. Henry and El crawled under the wagon and braced their slicker-covered backs against the upwind wheels.

Moose helped Miguel turn the oxen so that they faced away from the storm. The cart stopped some of the wind. They crouched between the cart and the oxen.

The horses milled nervously, hopping with front legs tied together, trying to place others between them and the approaching lightning. Moose's big bay bit and kicked until they were arranged in the order he wanted. El's buckskin stood apart, nostrils flared, looking into the wind. The bay paid no attention to him, as if they had an agreement.

The buckskin whirled when a lightning strike scattered dust only fifty yards from the encampment. There was an immediate, deafening crash. Horses and people alike, ducked as if to avoid its power.

Moose held Miguel's arm, although Miguel didn't give indication of wanting to leave their scant shelter.

A fierce gust pulled the windward side of the canvas loose from its ties, and it cracked like rifle shots until the buckboard's inhabitants wrestled it under control.

Lilia's pony, Bluebell, snorted as another flash of lightning struck closer. When the thunder clap shook the ground it jumped and began to run as well as it could on hobbled legs. A bolt of lightning connected the little horse to the clouds and, for a heartbeat, outlined it in silver. It pitched to the ground and lay still.

Large drops of rain rattled on the canvas, then hail. The sound increased to a roar, as a rush of rain covered them. Ruby had the sensation that they were in a boat moving under a waterfall.

Roz shivered and felt guilty about being inside the wagon while Moose, El, Henry, and Miguel were outside. His arm hurt and his teeth chattered while he tried to remember the last time he'd heard hail. It had been an afternoon when he, Moose, and Pit Gardner were talking inside the stage station in Mesa de Luna.

Over the years they'd lived there Roz had flattened tin cans with a hammer and used them as shingles to fix holes in the roof. He'd done it so many times that the roof was about half covered with cans of various sizes. On the rare occasions when it rained or hailed it was somewhat musical.

Pit had been about to leave when a quick summer hailstorm blew in. There was a thud when the first hail stone hit wood. The next one rang on a tin can. That set the pigeons to cooing and warbling. Hail fell with increasing frequency. It sounded like wooden drums under a several-octave scale of tin-can musical notes with sharps, flats, and warbled quarter-notes in between.

Pit had looked upward, almost reverently, with his mouth open. He began to smile and tap his foot. When the din quieted, he said, "Sounds just like a calliope I heard in a circus. Maybe better. That circus fella' couldn't play very well." Roz realized he missed Gardner's sense of humor. Then he thought of the men outside and felt guilty all over again.

Ruby glanced at Roz, Lilia, and Manuela as flashes of lightning continued to illuminate their canvas cave, but the bolts and thunder moved away to the east. Although thunder wasn't as loud as it had been, rain continued until it ran into the wagon and through the floor, soaking El and Henry below. The canvas couldn't shed all of the deluge. Drops collected on the underside and fell. Rivulets trickled on the inside of the cloth and then dropped into their hair and clothing. When all were thoroughly wet the cover served only to break the wind's force.

The cold downpour turned into a shower of rattling sleet, then back to rain. The wind died, the rain diminished and stopped, and the only sound was drops of water from the wagon-bed, falling into the puddles below. Bits of sleet floated in the puddles and lay in small piles against clumps of grass.

Moose and Miguel eased themselves up, shivering and blinking. Roz, Ruby and the others threw back the cover as Henry and El crawled stiffly from under the buckboard. They stared at the receding black wall spiked with lightning, moving to the east.

Manuela saw Bluebell and caught her breath as she shot a look at her daughter. Lilia noticed and followed her mother's gaze to where the little horse lay steaming in a sudden shaft of sunlight. She shook her head, but didn't cry. Her tears had been spent for a greater loss.

The mountains loomed, bright and sharp. New snow covered their peaks and flanks. They seemed closer, taller, in the crystal air.

The drenched travelers moved toward their horses, toward the dead pony, toward each other. It seemed they made no sound on the soaked soil, that the power of the storm had rendered them deaf and mute.

Intermittent sun scattered the remaining cloud tatters, and a breeze brought the smell of fresh-washed sage. The sleet melted. Grass blades shook off their load of drops. A meadowlark's song floated across the prairie, high, sweet, and clear.

Chapter Twenty Five

JOHN WESLEY HARDIN

Henry split some of the kindling they carried in a corner of the buckboard. It had become wet, but after splitting he was able to pare dry shavings from the core. He opened an oilskin pouch and removed a match stick. Then he rubbed a small, rough stone with his hand until it was dry. He kneeled and struck the match against it, but the head had already absorbed moisture from the air. He removed another match from the small store remaining, struck it, and it flared. He shielded it with his hat and carefully placed it on the rock. He fed shavings to the tiny flame until it was large enough to ignite the split kindling, which snapped and popped. Soon there was fire to heat the coffee pot.

"Now we can burn wet wood," he told the others as they stood watching him. "Long as we don't put too much on at one time."

El's buckskin nickered abruptly. They turned to see a rider coming from the south. As the horseman grew closer they saw that he rode a spirited black horse with four white stocking legs. The rider was wet in spite of a rain slicker, but sat tall and alert. He wore a dark wool coat and vest over striped trousers. His dripping hat was gray, dented on top and turned up on the sides in cowman style.

His coat tail was pushed back and revealed a blue-steel Colt Peacemaker in a tooled holster that matched his belt. The bottom of the holster was tied to his thigh with a leather thong. A loop of leather served to secure the revolver's hammer. The loop had been released.

El knew most riders left their weapons in their saddlebags unless they expected trouble, which didn't seem likely in a rainstorm. He shaded his eyes for a closer look at the man's face.

"Mornin'," the rider said quietly as he reined to a stop. He sat in such a way that the side arm was in plain view. "Mornin', ladies," he said to Ruby, Manuela, and Lilia, with a touch to his hat brim. His beard was neatly trimmed, and his dark eyes and smooth features caused the women to look at him in a way that made Roz straighten his collar and check his fingernails.

"Mind if I join you?"

He waited until Henry said, "Why, sure. We're about to make coffee. Come on over to the fire. Miguel, take the gentleman's horse."

"No. I'll hold him. I'd admire some coffee, however. Where you folks going?" He spoke in a soft drawl that suggested south Texas.

"Heading for Fort Union," Roz answered. "I'm Roz Wells," as he walked toward the rider, who hadn't dismounted. "Who might you be?" Roz asked as he extended his hand.

The black horse had backed away so Roz couldn't come close enough to shake hands. The rider didn't extend his, nor did he change expression when he replied, "I'm just a fellow who's been on the trail too long. I'm headed for the fort. Maybe I'll ride with you a ways."

"You can," Roz said, dropping his hand. "Do you want to come over by the fire?"

"I'll stay here." He swung his leg over the saddle horn and carefully slid down. "That way the horse won't get nervous." He looked around the horizon, dropped the reins and stepped on them. His horse began to crop the wet buffalo grass.

"Been to Fort Union before?"" he asked, staying back where he could see all of them at one time.

"I have," El replied. "How about you?"

"Once or twice. Where you bound?" He apparently knew they weren't staying at the fort for long. Civilians rarely did.

Moose peered more closely at him and then met El's eyes for a long moment. El nodded slightly, but the small movement didn't go unnoticed by the horseman. Moose replied, "Denver. Then we'll see."

"Never been there," the rider said.

"Where are you from?" Henry asked. When he didn't get an answer, he turned to El and shrugged.

"It don't matter," El replied.

"But…" Henry began.

"Henry!" El said, "If the coffee's ready, maybe we could offer some to this gent."

Henry had started to lean back and puff up like an angry cat, but El's tone made him thoughtful. He exhaled and turned to the pot.

"It'll be ready in a minute."

There was silence while the rider looked at them and at their makeshift camp. He glanced back the way he'd come.

When Henry brought a steaming mug of coffee, he said, "Thank you," in a sincere manner. He took it with his left hand, lifted the mug to them, and sipped without taking his eyes from them.

"Best to come in from the east or north," he said. "The commandant likes to fire the cannon about mid-day, and he always shoots toward that hogback. Happy Valley." He inclined his head toward the rocky ridge they'd been watching since it had come into view the day before.

"Do you know his name?" Roz asked.

"Armstrong, last I heard. Captain Armstrong, I think."

The stranger finished his coffee and put the mug on the ground. "That was good," he said. "I appreciate it." He mounted carefully, backed the horse a few more steps, touched his hat brim to the ladies, and rode around their camp before continuing in the general direction of the fort.

"Who the hell was that?" Henry asked when the rider was out of hearing range.

"John Wesley Hardin, I believe," Moose said as he released the breath he'd been holding.

"It sure was," El agreed. "I saw him in Julesburg. It was, I guess, three years ago."

"I'll be damned," Henry said, turning to El, "That's why you like to bit my head off."

"Better'n gettin' it shot off. He's killed more'n thirty men. Some say forty or more. Shot one fellow for snoring in the room next to him. Never laid eyes on him. Just shot him through the wall. He's crazy, they say, and you can't tell what he's going to do."

“He had mean eyes,” Roz said, “Or maybe dead eyes. I never saw him blink.”

“He said he might ride with us,” Henry said. “I’m glad he didn’t.”

“I believe he knew we recognized him, and he can’t afford to take chances,” Moose said. “There’s a sizeable reward on his head. Probably up to several thousand by now.”

“That’s why he can’t relax.” Roz said. “That’s a hell of a way to live.” Roz thought how it would feel to never be able to turn his back, never let down his guard. “How could you be happy like that?” he asked. There was no answer.

As the small procession started toward the fort, Moose noticed the downpour had already run off the hills and soaked into the sandy soil. “What’s that business about ridin’ in from the north? About Happy Valley, I believe is what he said.”

“I know what he was talkin’ about,” El replied. “It’s on account of the Army only lets married women or officer’s daughters stay on fort grounds. And liquor’s outlawed, although troopers sneak in a little. They ain’t supposed to get drunk on post, though. So they go to Happy Valley. It’s on the other side of that rocky ridge.

"When I was here last time, there was a regular' parade of off-duty bluecoats goin' back and forth. I guess the boss, Armstrong he said, don't like it. He has to shoot the cannon for trainin' anyway. Might as well shoot in that direction. Keeps the wh—, the camp-followers on the other side of the ridge and makes the fellers go the long way around."

"Sounds like he might be a hard man to get along with," Henry said.

"He is that," Roz stated with a glance at Moose, who didn't comment.

"Do you know this Captain Armstrong?" Lilia asked.

"We met. Did a little commerce. It was Lieutenant Armstrong when I met him. I didn't like him."

"Oh," Lilia replied without asking for details.

"Best to stay away from him," Ruby Lee said. She knew the whole story about the poker game and the upset chair.

Manuela looked from one to the other of them. It often happened that she didn't know what they were talking about. She decided to keep quiet. If they wanted her to know, they'd tell her, and there was a good chance Henry would tell her later. He always tried to see that she was included.

The first they saw of the fort was the flag, snapping in the wind atop a very tall pole. As they came over the hill more of the fort became visible. It was composed of two rows of buildings facing each other across a broad, bare earth parade ground. There were about twenty buildings, ten on a side. Two of them seemed to be large, two-story residences in the approximate middle of the two rows, opposite each other. The other buildings were one-story high and nearly identical in size. The first impression was of order and symmetry.

Large corrals held mules and horses at the end of the rows of buildings. A smaller corral kept a herd of cattle. The corrals served to close the far end of the quadrangle.

There was no stockade around the buildings, but a row of cannon crossed the nearer, open end, and more cannon could be seen strategically placed at the corners by the corrals. A watch tower in the center of the parade ground afforded a view in all directions. Figures moved in shadow beneath the roof of the tower, and one came down a long ladder and marched to one of the buildings that looked like a large home.

"We're bein' announced," El said.

They watched a group of six men march to one of the cannons at the entrance to the post. They swabbed, charged, and loaded the cannon with movements suggesting long practice. They formed rank as the gun captain touched a smoldering stick to the primer hole. The cannon bucked and roared. A cloud of blue-white smoke drifted from the muzzle and, nearly a half-mile away, the ball sent up a plume of dust where it hit the rocky ridge.

"Bet they heard *that* in Happy Valley," Roz said.

"Bet they was happier before Armstrong started shootin' at 'em," Henry added.

"Can we go there? To see Happy Valley?" Lilia asked.

"No!" The men said almost simultaneously.

"It ain't no place for a lady," El added while looking at the ground. Manuela said several sentences in rapid Spanish, and Lilia's expression changed from interest to surprise and a mixture of disappointment and pity.

"Happy Valley isn't a very good name," she said.

"That's a fact," El responded. "It sure enough isn't."

Chapter Twenty Six

FORT UNION

The fort spread over the landscape, unrestricted by natural features on the treeless plain. It resembled a small, neat town more than the typical military fort with stockades. Uniformed figures moved about purposefully. A train of three large freight wagons, each pulled by four teams of mules, slowly approached the far end of the complex.

Moose and Roz walked their horses forward to meet a young officer who came out of one of the two-story structures facing the parade ground. Miguel waited on his pony a few paces to the side of the others. Henry and El dismounted and stood talking with the women seated on the buckboard. The oxen and cart waited behind them.

"Lieutenant Stern," the uniformed figure said with a smart salute. "Good afternoon and welcome to Fort Union. The colonel sends his compliments. Sirs."

"Good afternoon to you, too," Roz responded with a smile and the beginning of a salute, which he thought better of and turned into a brief wave.

"And our compliments to your commanding officer," Moose added as he and Roz stepped down.

"Might that be Captain James J. Armstrong?" Roz asked.

"Indeed it is, gentlemen, except he's Colonel Armstrong now. He's our new commandant. As of April this year." The lieutenant shaded his eyes. "Might I have your names?"

"Of course, my apologies" Moose replied, before introducing Roz and himself.

The lieutenant gave a brief, knowing nod as he looked at the buckboard, the ox cart, and the tired horses. "I see you have womenfolk in your party."

"Yes," Moose replied. "There are three ladies traveling with us."

"Gentlemen, Mrs. Armstrong has a standing policy. Any escorted ladies visiting the fort are invited to bathe and rest and then have tea. That is, ladies traveling from a distance. What I mean is, uh…"

"We understand," Moose interjected. "We've all come a long way." It was clear that the residents of Happy Valley would not have received the same accommodation.

"Also, I'm to inform you the colonel would enjoy your company at dinner, after which he'll make the fort's amenities available to you. Such as they are."

"Please tell Mrs. Armstrong we will let the ladies know of her invitation straight away," Moose replied. "I'm sure they'll be glad to hear it, and will be along whenever it is convenient for Mrs. Armstrong to receive them. And please tell the colonel we will be delighted to accept his dinner invitation." Roz was silent, but he gave Moose a pained glance.

"It will be my pleasure," the lieutenant said. "The invitation includes the ladies, of course. They may use the visiting officer's quarters to freshen up. It's right over there. I'll see that hot water is brought around directly. You men are welcome to the bath house. It's the last building in this row, where you see the water tank. It shouldn't be too busy this time of day."

Moose cleared his throat and said, "I should tell you that two of the ladies, Mrs. Romero and her daughter, Lilia, lost their husband and father a short time ago. I believe they will want to come to dinner. "However, the boy, Miguel," Moose pointed to Miguel, who rested his horse apart from the group by the wagon and cart, "would probably rather explore the fort, if that is permissible."

"Certainly. He's free to look around as long as he stays near the buildings. I advise that he stays close to the compound, however. There are elements near every fort he is better off avoiding. By the way, I see three women. Is the third one, the one with red hair, married to one of you gentlemen?"

"No," Moose replied. "She's traveling with us. She had a business in Mesa de Luna but decided to close it and come with our party."

"You know. Safety in numbers," Roz added.

"I understand. I've heard that down where you're from there's good transportation east and west but not north and south. That will change. There will be a major effort to put the Indians on the reservation, where they belong. Next spring, that is. It's too late in the year to start a campaign now.

"There is a lad about the age of your boy, Miguel. I'll ask if he'll show him around. I suggest you take your animals to the corral on the right." He indicated an enclosure at the far end of the parade ground. "They'll be fed and watered and looked after. Ask for the smith if you need any shoeing."

Stern waved toward a one-story building near the entrance. "That's our post store. Supplies are somewhat limited, but you're welcome to see if we have anything you need. You can purchase from the sutler if you do. The colonel and his officers will be happy to give you travel information, directions, Indian activity, and the like. Can you join the colonel and Mrs. Armstrong around five o'clock?" He pulled a pocket watch from his tunic, flipped open the cover, and said, "I make it nearly two-thirty now," and looked at them for agreement as to the approximate time.

"Five o'clock is fine," said Moose, while checking and adjusting his own watch. "Please convey our gratitude for the colonel's kindness and for Mrs. Armstrong's thoughtfulness. It will certainly be our pleasure. Oh, and thank you for your help. We appreciate it."

"That we do," Roz added. He smiled and touched his hat with two fingers.

After the lieutenant had saluted, turned on his heel, and walked away, Roz said, "It sure ain't going to be *my* pleasure, though I don't seem to have much choice in the matter."

"I don't believe we can slight the colonel's invitation," Moose replied.

"And I don't intend to. I just wish I didn't have to go, is all. I'd almost pay back the twenty bucks to get out of it."

"A little late for that, don't you think?"

"Maybe. But I don't want to talk about it. Not yet, anyway."

"Welcome, gentlemen. I'm Colonel James J. Armstrong, at your service." He was of medium height, slim, and intense. He had dark hair, a neatly trimmed mustache, and piercing brown eyes that didn't seem to change as he smiled. After peering at Roz for a moment, he continued. "It's always good to meet people traveling this way, but a particular pleasure to renew old acquaintances."

Roz had hoped the colonel wouldn't recognize him. When it was clear that he did, Roz felt it was up to him to say something since he was the only one in their party the colonel knew.

"Why, we're pleased to be here," he said, "And I'd like to present Moose, uh, Morris Banner and Elwood Renfroe, and this here's Henry Atwater."

Armstrong's eyebrows went up when Roz said, "Elwood Renfroe," but he shook hands with each of them as if they were all dignitaries.

"Please, please, be seated," he said, pointing to chairs that were gathered around an oak table holding glasses, two decanters, and a large, oriental cigar humidor.

"I'm happy to make your acquaintance, as is Major Charles Reinholt." He indicated a short, heavily built officer with thinning, blond hair. "And Lieutenant Riley Stern," a tall, olive-skinned officer who didn't look as if he was old enough to vote or buy whiskey, not to mention lead men to fight Indians.

"Major Reinholt and I were together at Appomattox, and Lieutenant Stern joined us directly from West Point." As the major and lieutenant stepped forward and shook hands, Armstrong continued, "Our other officers are out on patrol. They'll be sorry they didn't see you. We don't always have as much time as we'd like to meet people like yourselves, but Mrs. Armstrong insists on entertaining parties traveling with ladies, and who am I to disagree?" He smiled. "It does make being here more pleasant."

He looked closely at Roz and then nodded and leaned back. "Before we have a cheroot and a glass of cordial," the colonel said as he turned to Roz, "I want to say it's good to see you again."

"And you, sir," Roz replied. "I've been hoping we'd run into you." The officer looked surprised. "As I believe I have something that belongs to you." The words seemed to come out by themselves. Roz hadn't planned to say anything in particular.

"Do you, indeed?" Armstrong replied thoughtfully. "Might it have anything to do with the card game we enjoyed?" he asked, with what appeared to be a genuine smile.

"It does. It surely does," Roz said, surprised by the colonel's friendly manner. "You left some money. And I'd hoped to be able to return it to you," he said with a smile at least as wide as the officer's.

"I see. I took you for a gentleman the first time we met," Colonel Armstrong said warmly. "And, as to money I may have left behind, you are all the more a gentleman for seeking me out. It couldn't have been a great deal, but you've gone to a great deal of trouble to return it."

"Not at all," Roz replied. "In matterrs of principle, specific amounts must be secondary to doing what's right. Wouldn't you agree, sir?" Roz's smile was beginning to hurt his cheeks.

"I'd agree that a trifling amount is nothing to be upset…" he looked into Roz's eyes, "…about. But a man wouldn't have a leg to stand on if he didn't try to do the right thing. Isn't that right, Mister Wells?"

Moose noticed Lieutenant Stern staring at Armstrong and Roz with curiosity. He concluded the young man had no idea what they were talking about, although his close attention suggested he knew their words meant more than was immediately evident.

Major Reinholt, on the other hand, wore a broad grin. Moose was sure Armstrong had thought the incident important enough to have related the story to him. He hadn't known Roz at first sight and must not have been in the game, but he realized who Roz was now, and he was enjoying the exchange.

"May I pour a libation for one who has come so far to return something to me?" Armstrong asked, bowing to Roz.

"I'd be genuinely honored," Roz replied, bowing even lower, as if he came in contact with cultured individuals every day. As he bowed, he wondered how to end the conversation. He'd started it, more or less, but he had no idea how to finish.

El looked from one to the other with a puzzled expression while Henry merely stood in one place with his mouth open. When Major Reinholt poured another glass and handed it to him, El said, "What? Oh. Thank you, sir," with a worried look.

"Please, gentlemen, be seated," Colonel Armstrong repeated as he lowered himself into a chair by the window. "Major, lieutenant, feel free to get chairs from the…" and he waved his hand toward the other rooms, "…wherever you can find them."

"Forgive me," the colonel said to El, Moose, and Henry. "I just think it's so unusual for a gentleman like Mister Wells to offer to return money he thinks I lost."

"It damned sure is," Henry replied.

"You have no idea," Moose said, and then quickly added, "how many times he's done that sort of thing."

Colonel Armstrong leaned back, smiled, and took a small sip of brandy. "Now," he said, "I assume you are the famous El Renfroe that my fellow officers talk about. They say you killed a savage a half-mile away with a rifle. Is that right?"

"Well, it's a Sharps buffalo gun, sir, if you see what I mean. An' I don't know how far it was that I shot, but it carries out a good piece, I will say."

"Had you heard that President Grant recently vetoed a bill to protect the bison? Guess you'll have to use that gun to wipe out Indians," the colonel said with a significant look at the other men.

"It appears President Grant just done that for us, didn't he?" El said.

"Sir?" Colonel Armstrong replied.

"The buffalo. If they ain't protected, they won't last five years. Maybe less. They'll disappear, and the Indians right behind 'em," El said.

"I thought you were an Indian fighter. You don't talk like one."

"I never shot an Indian I didn't have to shoot," El said.

"Neither have I," the colonel replied, "but I heard you were with my good friend, Captain Burt Wright, on the Big Muddy, and that you shot Bear

Stalking when he was almost too far away to see. You must have had a reason that day."

"We was trapped, and he was goin' for help. We'd a been wiped out. I was just tryin' to keep my hair."

"You're much too modest. Just like Mister Wells, who wants to repay me."

Roz was wondering what he had committed himself to do, how much he was going to have to offer to pay, while at the same time trying to maintain an interested appearance.

He heard Colonel Armstrong say, "But let's not talk about that right now. Mister Wells and I can settle the matter later. If that's satisfactory to you, Mister Wells?"

"It is, but please, call me Roz. I may not remember who you're addressing if you keep calling me Mister Wells."

Henry visibly relaxed when Roz reverted to his normal style of speaking, but Roz was even more worried than he had been. He didn't like the colonel's choice of words; "settle the Matter" and "satisfactory" sounded too much like words Roz had heard in connection with arrangements to duel. He began to wonder if the commander of an Army post was allowed to challenge someone to a duel. He guessed they weren't supposed to kill citizens they were charged with the responsibility of protecting, but he wasn't sure when a matter of honor was involved.

"As you wish. Roz." His smile grew even larger for a moment before he turned to the others and began to discuss where they had lived, where they were going, and why.

Moose led the explanation of finding the Romero family under siege only a two-day ride from the fort. They also discussed the Indian attack at the Mora River. Colonel Armstrong didn't think Mad Water was involved in either affair, as he'd recently been seen in Oklahoma.

Moose asked if John Wesley Hardin had appeared at the fort.

"Not here," The colonel said. "They tell me he goes to Happy Valley now and then, but he can only stay a day or two. Bounty hunters follow wherever he goes. Doubt if he lives long." They talked about the locusts, the dwindling buffalo herds, and other experiences since leaving Mesa de Luna. They skipped over Miguel's excavation of the dead Comanches.

Colonel Armstrong told them about some of the fort's history. It had been founded in the early 1850s at the western junction of the Mountain and Cimarron legs of the Santa Fe Trail. The mountain branch—which they planned to follow—led almost due north to Raton Pass and into Colorado Territory. The eastern route let to Fort Dodge, Kansas. Fort Union had served both as protection for the Santa Fe Trail and as a supply depot for other forts and military camps in the Southwest. In the early 1860s Kit Carson had mounted an expedition from Fort Union that pursued the Kiowa and Comanche Indians into what is now the Oklahoma Panhandle, and defeated them at the battle of Adobe Walls.

Later, during the Civil War, a Confederate Army brigade marched from Texas up the Rio Grande Valley. They captured Albuquerque and Santa Fe and prepared to continue north to rout the small, Civil War–depleted Fort Union garrison. Afterward, they'd planned to seize the gold fields and rich mining towns of Colorado. The South needed money to buy war materials: southern states didn't have the industrial capacity of the North. European nations would have supplied arms and other materials to the south, but insisted on being paid in gold. The Confederate dollar had depreciated to the point that it was almost worthless. Fort Union had sent a request for help to the Colorado Volunteer Army and hoped they could hurry to reinforce the Fort Union regulars.

The much smaller force of Fort Union soldiers, supported by New Mexico Territory volunteers, anxiously waited for the Confederate brigade at Glorietta Pass, about sixty-five miles west of Fort Union. They knew the superior numbers of Confederate soldiers would crush them if the Colorado volunteers, led by Major John Chivington, did not get there before the Confederates arrived at the pass.

Chivington's group of six hundred traveled an average of forty miles per day in January ice and snow. They arrived just as the Confederates prepared to attack. Chivington led the first charge, pistol in hand. A pitched battle raged in the canyon. Union forces circled back and destroyed the Confederate wagons, mules, and horses. The tide of battle turned; the larger Confederate force was defeated, and then learned they could not retreat except on foot. Their supplies and mounts were gone, and they were seven hundred miles from Texas over some of the worst desert terrain in the western territories.

Of the thirty-five hundred confederates who had started the mid-winter walk, nearly half died en route. Their dream of western conquest ended at the battle of Glorietta Pass and the horror of the march homeward.

The colonel was careful to assign no blame or credit to either faction. He sighed and said, "This place has seen some interesting history, but it will all be over soon. We hear the Denver and Rio Grande Railroad will build a line through here within two years. When they do, the fort's purpose will be at an end. Perhaps it's just as well.

"We should go in," the colonel said, "but first there is one more matter I'd like to mention." He looked at Moose and Roz. Both were quiet. "Three men came in a week ago, deputies from Albuquerque. They said they were looking for stage robbers, for you as a matter of fact; Banner, Wells, and a Mr. Borrega. I didn't believe them then, and I sure as hell don't now."

"Pablo Borrega died on the trip," Moose said, and described how Pablo had tried to help save the wagon. "He was a good young man," Moose said.

"Which way did they go?" El asked. "The three."

"Hard to say," the colonel replied. "Might have been any direction. Did you notice?" he asked the other officers.

"North, I think," Lieutenant Stern replied. "I watched them leave the gate, but I didn't take further interest. Sorry."

"I know Alcalde Juan Diego," the colonel said, "and I wouldn't trust him as far as I can spit. He's probably already spent the silver he says he's so worried about. You need to be careful. Juan Diego's deputies, if that's what they are, look more like cut-throat bandits. Keep your eyes open. Now, let us enjoy better topics." The colonel stood up. "Shall we join the ladies?"

While the others filed toward the women in the sitting room, Moose held back and quietly asked Major Reinholt if he'd heard of an officer named Parker DuPree.

"No," Reinholt said, "I don't know the name. Should I ask around?"

"No, no," Moose replied. "I was just wondering. It isn't important."

Juan Diego was genuinely worried, but not about spending silver. Carlos Mejia had just run in bowing, dropping his new hat, and stammering. "*T-the gobernador, es aqui—here,*" while pointing a shaking hand toward the courtyard where Juan Diego could hear the jingling of harness.

Already! Juan Diego thought. *Has he no patience? Is he concerned about the promised silver? Or is it something else?* Juan Diego began to sweat. He turned to Rosalinda who reclined on the horsehair settee, fanning herself.

"Upstairs," he said. "Hurry. Put something on."

"I have something on," she said with a pout.

"Get a shawl. And shoes. Hurry!" She languidly got up, stretched, and walked up the stairs, throwing him a smoldering look over her shoulder. His pulse quickened. What a woman, he thought. The door opened. Carlos Antonio Arajo de Chama y Las Animas swept in, followed by two aides. The governor was tall and slim. His full head of wavy white hair contrasted with his dark, well-shaped beard and his black eyes. His skin was light, suggesting more Castilian blood than Juan Diego could claim. "*Hola, Mi Amigo*," he said in a warm, rich voice. "How good to see you. *Como esta*?"

"*Bien, gracias, Excellencia*," Juan Diego replied, "and you?" while noticing that the governor spoke a mixture of Spanish and *Ingles*, as did most government officials.

"Fine, my friend, fine."

"What brings you to our humble town?" Juan Diego asked.

"A visit to my silver-bearing friend, of course," the governor replied.

It was as Juan Diego had feared. The governor couldn't wait until it had been recovered. His expression must have shown his thoughts because the governor's eyes hardened and his spine straightened. Now he was a full head taller than Juan Diego. "And it is safe?" he asked. "The silver?"

"It—will be, I am sure," Juan Diego replied. "Yes, I…"

"Perhaps," the governor interrupted in a silky tone, "you had better explain exactly what you mean." His two aides moved a little closer to him.

Juan Diego told what had happened. "But I have sent Lobo Alto and others to find Pablo Borrega and the men from Mesaluna. I am sure they will find the silver and bring it to me."

Rosalinda floated down the stairs, dressed all in black with a lace mantilla and long skirts that swept the floor. Her lips were rouged and, with her natural rose complexion Juan Diego couldn't help thinking about peaches and cream with the sweet black bean sauce he loved. But more important was the relief he felt at not having to hear the governor's response to his explanation. He had never been so glad to see her, even when she wasn't dressed at all.

"Ahh," the governor said, "and who is this?" He turned expressive eyes toward her and held out his hands.

"This is Rosalinda de—Corralles," Juan Pablo muttered, "my, ah, niece."

Rosalinda raised one eyebrow toward him, and then turned to the governor and took both of his hands in hers. She managed an impressive curtsy, even while holding hands. She slowly stood, her back straight and eyes downcast.

"*Muy Hermosa*," the governor murmered, "very beautiful."

"*Gracias excellencia*," she replied, as she looked up through thick, curved eyelashes and smiled. She and the governor stared at each other. The governor waited, seemed to come to a decision.

"How would you like to stay with me in the palace in Sante Fe?" He turned to Juan Diego without releasing her hands. "Until your—uncle brings something to me that he has promised?"

"But…" Juan Diego started to say.

"But of course," Rosalinda purred. "I am sure there are many things to see and do in your Sante Fe."

"I will endeavor to keep you occupied," The Governor replied. "So you see," he said, turning to Juan Diego, "a silver opportunity for you, and a golden opportunity for me. And for," he turned back, "*Señorita* Rosalinda. I believe you will be the toast of Sante Fe."

"*Gracias*," she said and curtsied again. "I will go pack."

The governor turned to Juan Diego after she'd hurried away. "I will take as good care of her as you will of our silver," he said. "Maybe even better." He smiled, briefly, turned on his heel and left the room.

Chapter Twenty Seven

DINNER AND FORGIVENESS

Following their cigars and brandy, the men joined Mrs. Armstrong, Ruby, Manuela, and Lilia in the sitting room. They conversed briefly before walking to the dining table where soldiers in clean uniforms waited to serve them.

The women had washed their hair and put on clean clothing. Ruby wore a plain, dark blue dress that Roz had never seen. Lilia had a white, long-sleeved gown. She'd placed a knitted shawl around her shoulders, and her hair was swept back and held by an ornate, tortoise shell comb. Ebony waves cascaded to her shoulders and sparkled when she moved. She looked the way Roz imagined a princess might look.

Manuela wore a black dress with a high lace collar and tight-fitting sleeves with a row of small pearl buttons at the wrists. Her hair was braided and coiled at the back of her head. She was an attractive woman and drew nearly as many admiring glances as her daughter, except from Lieutenant Stern who tripped on the coal scuttle when he saw Lilia. He recovered and bent to kiss her hand when he was introduced. Lilia colored slightly, and seemed to Roz to be delighted with the attention.

"May I escort you to dinner?" Stern asked. Lilia rose and took his arm. Roz felt a stab of jealousy, replaced by apprehension concerning the debt to Colonel Armstrong.

Moose offered Mrs. Armstrong his arm and escorted her into the dining room. Major Reinholt escorted Manuela. Roz offered his arm to Ruby, who took it with a slight smile and nod. Henry and El trailed along behind.

"Up here," Armstrong said to Roz and waved him to the chair at his left. Roz helped Ruby to the chair beside him. "Lieutenant, if you'd be so kind," and the colonel indicated the chair to his right for Lilia so that she sat directly across from Roz. The lieutenant assisted her and sat next to her. Mrs. Armstrong took the chair at the far end of the table and placed Moose on her right. She asked El to sit on her left. Henry seated himself between Moose and Ruby. The major sat next to El with Manuela on his left.

"There, now," Mrs. Armstrong said. "What an excellent gathering. I do so appreciate that you'd dine with us. It isn't often we have the honor of entertaining women."

"And such beautiful ones," Lieutenant Stern murmured as he lifted his wine glass. "I give you good health!"

"And quick passage," Colonel Armstrong added. Roz wasn't sure if there was hidden meaning in the colonel's toast. He liked the "good health" part better.

"Hear, hear," Major Reinholt said with a smile.

Colonel Armstrong looked at Ruby and said, "Miss Ahearn, I understand you had a business where you came from. I find that interesting. Can you tell us about it?"

Ruby opened her mouth to answer.

"She rented rooms," Moose said, "near the stage station."

"Really," the Colonel replied. "How many?"

"Now, James," Mrs. Armstrong interrupted, "we don't want to pry into our guests' private lives. Let's just be glad they are here. Please call me Lucy," she added. She told them about Pennsylvania, where she had grown up and where she would soon be visiting. She intended to travel with an escort of troops to Colorado Springs, where the Atchison, Topeka & Santa Fe Railroad had recently laid tracks linking that city to eastern Colorado towns and Kansas.

"I would go with you, but I am not scheduled to travel for another fortnight." She stole a quick glance at the colonel. "It will be good to see Colorado again. Did you know that Colorado is to be admitted as the thirty-eighth state next year?" she asked.

"The citizens have to vote before it's official," the colonel said.

"But they will, won't they, James? I hear they always do, and that there never has been a state where it wasn't voted in on the first try."

"I believe you are correct, my dear. Does anyone know? Roz?"

Roz didn't think he could name all the states, let alone tell whether they had all ratified on the first attempt. He shook his head.

"I think…" Moose began, just as the lieutenant raised his hand. They saw each other and leaned back, each waiting on the other.

"Mister Banner?" Lucy said.

"No, please," Moose replied, "I'd like to hear Lieutenant Stern," and he nodded to the lieutenant.

"Well, uh, we had a course on statehood and civic law. At the Point. I mean, West Point." He seemed nervous once he had begun to talk. He looked at his plate, cleared his throat, and continued.

"It was explained by our instructor that all areas proposed for statehood have to be approved by Congress and The President before they are eligible to draw up a state constitution and vote to ratify it. So far, each state has ratified its constitution by more than a two-thirds majority. On the first vote," he finished, with obvious discomfort.

"What if Congress doesn't agree?' Roz asked.

"Sir, you may have heard that there was a proposal to form the state of New Mexico at the same time that Colorado was brought to a vote. Congress declined. They didn't think New Mexico was ready to govern itself."

"What if citizens didn't vote for the state constitution that someone wrote up?" Moose asked.

"They would continue to be a territory," Stern replied, "and they might have to wait several years for Congress to be in the mood to approve them. I've heard that if Colorado voters don't approve it will be ten years until the question is brought up again as a congressional bill. But I'm not sure that's true. I'm really not much of an expert on these matters."

"Very interesting. I appreciate your knowledge of the process," Moose said.

"Lieutenant Stern does himself a disservice," Colonel Armstrong said. "Tell us where you finished in your class of graduates. Your grade standing, I mean."

"I was," the lieutenant reddened, "I was second."

"From the top," the colonel added, "and he was first in military strategy. We're very glad to have him in this command."

"That we are," the major said as he lifted his glass toward the embarrassed junior officer, "very glad."

Lilia glanced at the lieutenant, and dropped her eyes. Manuela watched her without seeming to.

"So you're going on to Denver," Armstrong said. "How long will you be able to stay with us?"

"We'd planned to come through here a month ago," Moose replied. "It's so late in the season that I think we'd better be leaving tomorrow, as soon as we can get ready."

"Is there anything we can do to help you? Anything you need?"

"We're a little short of rifle ammunition. And we need salt and coffee. We'll gladly pay. With coin, not silver bars," he said, smiling at the colonel who smiled back.

"And matches," Henry added.

"Salt, coffee, and matches will be no problem. Major Reinholt will see to it. However, ammunition is another thing. We're only given ninety rounds per man per year for target practice. Can you believe that! And we don't receive a great deal more for patrols and post defense.

"We get all the cannon rounds we can store, but ninety rifle shots per year? One shot every four days! If the men want more, they have to buy their own. It's not right. It's a wonder some of these lads learn to shoot at all." The major and lieutenant nodded agreement but looked away, signaling that they had heard the argument before.

"The government is broke," Armstrong continued. "Insolvent. The Civil War took all the money we could print. Did you know there were a million-and-a-half men in uniform in 1864? A million-and-a-half! Two years later, it was down to twenty-five thousand, spread all over the country. A little more now, due to Indian trouble, but we still don't have what we need." He grimaced, then pushed his plate away.

"However, you didn't come here to listen to our problems with Congress. I'll just say this. One of these days we're going to have a real massacre out in these territories, and the boys in blue are going to be in trouble if they run out of ammunition just because some fat-backed...well, you have problems of your own. Anyway, we'll help as much as we can."

"Are your animals in good shape?" the major interrupted.

"They are," Moose said, "though that reminds me, we could use a bit of axle grease if you have it to spare."

"We do, and you shall have it first thing in the morning," the colonel said with regained control.

"Now, to some unfinished business. Roz? Are you ready for a proposition?"

"Why, uh, yes. I am," Roz said with a sinking feeling. He'd heard that challenges to a duel were often issued in front of witnesses so that seconds could be chosen, a place selected, and weapons named. He'd heard about the Old Spreading Oak in New Orleans, where so many men had died, and his imagination took him through several possible outcomes before Colonel Armstrong spoke again.

"Well, sir, I propose to forget the whole thing."

"You do!"

"On one condition. That you'll stop and have a glass with me before you go."

"Now, that," Roz replied, "would be an honor."

"Then it's done. Shall we retire to the parlor? I'd like Major Reinholt to explain the best route to Wagon Mound and Raton Pass. In fact, I'd like the major to accompany you for a few miles tomorrow. He can show you the way."

"Thank you," Moose said. "That is very helpful."

“I'd like to volunteer to go along, sir,” the lieutenant said.

“Won't be necessary, my boy,” Armstrong replied. “Perhaps next time.” The young man looked at his boots. “Yes, sir,” he said.

The moon was up when they walked back to the wagon. The men had been offered the bunks of soldiers out on patrol. They declined, preferring their own bedroll to the uncertainty of military accommodations where lice and other vermin sometimes got out of control.

When their eyes adjusted and they reached the wagon, Miguel was nowhere to be seen. They didn't worry about it a great deal. They were used to his nocturnal wanderings and assumed he'd found interesting things to look at and, hopefully, someone his own age to talk with.

Lilia, Manuela, and Ruby accepted Mrs. Armstrong's offer of beds in the house. They found night clothes and other articles they'd need and walked back to the colonel's home with the close escort and attention of Lieutenant Stern. Roz was glad Stern wouldn't be going with them the following day.

When they were out of hearing, he said to Moose, “Now, that Colonel Armstrong wasn't as bad a fella as I thought he might be.”

“Maybe not, but there isn't much he can do, what with the women around and troops and such.”

"Don't you take him for being sincere? I thought he was right nice, considering."

"Maybe. I'm just saying you can't call him your best friend yet."

"Why, hell, Moose. He doesn't have to be a friend at all, long as he doesn't shoot me. Which I thought for a while he might be planning to do. I'll just enjoy that farewell drink in the morning. Then we'll be on our way. With an escort of soldiers, no less. I'll be able to relax and enjoy the scenery, with a cool breeze blowing and the warm sun on my backside."

"That you will," Moose replied. "Now, let's get some sleep before that warm sun comes up and finds you sleeping under this wagon while everyone else is up and busy."

"I kind of like the sound of that, Moose. Someday I'm going to hire somebody to work while I rest, preferably where I can watch 'em do it."

"Maybe you should just marry a quiet, hard-working woman. Did you ever think of that?"

"Matter of fact, I have."

Moose thought he was on the wrong track if he was thinking of the individual Moose thought he was thinking about. Hard working, maybe. Quiet? Possibly. In any case, it wasn't his business to say.

Moose was drifting into sleep when Roz sat up and said, “Don't you think sun-up's a little soon to start drinkin'?”

Chapter Twenty Eight

CANCELLED DEBT

Breakfast was early, in keeping with military tradition. By nine o'clock provisions had been loaded, a loose ox shoe had been tightened by the post farrier, and the group was gathered at the entrance. Major Reinholt and six mounted troopers waited in escort formation. Flags snapped on the flagpole in the morning breeze.

A sentry once again left the watch tower, strode to the Post Commander's quarters, entered, and returned, followed by the colonel who was, in turn, followed by an orderly carrying a silver tray with several half-filled cordial glasses and a brandy decanter.

"My compliments on a beautiful morning," the colonel said. "Are you ready to go?"

"We are indeed, sir," Moose replied, "And we very much appreciate the escort, although it doesn't seem entirely necessary." Then, afraid he might imply that the offer had no value to them, he added, "But, of course, if they have the time to help us…"

"We make time, for good friends."

Roz looked relieved to hear the word "friends" again. Henry grinned. El was conversing with the major. Moose wondered how they could have become "good friends" in so short a span of time.

"And so," the colonel continued as he carefully selected a glass for Roz and the others, "I give you good health and prosperity. I'm sure you shall have all that you deserve," and he downed his glass and held it aloft as the others finished theirs.

"Now, may the Lord bless you and give you good speed."

The bugler blew the notes of the leaving-post signal, and they followed Major Reinholt and six troopers up the trail to the northeast. The escort rode ahead, followed by the wagon and the ox cart. Moose and Roz rode on one side of the wagon, El and Henry on the other.

Miguel and Lilia, who had once again decided to ride one of the remaining ponies, rode beside the ox cart and conversed quietly. Lilia was the only one Miguel had talked to for two days, and she was riding partly to keep an open line of communication with him.

All had to adapt to the oxen's slow but steady pace. Settlers crossing the plains in the 1840s and '50s had learned that oxen were able to forage better and work longer than horses. Many parties had turned back or simply waited until oxen could be brought to their wagons so they could continue. Horses set a quicker initial pace but wore out much sooner.

"That wasn't very good whiskey," Roz said.

"Brandy, I believe. Didn't you like it? I thought it was fine, and you liked it well enough after dinner last night."

"Maybe it doesn't follow my breakfast any too well. Anyhow, I didn't like it this morning."

"Hmmph," Moose grunted. There didn't seem to be much to say.

They rode quietly for an hour before Roz said, "I sure am anxious to see Wagon Mound. Old Quanah gave 'em hell about this time last year, didn't he?"

"I believe it was Adobe Walls, but, yes, he did. He finally caught a big bunch of buffalo hunters, but he caught them in the wrong place."

"Wrong place?"

"If they hadn't fought their way into Bent's old fort, Quanah would have wiped them out."

"Guess so. Did you know that Bat Masterton…"

"Masterson."

"Yeah, Masterson. He was with 'em. He's a lawman now. Somewhere in Arizona Territory."

"I heard."

"Funny who ends up being a lawman, ain't it? I wouldn't be surprised if old John Wesley became a sheriff one of these days."

"I heard he was a gambler, a buffalo hunter, then an Indian fighter, and now a sheriff."

"John Wesley Hardin?"

"No, Roz. Masterson."

"Well, don't snap at me."

"I didn't."

"You did. And I don't feel too good, anyway. Your snapping just makes it worse."

"So, how don't you feel too good?"

"You mean where?"

"All right, where! For crissake, Rozier . . ."

"Y'see, there you go again," Roz said. His words were followed by a tremendous belch.

"That ought to make you feel better."

“I believe I do, or, maybe I’m not sure. I, uh…” Roz clutched his belly. “Excuse me. I’m goin’ over that ridge,” and he reined Buster around and kicked him into a lope. Buster shied at a patch of yucca and nearly unseated Roz, who hung onto the saddle horn grimly with one hand while he held his stomach with the other.

The cavalry troop stopped, followed by the wagon, the cart, and the other riders. Major Reinholt came back and asked if all was well.

“Roz is a bit inconvenienced, but otherwise we seem to be doing fine,” Moose replied.

“We’ll probably leave you in a few minutes,” the major said. “Now, let me tell you what signs to look for as you go. It might save you a few miles.”

He explained what the soldiers had learned about following Tickle Creek until it turned south. There the group should proceed northeast over several rolling hills before cutting the Wagon Mound Trail along the Republican River.

“If you’re in sand, you’re south of it. If you’re in rocks, you’re north.” Moose, Ruby Lee, and El nodded. Henry had no sense of the compass and didn’t try to understand anyone’s directions. He trusted the others to get him there.

The major told them where good water could be found and where they might spot game for the camp's meals. He described the trail from Wagon Mound to Raton Pass and Colorado.

"We appreciate all you've done," Moose said. His statement brought a grin from the major.

"And I've enjoyed doing it. Be on the lookout for Juan Diego's 'posse', if that's what it is. They looked more like a gang of bandits to me. Let's go see if your man is all right."

"It does seem he should have been back by now," Moose said.

When they rode over the ridge, they found Roz, swearing, sweating, and straining against waves of nausea, followed by diarrhea. He was pale and angry.

"I believe—that—that son-of-a-bitch—poisoned me," he said to Moose, too miserable to care that Major Reinholt sat on his horse watching and grinning.

"Naw, he didn't," the major said. "Could be some of that mule medicine got mixed up in your glass, though. It happens, now and again," he said with a chuckle. "Now I ain't saying it did or it didn't. But the colonel gave me this message for you. I was to give it to you if you began to feel poorly, and report back to him immediately."

He urged his horse two steps closer to Roz and handed a note down to him. Roz reached up and took it, broke the seal, and read with watery eyes. He grimaced and swore before another spasm doubled him over. When he could straighten, he handed the note up to Moose with a trembling hand. Moose read the words:

Fort Union

New Mexico Territory

Sept. 10, 1875

Dear Mr. Wells:

I'm so glad you stopped by. When we played in Mesa de Luna, you cleaned me out. I want to return the favor.

Sincerely,

James J. Armstrong

Colonel, U. S. Army

Chapter Twenty Nine

TRAGEDY AT TICKLE CREEK

When Roz was able to climb into the saddle, they slowly followed Tickle Creek, which wound back and forth through meadows of tall, drying grass. Pink tamarisk and light green willow trees alternated with cottonwoods and pin oaks along its banks.

They traveled on the bench land above the creek to save time. Roz made several side trips into the trees during the first day and then hurried to catch up. In the late afternoons they went down to the creek bottom and built their small fires in groves of cottonwoods, partly because of the firewood supply, and partly for cover from Indian bands that might be in the area.

Fires were made from the driest branches they could gather to make as little smoke as possible, and they built them under trees where the branches above spread the smoke. They encountered no Indians and saw no recent signs of them.

At one point, where red sandstone sloped into the creek from the hill above, they found many conical holes in the flat rock. Two of them had long, cylindrical pieces of granite protruding from them.

"Mortars," El said. "Indians used to grind acorns or other nuts with those."

"Aren't many oak trees around here," Henry said. "Wonder what they ate."

"There might have been once," El replied, "Or it could have been *piñon* nuts, or grains. Corn or such. They could have farmed this valley a long time ago. Even before the horse."

"Farming does pale beside chasing buffalo, doesn't it?" Roz said.

"They may be farmin' again," El replied.

"If settlers don't get all the land first," Moose added.

"Moose, you aren't making sense. This country's so big, it won't be settled in a thousand years, if it ever is," Henry retorted.

"Maybe so, but the railroads are making it smaller, easier to get to. And I read there are a lot of immigrants coming in from Europe. I think we need to find the land we want as soon as possible.

"Look at Oregon. Twenty years ago nobody wanted it, so President Andrew Johnson gave it to the Nez Perce. Now everybody wants to go there, so Grant takes it back. And last month I heard gold was discovered in the Black Hills of Dakota, smack in the heart of Sioux country. How long do you think those treaty reserves are going to last? Not long, I'd say."

"Some of it isn't fit to farm, anyway," El said.

Whenever they talked about farming, Manuela turned her head away.

Miguel was silent as usual, but as days went by Lilia took more and more interest in the conversations. She began to ask questions and venture an occasional opinion, while Miguel just watched.

Lilia liked to hear El play the harmonica and asked him to play "Camptown Races" and "Dixie" over and over. Manuela brightened when he did. The lively melodies picked up her spirits and helped her forget the pain of recent weeks. But often, after playing the brisk tunes that Lilia and Manuela preferred, he walked away from the camp and played sweet, sad music that seemed to answer a need of his own.

After listening to the distant, plaintive melodies, Manuela felt more alone than she had before Lilia asked him to play. But the music did mirror her feelings and, in a way, the songs seemed to draw the sadness out of her. Sometimes she cried; sometimes she just felt a great loss. Almost always she felt unburdened the following morning, as if the weight of her sadness had been worn away, at least a little.

One night when El came back to the embers of the fire Roz said, “El, that was real pretty playing. What was the name of that last tune?”

“Oh. It don't have a name,” El replied.

“Why not? I thought all songs had names.”

“Sometimes I just play what wants to come out. Whatever…I think of.”

“You mean you just make it up as you go along?” El nodded. “Well, I'll be damned. You're full of surprises. I'll say that.”

“What do you mean, Roz?”

“It's just, I don't know, you just seem to…oh, forget it.”

El blinked at him a few times, shrugged and went to unroll his blankets.

Early the next morning Roz dreamed a beautiful girl was nuzzling his cheek. Her breath was warm. Her skin felt like velvet, and she was planting wet kisses on his forehead. Then she snorted! Roz’s eyes flew open.

“Goddamn it, Buster,” he said. “Get away from my bedroll.” Buster jumped as if he had been frightened and spun away to run a few steps. He stopped and looked back to see if Roz was watching him. When Roz didn’t throw a boot he put his head down and began to crop grass. “Knot-head,” Roz said under his breath. "Now I have to wash my face." He hid a smile as he stood up and went to the creek.

They left Tickle Creek where it bent to the south. They continued in a northeasterly direction. Major Reinholt had told them it was a two-day drive with an ox cart from the bend to the Republican River. They were to follow the Wagon Mound Trail along the river bank northwest to Raton Pass.

The major had said there were plenty of fish and game along the Canadian, and El remembered it that way, too. However, he had mostly stayed many miles west of the river on his trip to Mesa de Luna, as he had wanted to be closer to the mountains. They all looked forward to the Canadian's abundant water, fuel, and food supply. First, they had to get there.

"Damn," Roz said on the morning of the third day when they hadn't encountered the Canadian's banks, "I think maybe we're lost."

They had been rumbling over fairly level grassland until a series of low, rough hills rolled up over the horizon in front of them. The hills were cut with small arroyos where rains had run off. They were passable by horse and rider but not by anything with wheels.

"We ain't lost," El replied. "I know exactly where we are. It's the danged river that ain't where it should be. What I mean is," he continued, "we must have headed too much east. We can't take the wagon and cart through those hills. We gotta' go west and then north around 'em."

They made a dry camp that night and hoped to find the river the following day. After a hasty breakfast of cornmeal mush and black coffee, they continued along the west side of the hills, struggling up one grade and down the other side, detouring where they had to. They followed the route that El scouted on the big buckskin, which carried him at least twice as far each day as anyone else had to travel.

At mid-morning, when there was no sign of the Canadian, El stopped the group and said, "I think I'd better go find that river. We'll have to have water." Henry, Moose, and Roz nodded. The memory of the dry trip to the Mora was fresh in their minds.

Miguel surprised everyone by asking if he could ride with El. Manuela was pleased that he showed interest in something of importance to them, and agreed.

"Glad to have you," El said. "We can both look." He told the others they'd rejoin them either that evening on high ground alongside the hills; or, if the river hadn't been found, they would meet the following day where the Canadian entered the hills they were skirting. "We'll cut it by then, for sure," he said. "You can keep going. We'll find you." He and Miguel rolled their blankets and tied them behind the saddles. They mounted and rode out of sight.

At mid-afternoon of the fourth day away from Tickle Creek, the others rode up and over a long shoulder of the hills they were skirting. They thought they might see the river, since they had followed the edge of the hills and were proceeding northwest at last. What appeared instead was a relatively small creek with red-stemmed scrub willow along its edge.

As they drew closer, Roz said, “Look. There’s a field of some sort.” They followed his gaze and saw a rectangle of cultivated crop that had either dried up or had been picked and the stalks left to rot over the winter. It had a ragged look as if it had been harvested haphazardly, or had been abandoned.

“Curious, it being way out here,” Roz added, as he reined Buster toward the field. When he grew closer, Buster snorted and jumped sideways with uncommon vigor. Roz held the saddle horn with both hands and started to swear.

A grizzled head rose out the grass in front of him and shaded its eyes with a trembling hand.

“What the hell…” Roz exclaimed. “Who are you?”

The head didn’t say anything for a long minute. Then, “L—look out. You’ll—stove in—my roof.”

The words came out of a mass of gray whiskers. A long nose pointed at the toothless mouth, and above the nose, close-set watery red eyes peered out from under bushy gray eyebrows. Above them was a haystack of hair the same color as the beard.

The figure stepped back, and Roz saw that he had almost ridden onto the roof of a soddy built into the side of the stream's bank. The roof had grassed over and looked just like the surrounding hillside.

The figure continued to stumble backward, and Moose and Lilia, who had stopped beside Roz, saw a painfully thin man dressed in filthy overalls that showed old patches as well as more places that needed mending. He had no hat, shoes, or shirt, and was deeply tanned where the overalls exposed wrinkled flesh.

The figure pointed to the right and said, with words that sounded as if they came out of a long pipe, "This way. C—come."

Roz motioned to the others and rode a safe distance around the hidden structure and down to the level of the stream. The dugout had no window. The "door" was a piece of fabric, torn at one side and tattered above ground-level. The skeleton of a horse lay at one side of the packed-earth yard. A pile of rusted metal and broken glass, not far from the entrance, indicated where junk had been discarded. A path was evident from the yard to the stream.

As they rode closer another figure, seated on an up-ended wooden box, gave no indication that it heard or saw them. Arms were clutched across a thin chest, and the individual, who appeared to be a woman by the lack of facial hair, rocked back and forth on the box and stared into the distance. A glass jar, half-full of water, sat next to the rocking figure.

"Emma, it's—company," the man said. "It's—uh. Emma—Em," the man said as he looked up at Roz and Lilia.

"*Madre de Dios*," Lilia said under her breath. Roz followed her gaze and choked. Flies walked across the woman's face and in and out of her open mouth. Wounds in her scalp drained a slick, bloody path through her hair, down in front of one ear, to disappear into the neck of the thin shift she wore. Lice moved at the edges of the scabs on her head. She, too, had no shoes or hat.

As they watched, she raised a claw-like hand with bloody fingertips and scratched at her scalp where a scab replaced the hair that had grown there. She seemed not to notice as the area began to seep blood that joined the trickle by her ear.

"Can't—can't make her…", the man started to say.

"Who are you?" Roz asked, unable to think of anything else.

"Can't—make her . . ."

"What?" Roz said. "Can't make her what?"

"She—she won't—listen."

"What's your name?" There was no response.

"What's *her* name?"

"Emma. That's—her..."

"I think they're starving," Lilia said. "Ask him if they want something to eat."

"Do you?" Roz said as the others in their party approached. "Do you want something to eat?"

"Emma won't—won't, eat. She won't..."

Roz looked at the others, at a loss concerning what to do. Ruby Lee climbed down from the buckboard and approached the woman. She clucked sympathetically and reached out to touch the woman's shoulder. The woman shrieked and whipped her shoulders back and forth. She struck at Ruby's hand, then clutched her chest once again and resumed rocking.

"Henry," Roz said, "is there something we can give them?"

Henry looked into the back of the buckboard, reached in and drew two apples from a sack they had bought at Fort Union. He handed them to Roz, who passed one to the ragged man.

The man peered at it, and slowly extended it to Roz. “Can—can you cut?”

Roz pulled his pen knife from his pocket, cut off a small piece of apple, and handed it to the man, who turned and carefully put it in the woman’s mouth. She chewed tentatively for a moment before letting it fall to the ground.

“Won’t eat,” the man said. “Price. Name is Price. Carl—Price.” He slowly chewed another apple piece that Roz gave him. When he swallowed it, he reached for another, which Roz cut and handed to him. Roz gave him the knife, also.

“Won’t eat anything,” he said. “She won’t.” He sat down on a piece of white cottonwood log. Parts of it had been chopped away. A broken axe lay beside it.

“How long have you been here?” Moose asked quietly.

“Oh. Long time,” he said, blinking. “Ten years. Twelve.”

“What are we going to do?” Roz asked Moose and Ruby. They shook their heads. Moose started to say something, stopped.

“I guess, try to get some food into them,” Roz answered himself, but he didn’t move, as if mesmerized by the sight of the woman who didn’t seem to know they were there and the man who seemed to have only a few words.

Roz had met prospectors and hermits, people who had lived away from conversation for months at a time. They usually had trouble articulating, and Roz knew language needed constant practice to be used easily. He began to wonder how long it had been since the couple had talked with others, and how long the woman had been incapacitated.

"What—what do you eat?" Moose asked. The man pointed to a pile of millet plants that had been pulled up by the roots and thrown beside the door of the soddy. Millet was what had been planted in the odd-looking field.

"Is that all?" Moose asked, tears starting in his eyes.

The man nodded and said, "But, Emma won't—won't eat," and the words trailed away.

"Here," Henry said. He'd found some biscuits left over from their previous meal. The scarecrow figure took one, broke it in half, and put half in the pocket of his overalls. He started to chew on the other.

"Shall I give one to Emma?" Henry asked. The man shook his head and kept eating.

When he'd finished and didn't take the other half from his pocket, Moose asked, "Where did you come from?"

"Lawrence. Kansas. Eighteen and sixty-three. Chased us out. Quantrill's raiders. Chased us…away."

Moose remembered that abolitionists had founded Lawrence, Kansas to try to insure that Kansas would enter the Union as a free state. They'd abhorred slavery, and hoped Kansas would elect to prohibit the practice in the state constitution when it was submitted for approval and voted upon. Pro-slavery factions made guerilla warfare on Union soldiers as well as private citizens in Kansas towns in an attempt to frighten the voters into voting for slavery.

On an early morning of August, 1863, a band of between two and three hundred pro-slavery raiders entered Lawrence, Kansas from their headquarters in Missouri. Quantrill's orders to his raiders were, "kill every man and burn every house." When they finally left, over 120 homes had been burned, as well as all of the town's businesses. Citizens had been shot down when they came out of their burning homes. Others lost everything they had, and many fled to western territories to avoid further bloodshed.

"We came—here," the old man continued.

"Just you two?"

"And poor Benny." Price glanced at the dugout.

"Who is Benny?" Moose asked.

"Benny? Emma's brother!" Price said with more force than he had been using, as though Moose should have known.

"Where is he?" Moose asked gently. "Where is Benny?"

"Poor Benny," the man repeated. He pointed a trembling hand toward the dugout.

Roz walked to the opening, started to move the cloth, which had once been a piece of blanket, and stopped as an overpowering stench came from inside. He turned away and gagged. Moose walked toward him. "Don't go in there," Roz said.

Moose pulled the blanket aside and stepped partly in, holding his breath. He waited a few seconds for his eyes to adjust to the dim light. He spun on his heel, walked to the side of the door, and was sick.

"God-a-mighty," he gasped, when he had caught his breath.

"Poor Benny," the man said in a monotone. "Couldn't feed…"

Benny's sightless eyes had stared at Moose from a pile of animal skins. His body was badly decomposed. Most of the room was in darkness. Moose had noticed a small table and a rough bench, but he hadn't seen a stove or fireplace. There was no chimney protruding through the grassed-over roof.

"What are we going to do with these people?" Moose said, when he could talk. "We've got to move them."

"But how?" Roz asked.

"I don't know. But we can't leave them here."

"Mister Price, do you have relatives?" Roz asked.

"What?"

"Do you have family?"

"No. All dead. In Kansas."

"I was afraid of that," Roz muttered to himself.

"Quantrill's raiders. All of them. Lawrence. Eighteen and sixty-three. They…"

"Do you want to come with us?" Moose asked.

"No." He shook his shaggy head.

"Why not?"

"Emma. She—won't go."

Moose and Roz looked at Ruby and Manuela as though they could do something men couldn't. Manuela shrugged and approached the woman gently. When she was only three or four feet from her, the ragged woman shrieked again and kicked out with surprising quickness. Manuela jumped back.

"Do you want to ride in the wagon?" Henry asked the woman. There was no response as she continued to rock. "Are you hungry?" There was no answer.

"Can I help you?" Lilia asked. Emma ignored her.

"Mister Price?" The man looked up at Roz. "Shall I call you Carl?" Roz asked with a smile.

"Don't matter."

"What can we do to help you?" Moose asked.

"Nothing. One thing."

"What's that?"

"Deer come."

"What?" Moose looked at Roz and the others.

"Deer. At night," and Price pointed at the millet field.

"Deer come to eat? There?" Moose asked, nodding toward the field.

"Yes. Need—to shoot."

"Well, I don't know about that," Roz quietly said to Moose. "It don't seem like he's able. We ought to take them somewhere."

"In your own words, how are we going to do that? She won't let anybody near her."

"I don't know." Then to Price, "Emma needs a doctor. Can we take her to a doctor?"

"Never had no doctor. Never."

"She needs a doctor, Mister Price."

"She won't—go." He looked down and was silent.

"Come over here a minute," Moose said to the others, and he walked a few yards beyond the oxen where Carl Price and Emma couldn't hear them. Neither seemed to take much interest.

"What the hell is going on here?" Henry asked. "Are they both nuts?"

"In a way, I think," Moose replied. "Probably always have been. Did you see that dugout? They never even had a window nor a chimney. And they've been here twelve years or more, to hear him tell it."

"I believe they have," Roz said. "All the junk laying around."

"What shall we do?" Ruby asked. "I don't think I can touch her."

"Should we tie her up?" Henry asked.

"I don't feel good about that," Roz replied.

"Not like an animal," Lilia said with vehemence that surprised them.

There was silence until Henry said, "We got to do somethin'. We can't just ride away."

"What about giving them a gun, so maybe he can shoot a deer. Then go to, uh, Springer is the next town I believe, to get a doctor to come down here."

"Do you seriously think a doctor is going to come all the way out here?" Roz asked.

"Goddamn it, Rozier! What's *your* solution?"

"I'm sorry. I didn't mean it that way, Moose."

"Neither did I. I apologize. Now, what shall we do?"

"How about the Army?" Ruby asked.

"Maybe," Moose said. "We have to tell someone. It may as well be them, I suppose." He took a deep breath, "All the way back to Fort Union."

Señores," Lilia said. "Perhaps we should go to the nearest town. Springer? There we could tell the doctor, the sheriff, the Army if they are there, or the others could tell them. Perhaps someone will come."

Moose said, "I believe she's making sense. That does sound like the best thing."

"I guess so," Roz replied. "it's probably quickest." Henry and Manuela nodded.

"All right," Moose said. "Now. How about a gun?"

"I suppose it ain't goin' to hurt anything," Henry said, "whether or not he can shoot a deer. Maybe he can, and all the better. If not, well . . . "

"Then it's settled," Moose replied. "Let's go tell them, and then try to get some help."

They told Mister Price what they planned to do. He seemed only partially interested.

Emma gave no sign that she heard them. The half-biscuit that Mister Price had put in his pocket was crumbled at her feet. There were crumbs on her crossed arms. They fell off a few at a time as she rocked.

Price said, "What—what about them deer?"

Moose handed him the .30 caliber carbine he hadn't wanted to carry anyway. He extended it to Price, who looked at it but didn't take it. Moose laid it at his feet and put a box of shells beside it.

"It's empty. Do you know how to load it?"

Price nodded. "Thank you," he said quietly.

"We'll send someone to you. Soon as we can."

"Here's a bag of cornmeal," Henry said, placing the bag beside the gun. "Soak it in water. Maybe Emma'll eat some."

They stood uncertainly until Moose mounted and began to ride slowly out of the yard. The others followed.

"That's the worst thing I ever seen," Henry said to Ruby after they were out of sight. Ruby nodded but didn't reply. There was a lump in her throat.

Manuela was thinking how hard it is to help some people, and Moose was planning how to convey the gravity of the situation when they reached a settlement. They'd gone only a few hundred yards when a shot rang out, followed by another that seemed muffled.

"Oh, Christ," Moose said, as he reined the bay around and raced toward the soddy. Roz, Henry, and Lilia followed at a gallop. Manuela and Ruby stayed in the buckboard.

As they rounded the corner and could see into the yard, they found Emma face down with a new wound in the back of her head. A thread of blood ran down and formed a large, bright drop in the dust by her temple.

Carl Price lay beside her. He had placed the muzzle under his chin and pushed the trigger. The top of his head was gone.

The box of shells and Roz's pen knife were placed neatly on top of the cornmeal sack, which hadn't been moved. A china plate, two spoons, a rusted shovel, and a cup without a handle rested on the ground beside the sack.

"Holy Jesus," Moose choked, tears streaming down his cheeks. "Oh, Holy Jesus."

Roz pulled Lilia aside. He forced himself to breathe deeply.

"Go back and ask your ma to tether the animals," he said to her gently. "Tell her we have some burying to do."

Lilia put her hand over his. "Yes," is all she said.

Chapter Thirty

HENRY

They rode silently through gathering shadows, each lost in thought. None wanted to discuss the experience at the soddy. Their impressions were too vivid. They attempted to get the images under control as they moved across the waving grass. An early moon rose behind them, thin and silver, distant and cold.

The next day they found the river. A faint game trail bordered the south side of the shallow stream. They kept as near to the trail as possible, knowing El would find them before many days passed.

Roz stayed in the lead, closer to the wagon than usual. Moose and Lilia followed. Henry rode beside the wagon and listened to the rhythmic creak of the ox cart wheels to be certain that the beasts were following Ruby and Manuela in the buckboard. He was attuned to the sound, as Manuela was, without being conscious of it. The only time they heard it was when the oxen dropped behind or, on rare occasions, forgot what they were about and stopped to graze beside the trail. When the cart's sounds faded Henry went back to urge the gentle creatures. He'd developed affection for them. Manuela had told him their names were *Acaro* and *Nieve*, which meant Mite and Snow. She'd said Miguel had named Mite and Lilia, Snow, when Juan had brought the oxen from Taos where he had purchased them.

"Mite because he is so big," Manuela said with a soft laugh. "That Miguel!" Then she sobered.

Henry thought how unlike this silent, brooding Miguel the boy must have been. There appeared to be no vestige of humor left in him.

"Has Lilia ever seen snow?" he asked. Manuela shook her head.

"How did…?" Henry started to ask.

"I told her of the snow I saw when I was a child," Manuela answered. "In the Sangre de Cristos."

Nieve was snow-white with honey-colored spots, whereas Mite was brindle, striped caramel and black. Both had short, curved horns rather than long ones such as Henry had seen in Albuquerque. They had great, dark eyes and hooves as broad as the crown of a man's hat. They were in their prime, strong and healthy.

They seemed to like people, and Henry made sure that he scratched each broad forehead as he unhitched them in the evening. Manuela often joined him, patted the beasts, and talked to them. Henry began to look forward to those minutes at the end of the day.

One evening, after taking care of the oxen, as they were walking toward the fire Moose had prepared, Manuela turned and said, "You are a good man, Henree At-wat-er." She emphasized "wat" instead of "At" as others did.

Henry thought it was one of the prettiest things he had ever heard, and he carried the sound of it in his mind like a secret. He said it to himself again and again. It was comforting, partly because Manuela had said it and partly because he had never thought of himself that way. He liked what she said, although he wasn't sure what it meant.

He knew he was steady, and kind to animals. But sometimes he talked to people, men in particular, in a way that was impatient and conveyed an impression of disinterest. That had sometimes made it hard to be a saloon-keeper. His best customers were ones who knew him and weren't offended if he wanted to be quiet. Usually he tried to stay busy to cover any discomfort he felt.

She had said, “You are a good man,” and then his name. He repeated it to himself many times before it began to fade. Then he was unable to remember the exact sound of her voice saying it. He imagined only his own voice saying the words, and that wasn’t satisfying.

He hoped she’d say it again, but thought she might not. He didn’t know why she had done it the first time. He wished he could ask, but knew he wouldn’t. He’d never known how to communicate easily with women, not even with his mother.

After they’d stopped to build a small fire and cook a simple meal, Henry sat and warmed the coffee pot by putting small twigs on the coals. He watched the bed of coals grow brighter each time a breeze came. When they cooled, he stirred them with a green willow branch. He watched the fire and thought how far he had come and how far he wanted to go.

Henry’s father, Liam Atwater, had been a ferryman on the Clyde River, as had his grandfather and other ancestors as far back as anyone could remember. But then Sybolt Towne on the south bank, and Harney on the opposite, decided to build a five-span stone bridge. When it was done, and when spring floods didn’t wash it away as Liam had hoped and predicted, he walked to London in search of income. He regretted that he was the one to lose the family legacy, but at the same time he felt a sense of freedom from not knowing exactly what he'd be doing for the next twenty to thirty years.

Liam found work in a tannery and rented a second-floor room. The owner charged tuppence a week to let him sleep out of the rain. When he had been there only a few months, Rosalie Cartwright was hired to do sums in the office. Liam first saw her in the common room where employees took their lunches. He watched her thin figure, dark brown hair, and serious eyes for several days before he worked up the courage to sit next to her and engage her in conversation before someone else did.

Rosalie saw a tall young man who smiled when she didn't feel like it, and whom everyone seemed to enjoy. He was kind to her and exhibited an optimistic curiosity that contrasted favorably with the grim circumstances she'd grown up in near the mines at Newcastle. She hoped he would fill gaps in her ability to deal with a changing world, and she imagined she might even be able to love him someday.

Within six weeks they had begun to plan a one-way trip to America, and what first seemed like an improbable dream became an arrangement for passage. For deposit, they used a bit of money Rosalie had been given by her mother before moving to London to make room for younger, hungrier mouths.

They agreed to be married in the new land, and the fact that Rosalie, or "Rose," as Liam always called her, was pregnant only made the couple work and save more vigorously in a contest with time before the mother-to-be became unable to walk up the stairs to the tannery's office.

"We've na' but three bob," Liam exclaimed one evening, with a mildly discouraged expression. "Do you think…?"

"We can make it, Liam," she said fiercely. "I know we can."

The cheapest ship accommodations were arranged. Liam and Rose traveled steerage in a cattle boat primarily employed to haul Hereford stock for the grasslands of the United States.

Rose was ill the entire five weeks the Atlantic crossing required. She had little help. The ship's crew paid a good deal more attention to the livestock which had generated more revenue per head than the human passengers in steerage.

Rose and Liam lay at night on straw pallets in the ship's hold. It smelled of urine, mildew, and rotting vegetable matter. In daylight hours, Liam climbed up and took a turn on deck to smoke his pipe. Rose laboriously followed and sat on a bench to watch the never-ending waves. She was unable to safely keep her feet due to her girth. Then, after a few days, she became too weak to make the attempt, even when the ocean was less rough.

Liam sat with her in the hold, hour after hour, day after day while she grew more despondent. He began to wish he hadn't taken such pleasure in her young body. Pregnancy mystified him, and he imagined that it made her doubly vulnerable to illness and other infirmities.

One morning during their third week at sea, Rose shook him awake and said he must determine whether there was a minister of the church on board. If there was not, he was to speak to the ship's captain.

When Liam asked why, she said she might not live through the voyage, and if she gave birth before she died she'd like their child to have a father and a name.

"You will do that, won't you?" she said, gripping his arm with surprising strength.

Liam agreed, and hurried to find the captain. He explained their situation in urgent terms. Captain McVeigh smiled and said that, although there wasn't a man of the cloth on board, he'd performed several marriages and as far as he knew they held up well enough.

"Most particularly if you have it confirmed by the church when you've a chance," he added.

"Let's hurry," Liam said, and hoped as they descended into the bowels of the ship, that the captain hadn't taken too long to find his Bible and slick down his hair. He half-expected Rose to be unconscious, or worse.

When they reached the hold, Liam was relieved to see her propped up on one elbow. Maude Withrow, a woman they shared the cramped space with, was helping her to arrange herself more neatly while Maude's husband, Jonathan, turned his back.

Captain McVeigh asked about Rose's health, about how long it had been since she'd taken food, how long since she'd had fresh air. When he had the answers to those questions, he asked if the couple might prefer to be married on the open waist deck of the ship.

They said they didn't know how to get Rose safely up to that level. Furthermore, Rose added, she was afraid she'd roll off when the ship put its bow into the next wave.

The captain assured her that they could move her safely since they were used to moving livestock and barrels, "Beggin' your pardon, ma'am," and other freight that was hoisted into and out of the hold in heavy net slings.

It wasn't necessary for her to suffer that indignity. With the help of two large sailors, she was lifted up three steep flights of steps and into the fresh air. The welcome sun peeked intermittently between wooly cloud-columns that reached up from the surface of the sea.

Rose was given a chair and Liam stood beside her as the gray waters of the Atlantic slipped by. When the brief ceremony was over, the captain moved the purser from his small quarters that opened onto the deck. Then he convinced Rose to occupy the purser's bunk.

When Rose and Liam said they didn't know how to thank him, he replied, "By not dying on my ship." He broke into a broad smile. The experienced captain knew seasickness when he saw it.

Rose rapidly became better in the fresh air. Before the voyage was over, she had begun to enjoy the rise and fall of the ship and the figure-eights the stars scribed on the night sky outside the small porthole. She continued to be ill, but the nausea was of a magnitude she knew she could manage.

They became friends with Maude and Jonathan Withrow and confided that they didn't know what they would do, where Liam could work, after they arrived.

"That won't be problem," John said with a wink. "Leave that t'me."

They landed at the Port of New York and moved on to Liam's job at a dairy farm outside Trenton, New Jersey, where John Withrow's cousin was the delivery foreman. Liam began work by milking Jersey cows, a thing he had never done. When he showed promise, mainly by being on the job early and not getting drunk each weekend, he was promoted to delivery driver. Henry was born two months later.

Rose proved to be as healthy ashore as she had been ill aboard ship. Her color returned, and her figure filled out to an extent that caused Liam to wonder at his good fortune. Soon she was expecting a second child to follow Henry, who had learned to run faster than she could in her expanded condition.

Liam took Henry on delivery runs, and the youngster learned to talk to the drivers and peddlers who inhabited the pre-dawn hours. During winter months, Liam bundled him in sweaters and wrapped an old wool muffler around his head, pinned at his neck. Henry crowed happily, pointed at the horses, asked questions, and ate the apples and other fruits and vegetables the peddlers distributed.

They stayed in Trenton four years before Liam heard about land that might be homesteaded in a far-away place called Oklahoma Territory. Liam and Rose had dreamed of having their own property, a thing completely impossible for them in England. They made arrangements to leave with Henry and his infant sister. They were to take the train west as far as Cincinnati, then go by boat down the Ohio River to the Mississippi River and

Memphis. There they'd buy a wagon and team, and plod overland to Fort Smith, Arkansas. They were part of the group that settled on parcels of Indian Territory land years before government programs opened it to formal homesteading, as authorized by the 1862 Homestead Act. They, and others like them, were called "boomers" in Oklahoma Territory, and "squatters" in other parts of the West.

Unfortunately, Liam had no experience in selecting arable land, and he discovered he couldn't farm what he'd claimed unless it rained. It became evident by the condition of the soil and the general absence of plants taller than the two-inch-high buffalo grass that it seldom did so.

"Nice ranch you got there," someone said, "if only you had ten times as much." What the person meant was there weren't enough acres to support the number of cattle that would, in turn, support the Atwater family.

Liam and Rose were wondering what to do when a neighbor, who had a better claim and recognized their plight, said, "Tell you what. I'll pay you two hundred dollars cash right now. You give me a bill of sale but date it three years from now. At that time, if we ain't starved out, I'll record the sale and send another two hundred wherever you say."

Liam moved the family on to Tulsa, where he managed to start a small dairy farm that was forced out of business by a larger and better-financed dairy operation.

They moved to Amarillo, where he had better luck with a retail store. Henry grew up in the store and had a happy childhood, except when his sister contracted cholera and died in what seemed like an impossibly short time.

It was as if Rose had absorbed a heavy burden of sadness with the death of her daughter, one she couldn't lay down. Months and years passed without bringing her relief from the depression that weighed on her and, consequently, on Liam.

Henry heard his father ask more than one doctor as well as the preacher at the nearby church, "Why don't she get better? It's been more than five years." Or seven, or whatever the latest number was.

Basically, their answers had been the same. "People are different." Or, "The Lord moves in mysterious ways." The truth was, Henry figured, they simply didn't know.

Liam felt his wife could return to health, that she *would* return, if she loved him enough and really wanted to. He never stopped hoping. He smoked a pipe of Union Mail tobacco on the porch every evening. Afterward he came inside and sat by her.

Henry grew to be a responsible teenager. He helped when and as he could. He did much of the housework and meal preparation. He encouraged his mother to eat and to go outside. She seldom did either, but she maintained a stable kind of unresponsiveness, and the only sign of time passing was the increasing gray in her hair.

Then she began to show signs of physical illness that must have been lingering beneath the surface. She lost weight as well as the ability to dress and groom herself.

When she died one winter day, Liam was almost as surprised as he was disconsolate. He had continued to think she might once again recover, as she had on the ship, and he had been waiting for her to decide to get better. He was never fully convinced that she hadn't somehow willed herself to die.

"That's possible," their doctor said, "but I doubt it."

"You didn't know her like I did," Liam replied, as the doctor nodded and looked away.

Henry didn't feel as much loss as he thought he should. His mother hadn't been **involved** in his concerns, hadn't shown interest in his friends or his plans. She didn't laugh and seldom looked him in the eye. He felt as if the real mother who had nurtured him as a child had left many years before.

He wasn't shaken as much by his mother's death as he was on the evening that Liam cleared his throat and announced that he planned to return to England. He asked Henry if he'd take over the family store and let Liam go back with the cash they had saved.

"I'll send for you as soon as I'm settled," he said.

Henry loved his father, but he wasn't sure he wanted to follow. He knew most people who came from what they called, "the old country," didn't want to return. A few who had made the return trip came back to America as soon as they were able.

"I might like to visit someday," Henry had said. "We'll see."

Less than a year after his father left an uncle he'd never met sent a package with a letter saying Liam had died in a London hospital, victim of influenza. The package contained Liam's pipe, his watch, and the deed to a small house outside of Sybolt Towne. The uncle said he'd look after the house, sell it, or do as Henry wished.

Henry mailed a reply, saying that he'd like to keep the house if the uncle agreed to accept the rent it earned as payment for his trouble. There never was an answer. Henry wrote twice more without receiving a return letter. Finally he gave up, but kept the deed and address so he could look at the house if he ever had the chance to travel to England.

As time passed, he became more and more dissatisfied with Amarillo. He couldn't rid himself of thoughts of his father, mother, and even his sister. He felt he spent too much time thinking about what might have been, and he knew it wasn't a healthy way to live.

He needed a change and decided to move west, into New Mexico Territory, where he might have a better opportunity to make his fortune and go back to visit his parents' birthplace. The more he thought about it, the better it sounded. He wasn't willing to work his way to England, as his parents had worked their way to and across America. Their method seemed old-fashioned, unnecessary. He decided to go when he had enough money to get there as well as to come back if he didn't like it. That day had never arrived.

Now he was bumping along a trail in New Mexico Territory, getting farther from things and places he had known. It was all strange and new except for the friendships he valued and a growing feeling of admiration, and something more, for the slim, dark woman who sat beside him but who seemed to appreciate him about as much as she appreciated a pleasant view or the song of a bird.

Henry was happy and unhappy, satisfied on one level but bereft on another. He felt confused, and began to hope he was normal and not flawed in some mysterious way, like his mother must have been.

"Henry! I said, do you need more wood?" Moose asked with a concerned look.

"What? Oh, sorry. No. That's enough. I was thinkin' about something."

Moose shrugged.

Roz looked at Henry, glanced at Manuela, and hid a smile.

"Listen," Manuela said as she stared toward the dark line of trees. "I think I hear Miguelito. And El."

Chapter Thirty One

TOWARD RATON PASS

The small group waited in silence as the rhythmic crunch of hooves on gravel grew closer. Then the sound stopped. Moments later El Renfroe stepped into the firelight. He put his finger in front of his lips, turned, and disappeared into the shadows. Then he was back, leading his horse. Miguel followed.

"Quiet," El whispered. "There's a band of Indians just up river about half a mile. I almost walked into 'em. They have women and children. They ain't painted. Still, we got to be careful. No tellin' what they'll do." He kicked sand over the fire.

"How many?" Roz asked.

"I'd say about twenty-five or thirty. I counted seven lodges. Don't know that I could see them all. And they must be hungry."

"Why's that?" Henry asked.

"No dogs," El explained.

"No dogs?" Henry replied. "Oh, I see." He quietly explained to Manuela that some tribes ate their dogs when they could find nothing else.

"What tribe are they," asked Moose.

"Kiowa, I think. Can't be sure. Looked like it, the way the women was dressed."

"You don't think it's a war party?"

"No, but we don't want them to tell the next one they see. That we're here, I mean. Let's get away from the river. We'll go wide around 'em. They may not know about us."

"Damn!" Ruby whispered as she slowly rose from the blanket she'd been reclining on. "I was just getting to like this place."

"Anybody doesn't have a full canteen better do it now," El continued, "but don't make a sound if you can help it."

The group walked their horses downstream, and then away from the willows and cottonwoods that fringed the Canadian's banks. The wagon and cart followed. When the travelers were satisfied they were out of the danger area, they mounted and began a slow and cautious night ride west and gradually, north. Starlight gave scant illumination. Occasionally, one of the horses stumbled and grunted as it regained balance. The oxen and cart moved smoothly and almost silently. The only sounds were the dull plod of hooves and the snap of small brush and twigs under the wheels. Saddles gave the usual small, rhythmic creaks.

As they rode, Ruby thought, *Isn't this a hell of a place. We act like the Indians own it. They act like we own it. We try to avoid them except for the cavalry. They try to avoid us except for their pony soldiers. Fifty years ago it was all theirs. Fifty years from now, it'll be ours, and they'll likely be starved to death or in jail. And here we are, caught in the middle. I think I was born too soon, or maybe too late.*

A three-quarter moon rose and made their way easier. The horses relaxed and settled into a slow, steady walk, paced to stay with the oxen and cart. They paralleled the river for five hours before El led them on a course that would intersect the dark line of trees in the distance. No one had to be cautioned to keep noise at a minimum. They reached the river without incident, stripped and hobbled the horses, and fell into their blankets, aware the sun would rise long before they had rested to satisfaction.

The next two days were days of long travel. Henry made coffee over dry twig camp fires. He soaked and cooked pinto beans with the last of the salt pork they had purchased at Fort Union. He extinguished the fires as soon as he'd finished cooking. No one complained. All thought about the meal they'd ask for, if or when they could have anything they wanted.

On the morning of the third day by the Canadian, El stopped until the others drew abreast. "Now, if I recollect proper, those hills are where Raton Pass is. Uncle Dick Wooten charges folks to go through, but he's mostly interested in cattle droves. Ain't enough money in it for him to be worryin' about little outfits like ours. We'll ask him what he'll charge. If it's too much, we can take the Santa Fe cutoff and go over to Bent's Fort. But I'd like to save the time. Let's head for that cut in the hills. That's where the trail begins, if I'm right."

They didn't have to wait until they reached the low, *piñon*-covered hills to find the trail. Converging tracks of cattle and horses made clear paths long before they began the gradual climb.

"What makes this place so hard to get through?" Henry asked El when they stopped to let the horses blow and crop a few blades of dry grass. "Don't look that bad to me."

"There's a steep drop-off on the other side," El replied. "A canyon wall. Must be a thousand feet high. No way to get a wagon or cart over it except at Dick's. He's got a road he and his men built. Guess he figures he's got a right to charge."

"Hope it isn't much," Roz said. "I'm too broke to pay attention."

"I'm goin' to try to see that he don't charge at all," El replied. No one asked how he might do that.

They were on the trail, well inside the first low line of hills and *piñons*, when three riders came down the trail to meet them. "Howdy. Goin' to Pueblo?" the first rider asked. He spoke in a civil fashion, but his coat was tucked back and his side arm was easily reached. The others reined up beside him. They, too, were armed.

"We are," Moose replied. "My name is Moose Banner." He introduced the others. The riders didn't seem interested in their names, but they stayed quiet until Moose had finished.

"Jake Walters. This here's Caleb Stone. And Lefty Riess. We work for Uncle Dick Wooten. This is a toll road, as you may have heard. There's seven of you and ten head of animals. A buck apiece, man or beast," he said in a sing-song manner. "Ladies, too, of course." He grinned and tipped his hat, pleased with the small joke. "That'll be seventeen bucks."

"We'll pay what we owe, but I want to pay it to Dick his self," El said.

"That ain't the way it works here."

"Was the last time I came through," El replied.

"Well, it don't work that way now."

"I guess you ought to go back and tell him you wouldn't let Elwood Renfroe pass."

"Well, who the hell…" and then stopped as the name sank in. "You're the Indian fighter that worked here a while, ain't you?"

"I don't go out of my way to fight Indians. Or anybody," El replied in a level tone. "Only if I have to."

The leader stared, shrugged his shoulders and said, "Your funeral. Follow us. We were about to go back, anyway." They turned and started toward the distant ridge.

Ruby, Roz, and Moose were thinking similar thoughts, which was that El had changed. He seemed more calm and capable. Mesa de Luna had compressed him, shrunk him. They sensed, without forming words, that the little town probably had made each of them something less than they could become if they got the chance. They had the vague feeling they'd be better, stronger people if they managed to stay alive until they got where they were going. Each thought the others seemed to have done so already. They weren't aware that they had, also.

The trail rose. The air grew noticeably colder. They smelled wood smoke and saw log cabins and a chained gate across the trail.

A half-mile back a tall, ghost-like figure rode a smoke-colored horse and led another. He watched the ground. He reined the horse away from the road and began to ride through the forest. His horse's hooves made no sound in the duff on the forest floor.

Chapter Thirty Two

COLORADO

Uncle Dick Wooten appeared in the doorway of a low-roofed log house. He began to greet them cordially as well as cautiously, like a businessman expecting an argument. He relaxed when he saw El, and came and gave him a hearty handshake.

"Get down. Take some weight off your horses," he said with a smile. "Park your wagon and cart over there. Coffee's made and I might have something stronger out in the barn. El, what the hell are you doin' here? Thought you went to Idaho. Are you back already?"

El began to explain their trip, but Wooten interrupted. "Come in, come in. We can finish that later. Main thing is, you're here. Good to see you. You folks all come on in when animals are put away. Boys'll show you where."

When they were seated in the main room of the log house, Wooten explained how El had supplied the camp with venison three years earlier on El's trip south. He proposed that El do so again in exchange for the tolls. He offered free passage and a communal sleeping room if El was willing to bring in two mule deer. El agreed. Wooten talked about the pass and about building the toll road until the visitors suppressed yawns.

Moose guessed the tolls were reasonable, considering the work that had been required to build the road. Wooten had explained how the pass had been used by game and Indians for thousands of years, but the trail had been a narrow, single-file path, and wagons couldn't cross. The old wagon route had been many miles toward the east and involved more days of travel. Wooten and his crew had felled trees and dynamited granite to make a road. It was steep, but possible for a wagon to travel up or down if the team driver was careful.

Moose asked if Wooten had seen men who were looking for them, or had asked about them.

"Yeah," Wooten laughed, "I was going to mention that. I saw three that looked more like outlaws than the lawmen they said they were. I told them to get off my property. I didn't want 'em stealin' horses or makin' any other kind of trouble. Don't know if they were after you. I didn't give them a chance to name names. Why? You in trouble? You don't look like it." He told them how he'd asked his men to escort the three away from the pass, what they'd said, what he'd said, and on and on. Wooten could get full value out of a short story.

Moose waited for Wooten to stop talking long enough for Moose to explain. When he had, Wooten replied, "Hell, don't worry about it. They're fools if they go into Colorado. There's real law there, though I reckon if there's a sizeable reward they might decide to try."

He gave them a long description of the differences between Colorado and New Mexico. "Anyway, that's how it looks to me, standin' on the line between both. It'll all change someday," he concluded, "but probably not for a long while."

The next day Roz and Moose grazed their animals a mile distant from Wooten's headquarters while El hunted, accompanied by Miguel. Closer meadows had been "hayed" for Wooten's livestock. His hired hands had scythed the tall grass and let it dry for a day or two so it wouldn't rot in the stack. Then they'd hauled it with a hay wagon and stacked it just outside the corrals. Making hay was hard work, and hay was a valuable asset. There was none to spare. They'd need it in the heavy snows of winter.

"Wonder why they call him 'Uncle'?" Roz asked.

"El told me everybody from Santa Fe to Denver knows who he is, but not even his employees know where he got his name," Moose replied.

Roz was silent for a moment, and then said, "How'd you like to be called Uncle Moose?"

"No, Roz, I would not. 'Moose' is more than enough."

"Well," Roz replied, "I'm not too fond of my own. I guess we won't be having a name callin' contest."

The meadow grass where Moose and Roz watched the oxen and horses was frost-browned, but nutritious. The animals grazed, rested, and grazed again before being brought back to Wooten's for the night. When the sun went down the temperature dropped, and the animal's breath condensed into clouds of vapor as they were put into the corrals. Moose and Roz turned up their collars as they walked toward the log houses. A white moon rose over the blue-black serrated line of pines. A clear sky promised deep frost.

It felt good to open a door and smell hot food. El nodded and stepped aside while they stamped their feet and came in, removing coats and rubbing their hands. He went out, closed the door behind him, and walked in darkness toward the corral. The buckskin nickered. He let the horse smell his hands and coat. Then he saddled and bridled him, led him out of the corral, and closed the gate.

El had ridden half a mile from Wooten's buildings when he found the small clearing he'd selected. He climbed down, put a halter on the buckskin, and tied him to a lichen-covered stone. He checked to be sure the horse couldn't tangle the rope in lodgepole pines that surrounded the grassy clearing. He pulled a short carbine from the saddle scabbard and followed the trail he'd found the previous evening. After walking swiftly for thirty minutes he reached the glade where he'd found horse tracks and long moccasin prints. He dropped to his knees behind a lightning-scarred snag.

An hour later El felt, rather than heard, motion on the other side of the clearing. A horse appeared, almost as pale as the moonlight. Another horse followed, tethered to the first. A figure slid from the saddle and slipped shackles onto the horse's front legs. The man was tall and thin, wearing a poncho or cape, maybe some kind of blanket, and El knew their pursuer from the Pecos River had found them. The tall man lifted a lever action carbine from the saddle scabbard, checked to be sure there was a shell in the chamber, put it under the crook of his arm, and silently headed toward where El hid behind the snag. El had been pretty sure he'd walk this way; he'd studied the tracks from his previous night's foray.

"Far enough," El said, stepping from behind the snag and jamming his carbine into the man's belly. "Who the hell are you?"

There was silence as each sought the other's eyes hidden in the moon-shadow of their hat brims. El jabbed the barrel into the man's hard stomach.

"Alto," rumbled the gray figure.

"Alto what?"

"Just Alto," the thin figure said, with a voice sounding as if it came from a sewer pipe. His eyes were level with El's. He seemed wary, but not afraid.

"What do you want—Alto?" There was no answer. "You have about two seconds before I gut shoot you." El knew he wouldn't without more provocation, but it sounded right. He jabbed the rifle barrel. "One. T.."

"Silver."

"What silver?"

"Dos Osos silver. Pablo took it. Now you have it."

"I don't know nuthin' about no…" Lobo Alto twitched, moved his rifle. El jabbed him again; Lobo froze, "…silver," El said.

"Pablo rode shotgun."

"I know that."

"He took it. There was no one else. I'll have it back."

"Maybe he did, but he didn't bring it with him," El replied, thoughtfully. El hadn't fully accepted Pablo's story about the silver not being there.

"If Pablo had silver," El added, "he hid it. And if we had it I'd be in Colorado ridin' in a coach, not freezin' my ass off and pokin' you in the belly." El knew he wasn't telling the strict truth. He'd take a horse over a coach any day, but Alto didn't need to know that.

There was a long silence, then Lobo said, "Go ahead." A warm feeling coursed up the back of Lobo's neck. He almost smiled.

"Go ahead what?" El replied.

"Shoot."

Now things are getting dicey, El thought. Alto hadn't moved much, even when El had rammed the carbine into his hard stomach. He seemed to be betting El wouldn't shoot him at close range. El understood the ploy, the way things were balanced. The man was quiet. He was hoping El might give him a fair chance. He was probably quick. Quicker than himself? El didn't want to find out. Alto had trailed them for hundreds of miles without being seen. He'd found them, even after they had been lost. He didn't give up. He was dangerous.

Alto was thinking, also. He couldn't reach the carbine's trigger. So he'd gambled; offered the man a chance to shoot him, which he might or might not do. He knew the tall red-headed fellow was unusual, tireless, and a good shot. Lobo had thought he was better, more careful than the red-head, but he'd never been caught flat-footed. He'd never been in the predicament he was in now. Two or three had tried. They were dead. But this fellow…his only hope was the redhead wouldn't shoot him before there was some distance between them. He'd taken a risk, offering the challenge. Maybe the fellow would step back. If Lobo was given half a chance he'd strike like a snake. Then he realized he'd regret it. This man wasn't afraid. He was someone Lobo might have liked if he'd had a chance. He waited, motionless as stone.

"Drop the rifle. Now!" El's voice rang like a pistol shot. Alto reluctantly spread his arms and let the carbine fall. "Now turn around," El said.

Alto didn't want to do that. He'd lose any chance at retaliation. He swiftly reached for the handgun at his belt. Lobo's head seemed to explode. He thought he'd been shot: the pain was immense, shattering. His eyes blurred. He hit the ground, hard. The pistol was wrenched from his belt along with his knife. He was rolled onto his belly while the red-head went over him from hat to boots, finding one more knife concealed under a band on his ankle.

Lobo couldn't feel his own hands. Then he realized El was standing on them, straddled over Lobo with a rifle muzzle in Lobo's ear.

"Now, you dumb son-of-a-bitch," El said. "I might kill you right here. It depends on what you decide in about the next minute. You hear me?"

Alto nodded. "Lobo," he said.

"What?"

"Lobo Alto. That's my *nombré*—my name."

"Well, Lobo, hear this and hear it good. I got no silver, and I got no quarrel with you, other than you'd probably kill me right now if you could."

"*Si.*"

"Thought so, but you won't get that chance. I'm going to do you a favor, and you're going to do me one in return. *Comprende*?" Lobo nodded again.

"I'll keep your guns. You'll ride away from here. You'll tell anybody else chasin' us, and whoever sent 'em, that I'll kill the next one without even askin' who they are. Then I'll come huntin' *you*. You got that?" Alto nodded again. "Let me hear it."

"I—believe you," Lobo said, and he did.

"Fine. Get up. We'll go search your saddle bags. Make sure you ain't carryin' any more toad stickers. Then you get the hell out of here. I'll be checking at sunup to make sure you went straight south."

"What's your name?" Lobo asked as he slowly got up and brushed dirt and leaves off of his clothing and hat.

"Elwood Renfroe."

"Never heard of you, *señor*."

"No reason you should have, but you will if you ain't gone in one minute."

Lobo mounted. He touched the side of his head where El had struck him down with the rifle barrel. He looked at Renfroe. *I could like this man*, he thought. One corner of his mouth tilted up. "Go straight to hell, Elwood Renfroe," he said.

"Already have. Now, git'."

Lobo mounted, checked the pack horse rope, and rode through the dim trees. In moments he had vanished.

El felt a hollow, breathless sensation, as if he, too, was disappearing. He spread his hands to relax. There would soon be no room for men like Lobo Alto, he realized, nor like himself. Not in this country of locked gates, fences, and railroads.

Lobo rode south for fifteen minutes. Then he stopped, turned, and looked back the way he'd come. He had never been disarmed in his life. He'd never been beaten. He'd never had a friend who wasn't afraid of him. He'd never known a father, nor had a brother. He'd never known a man he could respect. Or trust. Or maybe more than trust. In spite of the pain in his head he began an actual smile.

Lobo considered options. He still had some money. Renfroe had seen it, but hadn't taken it. There was enough for a couple of guns, a knife, but he'd need more. He could go straight to Albuquerque, two weeks at most if he didn't waste time. He'd sell his hut by the Rio Grande, maybe get more money from Diaz, and then return. He'd find this Renfroe and the others in Colorado, probably in Denver. He was good at finding people. He squeezed the saddle with his knees and urged his horses south.

Chapter Thirty Three

THE LINE

Wooten was talking, as usual. "I'll tell you what to expect when you get across the Colorado line," he said, "but first I want to thank El for fixing us up with camp meat, and Henry and Mrs. Romero, thank you for cooking dinner last night. I'm no hand to cook, and the boys aren't much good at it, either." He paused, but not long enough for someone else to talk.

"The last cook ran out of whiskey. He went down the hill, looking for a job at a hotel in Pueblo. By the way, don't hire a cook in the morning. Look for him after sundown before you ask your questions. If he isn't too drunk to answer, he's your man. If you see a good one down there, send him up. I pay room and board and ten bucks a month. But you won't have time to be fiddlin' with cooks. I'll go down myself in a few days."

Wooten drew a deep breath and continued. "Now, are you going to winter over in Denver?" Wooten had a way of changing the subject without pausing.

"I think that would be best," Moose replied with a quick look at El, who remained impassive. "We'll need a place to stay, and we'll need work."

"You'd best keep moving," Wooten said. "There's already snow in the high country, though it'll be a month or so before it sticks down here. The boys tell me the skunk cabbage is higher than a man's head down in the valley. That's how we tell how deep the snow's going to be," he said with a smile at the ladies. "Well, not really.

"You'll probably get a few snow flurries from time to time, but I don't think it will bother you much. My advice is to get to Denver by November first. I wouldn't want to be traveling later than that. I think you can make it. What day is it? About the sixth? You have about three hundred miles to go, give or take. That's about fifteen miles a day, and it's pretty easy going compared to what you've been through.

"Another piece of advice. Get rid of those oxen and that cart. Slows you down. I'd be glad to buy them. I'd like to break some sod next spring, and they'd be just the thing to pull a plough."

Manuela slowly shook her head.

"We'll be keeping those," Henry stated in a quiet but firm voice.

"Have you heard if there's work?" Roz asked.

"In Denver City?" Wooten replied. "There's that, and not much else. They say it's already bigger than Boulder and just keeps growing. Denver is kind of in the middle of things in that part of the country. It's on the South Platte River, as you may know, where Cherry Creek dumps in and where they found gold in fifty-nine, though not much. More important, it's where the silver miners start for Central City, or go all the way up Clear Creek to Idaho Springs, Georgetown, Silver Plume, and those other places. I think you'll find plenty of work if you don't get the prospector's itch. Most of them don't make expenses."

"Good," Roz replied. "We'll need a way to make ends meet while we save for getting started in Oregon Territory or wherever we settle." Moose's eyebrows went up. They hadn't discussed other destinations.

"I'll tell you what I've been hearing," Wooten said. "Some folks are already coming back from the Northwest. They say the best land is taken. The coastal areas and river valleys are filled up. I guess you could stay east of the Cascades. Grant opened it to settlement. Took it away from the Nez Perce. Plenty of land there. Problem is it's hot and dry. Folks are coming back and looking for land in Colorado and Arizona. Even northern New Mexico. Now, about work. Let me think."

Wooten was uncharacteristically silent for a moment. "Fellow came through here last spring. Said he was going to build a hotel in Denver. Can't think of his name. French name. La—something or other. LaGarde, LaBorde, something like that. He'll be needing sober help if he really built it. Can't tell about that, though. People's plans don't always work out. Never thought I'd stay here ten years. Guess I don't know where else to go. I kind of envy you folks. You seem to know what you want. And here I sit. Thought I'd be married by now." The thought of marriage seemed to quiet him. He looked at the wall, then at the floor. He rubbed his whiskers, while the travelers reflected briefly on what they knew of their plans and destinations.

Ruby wanted to get to Denver, have a look, and decide whether to stay or go on to San Francisco. She had been thinking about getting older, and realized she needed to find a new livelihood or a husband, some means of security. She'd been asked to marry several times, by men much like El. She'd had no interest in any of them.

Henry was torn about wanting to see England. He was apprehensive about the rigors of such a trip, and he was uncertain whether he would enjoy it if and when he got there. There was no way to know if he still held title to property, which might not amount to much even if he did. Henry wondered if his father had been happy before he died. His uncle had to be elderly, if still alive. Perhaps most important was his growing appreciation for Manuela, and he thought he might rather go wherever she was going, but he didn't know if she would make room for him.

Manuela wanted to find her sister, Blanca, in Pueblo. She hoped to rest and heal her thoughts in the presence of family and the comfort of a Catholic Church where she could attend mass. It had been a long time. She was grateful to the others, but didn't feel a tie to them as she did to the sister she hadn't seen for years, and didn't know very well. She wondered if she could even find Blanca. She worried about the reception she and the children might receive.

Roz was surprised at his increasing wish to be off of the road, to settle somewhere and begin to build a future. It was a new feeling. He'd always let life and circumstances move him along. He knew he wasn't what people called a "drifter" because he'd worked and stayed in one or another place for months or years at a time. Still, he'd felt rootless and somehow inappropriate. He'd had no significant possessions and few skills. It felt like time to change. He'd caught himself looking at the soil several times on their journey, wondering what it might grow. Most of it hadn't received enough moisture to grow much of anything except mesquite, tumbleweeds, and tough, wiry grass. But this mountain country was different. The cool, bright air seemed to taste and feel better.

Moose was surprised Roz had brought up the subject of work. He was even more surprised at his sense that Roz's purpose seemed to be changing. Roz seemed distracted and pensive, as if he was thinking about alternatives. Whether Roz was consciously aware of this, Moose couldn't tell. Moose had always expected to work while it seemed that Roz had often expected not to. It appeared that Roz might be maturing. It was an interesting thought.

El knew he grew uncomfortable whenever they neared civilized areas. He wasn't looking forward to the towns and cities of Colorado, and statehood would bring more people and fewer quiet places. He still warmed when he thought about Ruby Lee, but she seemed to regard him with mild appreciation, as she would have a friendly dog or a comfortable winter coat. His feeling of loneliness had begun to increase.

Lilia trusted her mother to make the best decisions possible under the circumstances. The pain of loss of her father was receding. There were days when she didn't think of it for hours at a time. She was glad they had left the farm; she didn't think she ever would have been able to find peace there.

Once in a while she remembered how Lieutenant Stern had laughed and blushed when he spoke. He had dark eyes and smooth skin. She thought she would have enjoyed talking to him. He was far away, but maybe she'd see him again.

Miguel said almost nothing, but others could sense a deep, abiding anger. His mother seemed powerless to diminish it, and she waited and hoped that he would become more like his former self. He related best to El. Sometimes they spent half a day in each other's company without saying anything at all.

"You don't have to worry much about Indians now," Wooten continued. "There aren't many between here and Cheyenne. The Union Pacific has pushed them back, and their hunting grounds are being settled. They're mostly south of Fort Union or north of the U. P. Line. There's plenty of them up along the upper Missouri River and the Wind River Range. Yellowstone country. Old Sittin' Bull's sittin' up there right now, they tell me."

"Sounds like they're under control," Roz said.

"Wouldn't be too sure about that," Wooten replied. "We've shoved them out of the Dakotas, out of Nebraska, and now folks are pushing to get them out of the Northwest. If we squeeze too hard, the Cheyenne and the

Sioux could make real trouble. They used to be enemies until they found a bigger one—us. Funny how old enemies become friends when they're both threatened. Could be trouble."

"Let's hope there isn't," El said. "No sense in them or us gettin' killed."

"Anyway," Wooten continued, "weather's your main worry. You got a long way to go."

"That we do," Roz replied. "That we do. We'd best get going."

Wooten's dogs were quiet when the travelers came outside. The morning was crisp, and the crystal-clear air had a pleasant, acidic tang. Heavy frost covered the barn roof and corral poles. Horses stamped and snorted. Saddle leather creaked, and the ox cart wheels popped and squealed as the oxen began to move them.

A raven croaked from a dead ponderosa at the top of the trail. Another answered far below. The first raven left its perch and soared down out of sight.

The early morning sun felt good on their faces as they said goodbye to Wooten. Then they were through the unlocked gate and into shadow as they started down the steep trail.

The terrain changed as they lost altitude. Glades were thick with frosted grass. Remnants of lupine, Indian paintbrush, and columbine stood frozen at the edge of the spruce forest. Marmots whistled from old rock slides. Golden-yellow aspens had shed most of their leaves and carpeted parts of the trail. Snow-capped peaks appeared in the west while vast sun-lit plains stretched away east toward the morning sun.

The animals snorted clouds of vapor as they carefully made their way down. The hand-brake on the wagon squeaked at the steepest spots, and the oxen labored to push back on the heavy cart. No one spoke. It felt as if they were moving down and down, into a new land. They were too busy watching and waiting to talk about it.

The trail grew easier as they reached the valley floor. They followed it to a clear, cold stream. El didn't remember the name. They asked a prospector coming the other way and learned it was the Purgatoire River. A ford led to a village called Trinidad where they bought supplies and camped north of the village, having come twenty-five miles, a distance that had tired the horses and oxen, even though most of it was downhill.

"Nice to be in Colorado," Roz said, "and those mountains are as high as you said they'd be, El. They're pretty, but they look cold."

"Not as cold as they'll be in a month or two, I'd guess," Moose responded.

"You think anybody is still followin' us?" Roz asked El.

"I'm pretty sure they aint', but I'll keep an eye on our back-trail for a day or two."

"Thanks. We appreciate it."

The next morning, Henry broke a thin sheet of ice on the water bucket. Roz was slow to get out of his warm bedroll. Moose roused as soon as he heard Henry start the fire. Manuela and Ruby were up. Two gray "camp robber" jays perched on a low limb and watched them, hoping for scraps or the opportunity to take food from an unguarded plate. Miguel came walking in from the cottonwood grove near the stream close to camp. Cold didn't seem to bother him. When Manuela asked where he'd been, he replied that he thought he'd heard something.

"See anything?" El asked. Miguel shook his head.

El knew Miguel required relatively little sleep, just as he did, and that Miguel sometimes went walking in the dark to listen to the sounds of the night. El had learned Miguel could come and go without making much noise, even in dry weather. They were much alike.

Everyone put on more clothing against the chill, ate breakfast, and then moved to their usual morning tasks. Roz inspected equipment and harness. Moose brought the horses while Manuela and Lilia put the oxen into the yolk and hitched them to the cart. Henry cleaned pans and pots. Ruby put bedrolls away and helped Henry in whatever was required. El doused the fire with sand before deciding how they would proceed. Sometimes he rode a mile or more ahead or behind, to be sure they were on the right road or trail, and to see that the trail behind them was clear. Meanwhile Miguel cleaned the camp site, sweeping it with a branch if there was one available. Afterward he'd hide the branch where it wouldn't be noticed. Caution had become a habit.

By each sun-up they were moving. The horses were more energetic in the cool air, and adequate forage had made them look less gaunt. The oxen never changed. Miles melted away as they plodded on. El explained the pioneers had needed to sell their horses and buy oxen in order to make the long journey from the Missouri River to Oregon Territory. Horses couldn't continue to pull the heavy Conestoga and Studebaker wagons, loaded with provisions and whatever else the pioneers had decided to carry. They became fatigued and failed after a few weeks. Oxen were slow, but seemed always to go on.

At Pueblo, Manuela learned her sister had moved to Fort Collins where her husband opened a feed and livery company. Friends in Pueblo had received letters from her. Manuela had had none for over two years. She supposed it was because she'd lived so remotely on Mora Creek, and that the letters were waiting on a dusty shelf somewhere in Wagon Mound or Valmora, or maybe even in Santa Fe. She doubted she'd ever see them. There was little reason for her to stay in Pueblo, and she asked to continue. The others looked at her as if she was asking for something she already had.

The group decided to take an evening meal and rooms for one night in Pueblo's Fremont Hotel. After dinner they sat by the fireplace in the lobby, where crackling piñon-wood logs filled the room with warmth and pleasant incense. Roz picked a copy of the *Colorado Daily Chieftain* out of the wood box while he rocked in an oak chair. He scanned through the newspaper and gave pages he wasn't interested in to Moose.

"Says here, this daily is printed every morning except Monday," Roz said. "Guess it's not quite a daily. Here's an interesting piece. It reports the sale of stamps in the Denver post office last month totaled $1,937.81. Wonder why anybody in the world would care about…?"

"Listen to this," Moose interrupted. "The U.S. House of Representatives passed a bill by a vote of one hundred and sixty-four in favor to seventy-six against that allows Colorado to become a state, if the citizens agree. First a constitution has to be drawn up. Then folks will vote on it. There will be a constitutional committee at work on the drafting commencing during the month of September—well, this is a really old paper—says here, printed on July 12, 1875, over two months ago. Anyway, they're drawing up a constitution modeled on those of the eastern states. I guess that's happening right now. You know how politicians are when they get together. Reminds me of flies on… well, anyway, it says the vote will be early next spring or summer, and that Colorado will be called the 'Centennial State' on account of it being a hundred years since the United States was formed. Says there are about 150,000 people in Colorado now, and a lot more to come."

El flinched. Miguel noticed and tried to match El's expression.

Roz put the paper down. "I guess if you want land, it's best to get it while you can. I wonder what advantages there are in being a state or not being one?"

Moose considered for a moment and then said, "Well, for one thing, they'll be able to vote for their own representatives, state and local. Now it's all done by federal appointment. There will probably be new taxes, but I expect they think growth will make up for it. One thing they'll probably do is tax businesses, like railroads. Then they can build better roads, get streetcars, and the like. I suppose there are points for and against. We'll probably hear about it when we get to Denver."

"Guess so," Roz replied, reaching for the page Moose had read. "Let's see. Says here New Mexico and Colorado petitioned for statehood at the same time, and both were written into a congressional bill for vote. The bill was amended, at the end of a long debate, to the effect that Colorado was passed, but New Mexico wasn't. Just like Wooten said. I'll bet if New Mexico had gold and silver mines it would be approved right now."

El scratched his chin. He wasn't interested in political news, and he certainly didn't want to hear about population growth. He went outside to get his bedroll. Miguel followed.

The next day they continued north toward Manitou Springs, with strange and beautiful red sandstone formations revered by local Indians as a place of great spiritual value. They traveled over relatively level terrain on the road used by the Butterfield Stage, and camped by the trail at night. They saw a coach going north or south nearly every day. They had to wave the stagecoach to a stop if they wanted news or information about the road ahead. Butterfield drivers were terse. They were expected to keep moving and stay on time.

When Pikes Peak loomed on their left, it seemed impossibly high. El reminded them of the conversation in Mesa de Luna considering mountains too high to climb.

"You were right," Roz said to El. "I doubt I could climb it, and probably no one has." He was wrong; young Indian men had struggled to the top in search of visions from which they often took their adult names. The air was thin at fourteen thousand feet, and visions came after a day or two of fasting. It was considered 'good medicine' to make it to the top of one of the large Colorado Territory mountains, visible from the plains. Pikes Peak was the tallest in that area. Each tribe had different names for it as well as for other prominent peaks.

The group encountered few other travelers, and saw no Indians except those who stayed close to the trading posts and whiskey joints of Pueblo and Manitou Springs. They traded for needed supplies at Butterfield change stations or at trapper's trading posts. They passed an area called Monument for the upright stone formations. They stayed one night at Castle Rock, named for the citadel-like monolith that sat on the top edge of a steep hill and seemed ready to crush the scattering of buildings below.

At last, on October 12, 1875, three days ahead of Wooten's estimate, they found Cherry Creek and followed it toward Denver City. The horses were tired and thin, but trail-tough. The wagon was worn out. Their clothing was patched and soiled. Saddles and harness needed repair. The oxen looked as if they could go another thousand miles.

"Those critters just don't quit, do they?" Roz said.

"Nope," Henry replied. "They're slow, but they go."

Manuela smiled. "Soon they will have done their work for us. I think they must go to someone new." All eyes turned to her. "We will not need them. They should work, maybe on a farm. The children and I, we will not be going back."

"What about your sister?" Moose asked.

"I will try to find her," Manuela answered. "We are close now. We will see. I will write to her or go there. Maybe there is work for us in Fort Collins or Denver."

"I guess we all need to do something to earn money," Roz replied, while carefully not looking at Ruby.

El was thinking of a place he'd heard about, high in the Rocky Mountains. Estes Park had been found by a beaver trapper in the early 1800s, and by Indians long before that. El thought it likely the beaver had been trapped out, but he'd heard that deer, elk, and other game abounded. He knew he wouldn't stay in Denver, couldn't, and he'd begun to resign himself to the fact that Ruby would, or that she'd travel on to some other large town. She needed and wanted city life. He couldn't stand the thought of it.

El realized Mesa de Luna, that unlikely, semi-civilized half-village, was the only kind of place they could have met. It saddened him. He felt trapped by his own preferences. He knew the railroads, the stage lines, the increasing number of homesteads, and the growth of towns they had seen and heard about were closing in. There was a great deal of open space still, but the trend was evident.

He'd seen barbed wire for the first time as he scouted for a campsite near Castle Rock while the others waited on the road. It was strung on posts by a small lake and clearly was intended to keep something in or out. He passed it by and didn't mention it to the others. He eventually found a site near a clear stream and wondered how long before it and others like it would be fenced.

Indians were being pushed to the most remote areas, and he began to feel like one of them. He thought again about Estes Park. Remote and bountiful, he had heard. Three or four days' ride from Denver, and often snowbound in winter. Miguel might want to come. There were things El could teach him, or maybe just show him. Miguel didn't talk too much, and they understood each other. "C'mon, Buck" he muttered. "We've a long ways to go."

They traveled through scrub willows and cottonwood trees on a muddy, rutted road on the north side of Cherry Creek, to the bench land where it fed into the South Platte River. Denver City didn't look like much at first glance. Most of the clapboard buildings were single story. Few were painted. Streets were water-filled wagon-wheel ruts with mud holes at the intersections. Homes were small board-and-batten affairs with a woodpile and a privy out back. Some had corrals and a lean-to for a horse or cow. The city had a raw, transplanted look, unlike Pueblo which was larger and seemed more finished. They followed the main road to the Butterfield Stage station.

"Need any help here?" Moose asked the station manager.

"Nope. Full up. Lookin' for work, are ye'? Might stop at the newspaper office. *Rocky Mountain News*, just down the way. They've got jobs posted. Carpenters mostly, I think. Stone masons. Tough work in the winter, but some will do it. Anyway, check over there. Might be something for you."

"Much obliged," Moose said. "We'll go by. How often do you go to Fort Collins? Some of our party needs to get there."

"Every third day," the manager replied. "We go there and Bellvue on the way to Laramie. Not much in Fort Collins. About a week's round trip. Stage leaves day after tomorrow. We carry mail, too, and light freight if that helps."

"Thanks. We'll discuss it. Which way is the newspaper office?"

"Back up Speer Trail, the way you came from, to where you see that windmill. Left on California Street, about fifty yards. You can't miss it."

"Thanks, again," Moose replied. "One more thing. We'll be needing a place to stay. Any suggestions?"

"Well, there's a few rooms here and there. Two hotels, but one's full and the other isn't finished. They're over by the newspaper."

"Let's have a look at that empty hotel," Roz said as the manager went back inside.

"What for?" Henry asked.

"He didn't say 'empty,' Roz," Moose replied.

"Not finished, then. Let's go over there." Roz moved Buster on down the street.

"What's he tryin' to do?" Henry asked.

"Well," Moose replied, "I think he may be trying to solve several problems at once. Let's go see."

They found a thin, discouraged-looking fellow in a dirty white shirt and buckskin vest over black wool trousers perched precariously on a rough-made ladder, trying to hang a painted sign that said, "HOTEL LAGARDE" and, hand-printed under that, "J. LaGarde, Proprietor." As the morose sign-hanger started to drive the first nail, the hammer missed and struck the sign; the other end of the sign slipped off a prop and fell to the board porch with a crash. J. LaGarde slipped off the ladder and bounced on his backside next to the sign. Ladder, hammer, and nails clattered from the porch to the street below.

"*Merde*!" the figure exclaimed. "*Sacre blieu*! That stinking, no good…" He stood up, dusted himself off, and stared at the entourage that stopped in front of his building.

"Roz Wells is my name. This is Moose Banner," and Roz began to introduce the others.

"*Mon dieu, messieurs*, ze hotel ees not ready. Eet is not finish."

"I know that," Roz replied as Moose nodded. "We've come to finish it."

"But, but, there is no beds."

"There will be," Roz said. "We'll make them."

"There is no *chef*—no *kook*."

"Yes, there is," Roz replied. "Let's go inside and talk."

They learned Jean-Claude LaGarde had found labor to get the two-story building framed and roofed during the summer months. But then Indian scares, more lucrative offers, and the promise of riches in the silver mines had taken his workers, one by one. He'd struggled on by himself but, by his own admission, hadn't the skills for the project and wouldn't have finished for years. Rooms still needed to be divided and corner bunk beds made until free-standing beds could be purchased. LaGarde had a rough kitchen and basic foodstuffs, but no one to cook and little to cook in or on.

They made a bargain to build walls, beds, a front desk, tables, and benches. They agreed to help run the establishment when it was operational and to finish and rent rooms as soon as each room was ready. In exchange, they would receive bed and board and either wages or a small share of profit if and when there was some.

Ruby said she'd make beds and build furniture.

"Can you do that?" Roz asked.

"What?"

"Build furniture."

"Of course, I can…if I need to," she said with a smile. Roz didn't ask why she hadn't made the door to her adobe in Mesa de Luna or the other things he'd built for her. He'd started to ask, and then realized he was tired of banter, at least for the time being. *Good Lord*, he thought, *I'm losing my sense of humor on top of everything else. I hope I'm just tired.*

Henry and Manuela cooked. Lilia assisted with cooking, serving, and sweeping up after the day's carpentry was done. Roz built a three-holer for the men and, in the opposite corner of the lot, a single for women. Moose helped organize pricing and bills of fare, and assisted LaGarde in other ways. LaGarde had even less hotel experience than Moose had gained in New Orleans. However, he was eager to learn and easy to get along with.

El paced and got in the way for several days. Then he left for Estes Park. Miguel had asked to go along. Manuela finally agreed after trying to dissuade him.

The others worked hard, seven days a week. They spent half their time finding supplies and construction materials. Fortunately LaGarde had accounts in most of the areas stores, and his credit was good. He paid his bills on time. He'd told them he was from a wealthy family in France, and had taken his portion of an inheritance in cash and letters of credit. He was the only family member who had wanted to come to the United States.

Weeks passed. Slowly the hotel began to take shape and look like a real business. People stopped and inquired about rooms. Rooms were rented as soon as they became ready, however there was no serviceable kitchen or dining room, and patrons took their meals elsewhere. Only LaGarde and the three men and three women from New Mexico used the half- finished kitchen.

LaGarde had paid them, just as he'd said he would. The group was able to buy clothing and other supplies for themselves. Roz, Moose, and Henry went to a clothing store named the Chicago Square Dealing House, A. Philby, Proprietor. The women visited clothing and millinery shops, and came back looking more respectable than they had in many months.

On winter afternoons the group sat together by lantern light and played cards or read newspapers and magazines. The *Rocky Mountain News* office was close by, and Moose often stopped and bought either the weekly world news edition, or the daily local.

One evening, as they distributed portions of the paper to those interested in reading, Ruby said, "Look at this. "We can buy wholesale grocery products from the Londoner & Brothers store. It will save money when we start serving food. They have maple syrup for $1.50 per gallon. Ten pounds of New Orleans sugar for a dollar. Eight cans of oysters for a dollar. That's a lot of oysters."

"Stew," Henry interjected. "You use celery, carrots, a little milk, salt and pepper…"

"Sounds good," Roz said. "I could use some now. Too bad we don't have any."

"Anyway," Ruby continued, "It says there's choice Japanese tea, forty cents a pound, and Key West cigars for $7.50 a hundred."

"Here's a good one," Roz interrupted. "This headline says, 'The Man Who Fell Into An Upholstery Machine Is Fully Recovered.'"

"What?" Moose exclaimed. "I think you made that up. Let me look."

"Later," Roz answered, while holding the page so they couldn't see his face. "I'm not done. Listen to this. The meanest dog on earth will be put on exhibition, right here in Denver. He has a wolf's head on one end, and a bulldog's head on the other. He eats anything."

"Rozier, that's ridiculous."

"But," Henry said, "if he eats anything, and he has a head on each end, then how does he…?"

"He can't," Roz crowed. "That's what makes him so mean," and he broke into a fit of laughter. Lilia whispered a few words to her mother. Manuela looked puzzled for a moment, looked down and smiled. Moose shook his head

"I'll tell you what else he is," Henry replied.

"What's that?" Roz answered.

"Confused."

"Why?"

"Because," Henry said with a cackle, "he doesn't know if he's coming or going."

This brought a roar of laughter from Moose. Ruby punched Henry on the shoulder. After Lilia's interpretation for Manuela, she laughed also.

"Got you that time, Roz," Moose laughed.

"That he did," Roz chuckled. "Henry, you surprise me. I didn't think I'd hear that from you."

"That's because you don't listen," Henry replied.

"Sometimes I don't, on account of I have so much to say."

"Listen to this," Moose interjected, "on November 3rd, that was last week, umm … I'll read it to you." Roz closed his eyes and pretended to snore.

Moose raised his voice. "A dispatch from Fort Laramie this morning said that the Council of Indian Treaty Commissioners have returned and will proceed to Cheyenne by the quickest possible means. Train, I guess. Their attempts to conclude a treaty with the Sioux were a total failure, and the latter are so much excited that there is great danger of war'. I'll skip some of the details. It goes on to say, 'The northern and southern bands are so much incensed against each other that a tribal war is imminent, in which case the white settlements and agencies will be likely to suffer from both parties. There is now no hope of opening The Black Hills, which causes bitter disappointment to all.'"

"That doesn't square with other news we've read," Roz said. "Miners have been going by the thousands."

"That's right," Moose answered. "General Custer went with a troop of cavalry in seventy-three to survey sites for military posts. He came out talking about gold. Those were treaty lands. Federals shouldn't have been there in the first place. The Sioux and Northern Cheyenne were furious, and who can blame them? Now the government has been trying to buy the whole area from the Black Hills on the east, to the Bighorn Mountains on the west, and from the Platte River south, to Canada, for six million dollars, according to what it says here.

"It says the Indians, I guess some of the reservation Indians, wanted sixty or seventy million. That's more than ten times as much. Some of the non-reservation, or free Indians, said 'no sale at any price.' Of course, you can never be sure you have the whole story when the facts come from the government. I think I'll go to bed. Reading this stuff tires me out."

In spite of rampant Indian-war rumors, the hotel continued to take shape. The industrial kitchen stove finally arrived by mule train from Omaha. Henry and Manuela shopped for foodstuffs and cooking utensils. Additional rooms were rented as quickly as they were ready, and others were reserved weeks in advance. Moose insisted on a week's advance payment.

People soon learned of the good food being served, and the tables and benches were full for all three meals. In only a few weeks there was enough cash to order curtains and carpets, as well as chamber pots and commodes to put them in. LaGarde relaxed after he decided his new partners wouldn't leave or steal, and by the middle of December they had a rough but running enterprise.

"I like this place," Moose told Roz one evening as they relaxed by the parlor stove. "The hotel reminds me of Mom's boarding house, but I like the people out here a lot better."

"Why is that, do you think?" Roz asked.

"Well, partly because everyone has an equal chance. There are no old, rich families calling the tune for everyone else. Every person has the chance to work, prosper, and marry anyone they choose. That's real freedom. Plus, Colorado is just getting started. New Orleans was settled a long time ago, and Mesaluna was going backward. Here, folks can even decide to be a state or not be one. I'd guess Territorial Governor John L. Routt will be the first state governor."

"Grant appointed him, didn't he?" Roz asked.

"To be territorial governor, yes. I read there have been seven. The other six were thrown out for one reason or another. Evans was doing fine until Chivington's Sand Creek massacre." He shook his head. "Two hundred unarmed men, women, and children, killed for no good reason. Chivington was the hero of Glorietta Pass, but now he and Evans are both out of favor. Hell of a thing. A genuine tragedy. Anyway, that's behind us. It seems a lot safer here now, for Indians as well as whites. And," he added, "I like the hotel business, meeting new people, hearing the news. I like all of it. How about you?"

"I'd rather have a small spread, do some farming, raise some animals, raise a family, make a real home for myself."

"You have any idea where you're going find someone to raise a family with?"

"I don't know, but the Good Lord didn't intend me to sleep alone," Roz said with a grin.

"Noticed you were a little late getting home last night. Up to your old tricks?"

"Why, Moose, I was just mindin' my own business. Course, I was helping one of those Silver Dollar girls mind hers, too."

"I'm glad you're yourself again—I think. And it seems we don't have to worry about the *Alcalde* any longer."

"I never did worry about him much, you know."

Moose started to reply, closed his mouth. Roz was probably right; he didn't worry about much of anything. It was one of his charming attributes, even if a bit unrealistic, and maybe a little dangerous.

Chapter Thirty Four

WINTER

"The Silver Dollar? I thought you might be over there. I also thought you might be settling down some."

"I wouldn't mind doing that, Moose. I'd like to find the right woman, make a family. You know?"

"I suppose I do, although you are kind of hard to keep up with. Six months ago," Moose lowered his voice, "you were chasin' after Ruby like a, like a . . ."

"Just having fun, Moose. We were friends. Still are."

"Then you were all steamed up about Lilia. Though I'll say you seem to have relaxed some on that idea."

"She's sixteen years old, or thereabout. She belongs with her ma for a year or two. I think I'm nearly twice as old as she is. Plus, sorting her out with her mother, Miguel, memories of her dad, relatives in Fort Collins…well, I'd just like things to be easier."

"I don't know if it ever gets easier," Moose replied. He stared at the flames flickering behind the pot-bellied stove's isinglass window for a full minute. "Roz, I'm going to tell you something I've never told anyone. You have a few minutes?"

Roz was slumped in his chair with his feet propped against the wood box. "Do I look like I'm in a hurry?" he said.

"Guess not. Why don't you go get that jug under my bunk. This may take a while."

Roz stood up slowly while looking at Moose, and then left the room. When he returned with the whiskey jug, Moose was deep in thought.

"This jug?" Roz asked.

"Of course, that jug. How many do you think I have?"

"I was just trying to get your attention. Don't get proddy."

"All right. Sorry." Moose took a swig, wiped his mouth with the back of his hand and pinched the bridge of his nose. Then he settled himself and began to speak slowly, softly.

"About five years ago, when I left New Orleans, I really didn't care much if I lived or died. I never told you why I left. There was a girl, a young woman. Her name was Suzanne Marie Pelletier. She's Mrs. Parker DuPree now. She was the most beautiful woman I've ever seen. I'm going to tell you what happened."

After Moose finished speaking he looked Roz in the eye. "I want to show you a letter," he said. Moose handed his copy of The Rubaiyat to Roz and asked him to read the enclosed letter folded inside the first page.

My Dearest Morris,

I must hurry to write this. I cannot leave you without some word of what has happened. It was arranged two years ago that I would marry Mister DuPree, my father's partner. I wasn't informed until later, and I postponed and postponed as I have no feelings for him. I wanted to wait until October, when I would have been a legal adult and able to do as I wished, but that is of no consequence now. My father learned of our courtship. He informed me that Mr. DuPree owns everything we have, including the business and this house, due to gambling debts of which I was not aware. If I do not marry as he wishes my father will have no home. Clarissa and Old Dave would have nowhere to go. Father will force me to leave on a packet boat tomorrow morning, for St. Louis where I must marry Mr. DuPree. We will travel to his assignment on some frontier post in the Dakotas where he will accept an appointment in The Army of the United States. Clarissa is not allowed to come with me and that, too, breaks my heart. Father knows she aided us and believes she should have told him.

Please do not follow. I couldn't bear that. It will be very difficult to do what I must, and much more difficult if you are near. I can only tell you this. I have loved you, and I do love you, most sincerely. I must hurry and pass this to Clarissa. I will tell her to take it to you after I am gone.

Unending love,

Suzanne

P.S. You can never know what you have given me.

When he'd finished reading Roz carefully folded and put the letter back. He placed the book on the table and looked at Moose.

"Roz, she didn't want to go. I know it. But she did. I guess she had to, and I couldn't do anything about it—or I *didn't* do anything about it. I don't know…"

"Where do you think she is now?" Roz asked.

"I wish I knew. Living at some fort up north, I guess."

"Well, Moose, the way I see it, you have two choices. You can get your head straightened out and find another woman, or you can go looking for her. There has to be records. Of where her husband is, I mean. I'll help you find her if you want me to."

"No, but thanks. Even if I knew where to look, I'm not keen on stealing other men's wives. She is married, you know."

"There is such a thing as legal divorce, and it seems to me like she was yours first."

"I've thought about that; too much probably. But one thing I could never do is break up a family. It isn't right. If I have to suffer for not doing so, I'd suffer even more if I did.

"That doesn't leave you much choice, does it?"

"No, it doesn't. Maybe I'll meet somebody someday, but I'll never forget her, and I'm afraid she'll always be first. I mean, I'm afraid her memory would mean more to me than the other woman. That would be a terrible thing."

"I have to agree with you on that. I'll tell you one thing I've learned, though."

"What's that?"

"You should never give up. Never."

Moose looked at him quizzically.

"Never," Roz repeated with force. "You can't tell what's going to happen."

"Maybe you're right. Here I am talking about her instead of letting it go. I'm going to try to get some sleep and try to forget it, at least for a while." *And hope I don't dream,* he said to himself.

Christmas came to Denver, escorted by another snow storm. Roz found a small blue-spruce tree and fashioned a stand for it with two pieces of crossed board nailed through the bottom of the trunk. He placed it in the corner of the dining room. They decorated it with paper chains made from strips of butcher paper and flour-and-water paste. Ruby and Manuela strung popcorn with needles and thread. Roz cut stars from pieces of tin cans. Moose punched a hole in one point of each star and handed them to Lilia, who hung them with thread.

El and Miguel surprised them by traveling through winter weather, arriving two days before Christmas with fresh venison and grouse. Henry and Manuela made a feast fit for royalty. They didn't exchange gifts, but El played the harmonica after much coaxing. A guest went to his room and came back with a violin. Henry surprised everyone by singing Christmas carols with a clear tenor voice. Manuela stood next to him and hummed the ones she knew.

"Henry, I didn't know you could sing," Roz exclaimed. "Why didn't you do it before?"

"Didn't feel like it," Henry answered, "and now I do."

New Year's Day dawned crystal clear and bitterly cold. The snow had melted and the hills west of Denver were brown, dry. Only the highest peaks wore white. El and Miguel said goodbye and rode through Boulder and Lyons, to Estes Park.

Lobo Alto, just back from Albuquerque, had been camping on Cherry Creek. He'd spotted the horses before he saw their owners. The buckskin, the large gray, the black horse, and Indian ponies loafed in a muddy corral behind a half-finished hotel building. He'd watched from a distance as guests came and went. On the first day of 1876 he noticed El packing the saddle bags on his buckskin, and helping the boy get ready to leave. Lobo almost smiled. He'd follow them, see where they were going. He wasn't sure what he'd do then, but he was determined to meet El face-to-face, and next time he'd be ready.

El and Miguel kicked snow from the door and stepped inside the Estes Park cabin. It seemed twice as cold inside as out. El hurried to make a fire in the potbellied stove while Miguel stood aside, shivering. When the inside temperature rose above freezing they banked the fire, blew out the lamp, and went to bed, exhausted from the long ride.

Lobo Alto stood in the open shed behind the big buckskin and the Indian pony. He watched smoke curl into the dawn air from the log cabin's chimney. Renfroe and the kid were inside with a warm stove and an oil lamp. Lobo saw yellow light through the small window. He'd never been so cold in his life.

Renfroe opened the door and walked through knee deep snow to the privy. He was unarmed. Lobo approached, carefully sliding his feet to avoid creaking footsteps on the snow. He stopped when he thought he might alert Renfroe. The privy door opened and Renfroe stepped out, cinching up his belt. Lobo quickly walked in front of him, revolver leveled at Renfroe's chest. "Inside," he said.

El looked at the pale eyes, the gun that didn't move, shrugged, and started toward the cabin's plank door. Lobo let him pass, and then followed. El opened the door and quickly gestured to the surprised Miguel who had started to reach for a rifle leaning against a corner. “Don’t,” El said. “Not now.” Miguel stepped back.

“Sit,” Lobo said, pointing to one of the two rough-made benches.

“Then what?” El said. “You plannin’ to kill us?”

Lobo didn’t answer as he eased himself onto the other bench across the table from El. He stared at El for a long moment. Then he carefully placed the revolver precisely between El and himself. He moved his hand away from the gun, about the same distance as El’s. Then he waited. Two minutes passed while the two tall men stared at each other. Neither blinked. The only sound was the popping of pine knots in the pot-bellied stove.

No,” Lobo replied, as he slowly leaned back and put his hands in his lap.

“What, then?”

There was a long silence. “First,” Lobo rumbled, “get warm. Then eat.”

“Eat?”

“Yes. Then talk.”

“Well, I’ll be damned,” El replied.

“Yes,” Lobo said. “You will.” He looked at Miguel. “There’s bacon on the pack horse. Left side pannier. Behind your shed.”

Miguel looked at El, who nodded. Miguel went out.

"Can he make biscuits?" Lobo asked. El shook his head. "Can you?"

"No."

Lobo sighed. "I'll teach you. You have beans?"

"Yes."

"Flour?"

"Yes."

"Venison?"

"No."

"Elk?"

"I was going hunting today."

"I'll go with you," Lobo said.

Chapter Thirty Five

ICE

Cherry Creek and the South Platte were frozen solid. Livestock owners broke six inches of ice in their watering tanks. The tanks froze again within thirty minutes. The bucket in the hotel kitchen had a quarter-inch of ice even though it was only six feet from the stove. Guests came to breakfast early, breathing clouds of vapor as they entered and sat down. Henry kept the coffee pot filled and listened to complaints about the weather but rarely about the hotel. Guests expected to be cold and were, in some measure, used to eating in heavy coats.

On January seventh, a blizzard howled down from the northeast plains and didn't stop until the tenth. Freight wagons couldn't get into or out of Denver for over a week. Residents shared dwindling supplies of food and firewood. A troop of U. S. Cavalry soldiers were welcomed into Denver homes until they could continue their travel. High winds drifted snow until it reached the eaves of some of the houses and businesses. Older horses died in their enclosures. Cattle died also, and the meat was quickly processed and sold. Some said it tasted as though a bit of horse meat might have been included, but no one complained.

A flu epidemic had broken out before Christmas. It stopped as soon as the blizzard started, as though frozen out of existence. Freighters asked if they could rent Manuela's oxen and cart to get supplies from sources at Fort

Morgan and Fort Collins. After consultation with Henry she politely declined, fearing they might be harmed by overwork or abuse.

One January day, after freight service had resumed, wagons brought a load of new beds and bureaus from the Cheyenne railroad depot to the LaGarde. They had been shipped by the Union Pacific from Chicago.

"What will we do with the old ones?" Manuela asked.

"I guess, burn them," Roz replied. "We're low on wood, anyway. Unless someone wants to buy them."

"Put them for sale in the newspaper," Moose suggested. They did, and within two days all had been sold.

"We're low on hay," Henry said.

"I know," Manuela replied. "When spring comes, we will sell the oxen. Farmers will want them for working the fields, for ploughing."

"That might be best," Roz agreed. "All the same, I'll hate to see them leave. They did quite a job for us."

"Yes," she replied, "but there are times to let things go."

Roz nodded, knowing she'd said more than was apparent.

In early February, the freeze was broken by a "chinook" wind, raising the temperature forty degrees in less than an hour. It melted the drifts and turned the streets into muddy bogs. Horses and mules walked in the fetlock-deep muck with a sucking, popping sound.

The South Platte River and Cherry Creek ran bank-full. Where they met, the water was the color of old coffee mixed with soured cream. Teacup-sized tufts of foam swirled in the backwater eddies of Cherry Creek. The Platte carried bloated carcasses of animals killed in the January blizzard, mixed with tree limbs, pieces of lumber, weeds, and grass. There were no fords available for miles in any direction. Travelers who wanted to go west toward the mountains had to wait and hope for low water.

The flood crested on the third day, and the water level started to drop. Then it rained for a day and snowed the following two. Again the river rose, but finally became shallow enough to cross after several dry days. Hotel guests left for the trail along Clear Creek, going toward Idaho Springs and the mining towns higher in the Rockies. Travelers who had been stranded on the west bank took their place. People moved through Denver, headed north toward the Union Pacific railroad in Cheyenne. Others came from Cheyenne and passed through, going south toward Santa Fe and Albuquerque. In all conditions, mud, rain, snow, or blowing dust, during day and night, Denver continued to grow in its noisy, hearty way.

The Rocky Mountain News editor had dubbed Denver, "The Queen City of the Plains," a generous appellation for the collection of tar-paper buildings, board-and-batten store fronts, double-wall tents, and scattered structures made of brick or stone. Moose guessed the residents would like the description and keep it.

April brought the first day that didn't require an overcoat, and in early May the mud began to dry. Two weeks later, the streets were again dusty, and coated one side or the other according to which way the wind blew. Freighters and travelers arrived and described the conditions they'd encountered on the rivers and plains. Cavalry troopers gave accounts of Indian activities in the Dakotas and Wyoming. It was rumored that a large contingent of Northern Cheyenne and Sioux were gathered around the headwaters of the Missouri River in Montana. Opinions were mixed about what should be done about "the Indian question," and it became a topic of political debate.

Moose told them what he'd heard, that a U.S. Army expedition was being organized to travel up the Missouri and give a show of force to Sitting Bull, Red Cloud, Crazy Horse, and other Cheyenne and Sioux leaders. Soon the news was all over town. Most level-headed people hoped the cavalry could contain the tribes and motivate them to move toward reservations without bloodshed. Not all citizens and soldiers hoped for peace, but the majority did. They wanted no more massacres such as the Sand Creek "battle", where Chivington's Colorado militia had killed scores of unarmed Indian men, women, and children. Chivington was in disgrace after a military tribunal had heard evidence from courageous officers under his command.

Roz noticed Moose talking with all the uniformed officers he met. He'd seen them shake their heads when Moose asked a question; a question that Roz couldn't hear, but was pretty sure he understood.

In mid-May El and Miguel came down from Estes Park, accompanied by a tall, thin rider who appeared to be at ease with them. He avoided talking with anyone except El and Miguel, and they seemed to communicate with gestures and facial expressions as much as with words. He declined an invitation to come into the hotel and said he'd sleep with the horses.

Then El learned of the expedition to the headwaters of the Missouri. He contacted the local army post and asked for an assignment to guide troops, even though he hadn't seen the country where they expected to find the Cheyenne and Sioux. His reputation as a moderate and careful scout, known and respected by at least some of the Sioux, was thought to be helpful. He asked for permission to bring two individuals with him and received approval.

His orders were to travel to Fort Abraham Lincoln in Dakota Territory near the junction of Big Muddy Creek and the Missouri River, and to be at the fort by the tenth of June. Fort "Abe" Lincoln was one of the largest military installations on the northern plains, garrisoned by three companies of infantry and six companies of the famed 7th Cavalry. He was to meet with the contingent headed by General George A. Custer.

"Why do you want to do that?" Moose asked. "I know you don't want to fight Indians."

"I don't, but maybe I can keep things calm while I earn a bit of money. Besides, I've always wanted to see that country where Lewis and Clark went. Lobo," he gestured in the direction of the corral, "wants to come along."

"Me, too," Miguel said.

"Miguelito!" Manuela exclaimed. "You are fourteen years. You are not going with soldiers."

Miguel gave her a level look and said in a quiet voice, "Mama, I am not going to stay here. I am old enough to go where I want to go. If El goes, I am going."

"There's work for boys," El added. "Stock work, bugling, and such. It's all right with me, but he'll, uh…you'll have to decide. I have to leave day after tomorrow."

"You are not going," Manuela declared.

“I am. I have already decided,” Miguel said to Manuela. “I am going.” He crossed his arms and stood as tall as possible.

Moose saw that Miguel was an inch or so taller than he’d been when they met him at the farm on the Mora. He didn’t weigh more than one hundred and twenty pounds, Moose guessed, but there was something very hard and resolved about him. He’d left childhood behind, if there had ever been one. He looked like a smaller, darker version of El, thin and whip-cord tough. Moose hoped they would have a successful campaign and return to settle somewhere nearby, although it was hard to imagine El settling anywhere.

El, Miguel, and Lobo, their silent companion, left on a bright morning. Miguel, on a full-sized horse Lobo had given him in Estes Park. Manuela had provided Juan’s saddle. Miguel leaned down and let his mother and Lilia hug him. “I’ll—be back,” he said as he turned his horse away.

El blushed and tipped his hat to Ruby, then nodded to the others. Something in his eyes told them he had already started the journey. He looked at them, but saw something else, something far away. The group stood in silence while El and Miguel mounted and rode side by side, up the street to the corner, turned north, and passed from view, Lobo close behind. His horse seemed to move without sound.

There was no breeze. Dust hung in the air. A thin brown dog trotted up to them, sniffed anxiously, and moved away. The faint sound of hammering came from the next street. Sparrows quarreled over nesting sites behind the hotel sign. The Rockies were pure white. The United States flag hung limp in front of the new post office. An old man dozed on the steps in the morning sun.

Ruby shook her head and went inside. Manuela crossed herself and followed Ruby, with Lilia close behind.

Roz turned and looked at Moose. Moose waited.

"I'm staying here," Roz said. "I mean, not right here, but in Colorado."

"I thought you might," Moose replied.

"I want to see that Fort Collins country we've been hearing about. Larimer County they're going to call it, when statehood passes. I want to see the Cache la Poudre River, Red Feather Lakes, Livermore, Virginia Dale. I like rim-rock country, like we saw down by Monument and Manitou Springs. I'll probably settle up there if it's as good as people say. It's only about forty miles from the railroad. The army is going to need beef and horses. Other folks will, too. I don't want to travel any more. I—guess I'm getting old, or just plain tired."

"Maybe you're getting smart," Moose replied.

Roz grinned and said, "Folks have accused me of a lot of things. I don't recall that being one of 'em."

Moose smiled with him, then sobered. "Well," he said, "I've decided I don't want to farm or ranch, and probably never did. I don't need to go all the way to the Northwest to learn that. I think I was trying to run away from—well—you know, but I don't think I need to anymore. Maybe I'll start a hotel in the country you're talking about." Moose also hoped against hope that he might find Suzanne living at Fort Collins. He knew it was irrational, but he needed to hope for something, however remote.

"Why don't we have a look? We could take a few days and see what we'd see. Henry and Manuela can take care of this place with a little help from Ruby and LaGarde."

"If he doesn't go to England while we're gone," Moose chuckled.

"Hell, Moose, Henry ain't going anywhere Manuela doesn't go, and she ain't going anywhere."

"How do you know?"

"Lilia told me Manuela's sister has written three letters asking them to come to Fort Collins. Manuela won't set a date. She has a paying job and she likes it. Won't even ask what the stage fare is. And I don't think she'll leave Henry, dumb as he is. If he asked her to marry him, I believe she might."

"Why don't you tell him…you know, 'put a bug in his ear?"

"No, Moose. I'm through butting into other people's lives. I hardly know what to do with my own. One thing I've learned on this trip is that I'm not as smart as I thought I was."

"You'll get by," Moose answered. "What about Ruby?"

"Ruby?" Roz rubbed the back of his neck. "I expect she'll be getting on the stage for Cheyenne one of these days, and take the U.P. to San Francisco.

"Who will?" Ruby said as she stuck her head out of the door. "Me?"

"I was just guessing," Roz replied.

"You guessed right, and I know exactly what I'm going to do when I get there. I'm going downtown. I'm going to rent two rooms. I'll sleep in the small one in the back, and I'll open Ruby Lee's Card Room in the front. I'm going to have gas lights and red carpets. I want to retire from my—former occupation, but not get too far from it, if you know what I mean. I like men, and I like money." She gave a toss of her head and disappeared.

"Well, Moose, I guess that leaves you and me and a world of opportunity, don't it."

"Yep. Looks like it does. Why don't we walk down to the Silver Dollar. I'll buy you one."

"That's the best idea you've had all day. I'm dry as a popcorn fart, if you'll pardon the expression."

As they stepped onto the downtown boardwalk Moose saw a tall woman with auburn hair pinned up under a stylish hat. The way she moved, the way she'd tilted her hat, caused Moose to hurry and catch a glimpse of the side of her face. But he'd never seen her before. He sighed, slowed, and let Roz catch up. Roz looked but made no comment.

As Moose and Roz seated themselves at the bar a pair of teamsters came in and elbowed to get room beside Roz. They leaned down and put grimy elbows on the bar. The closer, larger one had a cataract in the near eye. He had to turn his head half-around to see Roz clearly. "Why'n hell don't you move over?" he said between gapped, brown-stained teeth. His breath reeked of garlic.

"I'd be more than glad to do that," Roz replied, "except there's no more room on that side than there is on yours."

"Well, aren't you the smart ass," the freighter said. "What's your name, smart ass?"

"Roz Wells," Roz said carefully and looked the freighter up and down.

"I think that's a stupid name."

"I think a man's entitled to his own opinion," Roz said. He carefully drained his glass. He shoved it over and knocked the freighter's glass so that it spilled onto the bar.

"Now," Roz said, before the freighter's had time to respond, "What's yours?"

"What's my what?"

"You know what," Roz snapped while moving closer and standing to be a little higher than the slouching teamster.

"Al Williams," the teamster said truculently. "And I told you . . ."

"Aloysius, Alphonse, what?"

"Albert, but it's none of your goddamn business," the freighter said as he stood straight.

Roz turned to Moose, then turned back. "Albert Williams," Roz said thoughtfully. "I knew an Albert Williams back in Texas. Could that be…?" He looked at the freighter carefully. "Naw, he was a lot bigger than you. Dumb as a post. Ugly, too. No offense. I remember old dumb and ugly Al Williams. Tried to rile me. One day I thought to myself, I might as well knock some sense into this Albert Williams or I'm never going to get any peace." He stared into the teamster's good eye. "Broke him up pretty bad." The freighter looked confused. Moose was beginning to enjoy the exchange.

Roz looked thoughtful for a moment. He smiled without blinking while he flexed his hands and said, "Broke some of his ribs and most of his teeth. They say he didn't hear too well after that. Too bad about poor old stupid Albert. I guess sometimes I just get out of control."

The freighter glanced around the room, pulled at the collar of his shirt, and said to his partner, "Let's get out of here. I don't like this place. Too damn crowded." He looked back at Roz once as he walked away. Then they were gone.

"Now, you didn't really know an Al Williams, did you?" Moose asked.

"Course not," Roz replied, "but that fellow was big. Might have hurt me," Roz said with a grin. "I'd like another," he said to the bartender, and to Moose, "I want to toast you and me to good luck."

Moose smiled and waited for the bartender to fill Roz's glass. "To luck," he said as they clinked. "It's high time."

Carlos Antonio Arajo de Chama y Las Animas, *Gubernador* of New Mexico Territory, stood with his back to the fire burning in the small corner hearth of his bedroom suite. An even row of tall poplar trees whispered outside his window, sentinels nodding in the breeze. Yellow climbing roses scented the room, mingling with the governor's cigar and the remnants of Rosalinda's perfume. *Good*, he thought . *Every day is good.* He slowly toured the room, cigar hand behind his back while with the other hand he touched favorite objects of turquoise, gold, and silver.

How fortunate Juan Diego lost the silver. I don't need it. I can get more any time. Rosalinda is worth her weight in silver, in gold even. He smiled. *If the men find it, fine. If not, fine too. I will let them keep looking, but I really don't care. Juan Diego can rot. He makes too many promises anyway.*

Chapter Thirty Six

HOMESTEAD

Henry watched Moose and Roz saddle up as they prepared to leave Denver on a warm spring day. "Be careful," he said, "and watch what you eat. You don't cook well enough to avoid poisoning yourselves, and I don't want to have to come lookin' for you."

"Why, Henry," Roz replied with a grin, "I didn't know you cared."

"Hmmpf," Henry grunted with a sour expression and stomped back inside.

"Ready?" Moose asked.

"As I'll ever be." They mounted and turned the horses toward the Fort Lupton road, following the east bank of the Platte, between the water and the graded road for the new Denver Pacific tracks. The river had shrunk to its normal width of twenty-five to fifty yards and was rarely more than a few feet deep.

On the west side of the river farmers were growing corn, beans, and other crops that were difficult to identify at a distance. The east bank soil was sandy, too dry to farm while the west side was flourishing.

The road had been made on the higher and drier east side. It came close to drop-offs where winter floods had undermined the bank, and in a few places the road had been re-built where it had been washed away completely.

They stopped for a meal in a café at Brighton Corner, skirted old Fort Lupton by staying on the east side of the river, and decided to spend the night at Fort Vasquez. The "fort" was actually a private trading post, just as Bent's Fort and Fort Lupton had been; all built for the fur trade in the 1830s. The trading posts predated all of the military forts in the area, including Fort Morgan and Fort Collins. The post stock wrangler told them Fort Vasquez had closed in 1842, but was reopened as a Butterfield Stage station in the 1850s.

Vasquez had served as a safe haven for travelers during the 1860 to 1865 Indian uprising. It was square, one hundred feet on each side, and walled with adobe bricks; the walls approximately twelve feet high. Sentry posts were built into the northwest and southeast corners and large central gates allowed passage of stage coaches, livestock, and wagons. The fort included corrals and a barn, living quarters, sleeping rooms rented to travelers, and a trading and food sales room. It was still operating as a traveler's way-station when Moose and Roz arrived. It offered good food and reasonable accommodations. They ate and slept well.

The next morning they followed the Greeley road and forded at LaSalle, although they could have crossed the shallow river almost anywhere. They continued north to the town of Greeley, a communal farming and trade town organized by Nathan Meeker in 1869 and controlled by individual investors in a joint-stock company called 'The Union Colony'. It was an experiment in Western idealism. A large, carved billboard proclaimed Greeley to be the new "Utopian Garden". The board stated that owners and participants adhered to the ideals of temperance, religion, cooperation, and agriculture, along with "such other community services as may be required." A painted arrow pointed to a rain-proof box containing printed cards.

"Ever see anything like that?" Roz asked, pointing at the sign.

"Never," Moose replied. "Here, take one of these little cards. It tells more about what they're up to."

The colony had been inspired by Horace Greeley, the editor of the *New York Tribune,* and of "Go West, Young Man" fame. Meeker had been Greeley's agricultural editor, an important department in a nation where agronomy was the foremost growth industry. Meeker had learned of an opportunity to buy sixty thousand acres along the planned Denver Pacific Railway. The land was halfway between Denver and Cheyenne, which the railroad had connected one year later, in 1870. Meeker knew a good thing when he saw one, and he had the vision and administrative skills to make it happen. Each colonist was required to pay a $155 fee to The Union Colony for a city lot before they could settle and receive stock shares.

“It’s seems a little too confining for my taste,” Roz said after he’d finished reading. “But let’s ride through it anyway. Then we’ll go on.”

Greeley had been carefully planned and laid out. It had wide, tree-lined streets with curbs and gutters. City blocks were rectilinear, due north and south. It looked prosperous and quiet. There was something attractive about it, in a disconcerting way. It seemed almost too orderly to allow relaxed comfort.

“What that place needs is a few bars and dance halls,” Roz commented as they left. “I’ll bet they don’t even have a town drunk.”

They continued toward Fort Collins, following the south bank of the Cache la Poudre River, named by French-speaking beaver trappers who were caught in an early fall blizzard in 1836. Moose and Roz had read that the trappers dug a hole, a “cache,” in which they deposited supplies including gunpowder. The following spring, they found the cache of *poudre* intact. They’d named the river for their experience.

The Poudre flowed cold and clear from the foothills of the Rockies. The mountains grew closer as afternoon waned. The earth under their horse’s hooves changed from the warm, dry, open plains to moist ground. Cottonwood trees were numerous. Small lakes and ponds dotted the landscape. Waterfowl swam away from them, or took flight to land on other ponds in the distance. Deer bounded from red willow patches. Grouse and prairie chickens called from the sagebrush-covered hillsides. Trout darted from the shallows toward deeper pools.

The soil looked dark and rich. Farm crops and small houses indicated that settlers had homesteaded the river-bottom land. Barbed wire was used to fence haystacks away from cattle, deer, and elk.

They found the town of Fort Collins perched on a bluff above the Poudre. At first glance there seemed little reason for it to be there. The old fort commanded the river, but the small volume of water made travel unlikely, even by canoe. They knew the site had been chosen because of the junction of trails going west up the Poudre, south along the front range of the mountains, north to Cheyenne and the railroad town of Laramie, and east toward Greeley. Cheyenne was one long day's ride and Laramie, two or three.

They talked with the hotel clerk at the Fisk House where they had decided to room for a few days. He told them the fort had been founded in 1864 by General Robert A. Cameron, but was named Camp Collins for Cameron's superior officer, Colonel William O. Collins, Commandant of Fort Laramie.

Must have been suckin' up to the chief, Roz had almost said.

Fort Collins was built by federal troops, including a company of "galvanized rebels," captured Confederate soldiers who had been discharged from federal military prisons on condition that they pledge allegiance to the United States, enlist in the Union Army, and take assignment in western territories to defend settlers from Indian attack.

Camp Collins, later re-named Fort Collins, had housed two companies of 11th Ohio Volunteer Cavalry brought from Fort Laramie. The town grew beside it and adopted the name. However, most of the garrison had been relocated to Fort Laramie in March of 1867, almost ten years earlier.

Their room wasn't as clean as Moose would have liked, but it had a window that opened. Moose felt he could improve the way the hotel was run, but didn't plan to mention his ideas to the clerk or to the owner, whom the clerk had said was busy with another Fisk establishment, the Fisk General Merchandise Store that sold furniture, buggies, clothing, hay, grain, hats, tools, and sundries.

The following day Moose spoke to a number of merchants as well as the president of the Poudre Valley Bank. He inquired about the availability of business opportunities in the area and learned that nearly everyone was willing to sell what they had—for a price. However, most were waiting until the railroad spur to Fort Collins would be completed in 1877 when, they assumed, the city would grow even more rapidly. Moose concluded he'd have to start a business with borrowed capital, if it was available, or make a deal with an owner who was motivated to leave and would accept reasonable terms.

Roz found the federal land office where he studied large maps showing areas that had been homesteaded, or deeded by the government in some other manner. He was given brochures which explained that in 1841 the U.S. Government had passed the Pre-emption Law. The law allowed a person or family, popularly called "squatters", first claim to 160 acres of un-surveyed land. The fact that boundaries hadn't been surveyed made establishment of property lines a matter of debate, and battles had raged in the courts for decades. The price of $1.25 per acre was made easier by a provision allowing payment of only twenty-five cents per acre, with the balance due eighteen months later. Much of the best land had already been secured in that manner.

The Homestead Act, passed by Congress in 1862 and made effective on January 1, 1863, allowed each "bona fide" settler to obtain 160 acres of already-surveyed land owned by the government. The property was to be filed by legal description, and the person making the entry had to swear he or she had personally seen the property before filing. Thus, "squatting" lost all legal status, and settlers who had owned Pre-emption Act land were required to re-file under the Homestead Act. However, the requirements of living on the land for at least five years and for “making improvements” were waived for Pre-emption Act landowners.

Those who gained title under the Homestead Act were required to cultivate at least ten of the 160 acres. They had to build a permanent dwelling and live on the land for five years. At the end of that time, with two neighbors or friends who would vouch for the truth of their statements about the improvements then could sign the ‘proof’ document and take title.

One hundred sixty acres constituted a quarter of a section; a surveyed section was one mile square and encompassed 640 acres. Thus, the typical quarter-section was a one-half-mile by one-half-mile square. If the quarter was in rich river valley soil, or “bottom” land, it was adequate for farming, raising livestock, and raising a family. The same number of acres on the arid tablelands often would not provide a living, no matter how hard a family worked. Many homesteaders failed to “prove-up”, and left their filings to go elsewhere. These abrogated homesteads were again made available for filing, but there were few takers unless adult (age-twenty one or older) family members could file and attach the land to other acres already owned by the family, thereby making an effective economic unit. Some large families with several children over the age of twenty-one were able to claim and keep large family farms.

Roz had thought he might go north and look at the area around LaPorte and Bellvue. Land office maps showed most of the land near Fort Collins, and all of it along the Poudre River, had been taken many years earlier. North and west of Fort Collins, homesteads were continuous along the Poudre to where it entered the mountains. And most of the good land near Bellvue and LaPorte had been filed.

The maps showed that around Livermore, twenty or more miles north, the filings became less frequent. Plots that had been surveyed and filed were located near running water, but there were open areas, also. There appeared to be a few available sites near what Roz hoped were year-round streams, but he knew he'd have to see for himself. He carefully took notes and made crude maps of the areas he sought.

"I'll be interested to know if you find something good," Moose said. "But I'll stay in Fort Collins and talk with the townspeople about what they have and what they need."

"I'll be gone about three days," Roz said. "Maybe four. Are you sure you don't want to come along on this grand adventure? You might see things you've never seen before."

“I’ve seen enough things I never saw before, at least for a while. You go ahead.”

Roz left the following morning, alone for the first time in years. He would have preferred company, but was excited about the prospect of finding a place of his own. He listened to the musical rush of Poudre River as it tumbled over smooth stones and eddied into deep pools. His horse frightened grasshoppers, which sprang away. Some fell into the water where hungry trout gulped them with a splash.

Roz forded near LaPorte, and lunched near the general store in a grove of cottonwood trees with gnarled trunks four men could not have reached around. LaPorte pre-dated Fort Collins by several years, and had been the area’s first fur trading post.

He passed Bellvue by staying on the north side of the river. Bellvue seemed to consist of a large saloon surrounded by a scattering of small homes. He continued along the river road toward the mountains. He found the red sandstone hogback, the first line of up-tilted strata that marked the beginning of the Rockies. Ponderosas grew up the steep flanks of the foothills, their dark green branches contrasting with red-stone cliffs and light green grass.

He passed by the cut where the Poudre tumbled out of the foothills. It wasn't possible to travel west up the Cache la Poudre. A narrow gorge with deep, tumbling water prohibited going that direction. If one wanted to go to the headwaters, as many loggers did, it was necessary to go by way of Livermore and return to the Poudre many miles upstream. He turned north to continue on the stage road to Livermore, Virginia Dale, and Laramie.

As Roz rode between the first and second hogback the air became warm and dry. He continued past a ranch situated by a small stream that meandered toward the Poudre. The ranch appeared to have very little pasture or hay meadow. Roz was surprised at how quickly the landscape changed from the lush river bottom to dry-land pasture, studded with boulders fallen from the ridges above.

He traveled six more miles on the crushed-granite Butterfield Stage road toward a gap in the high ridge on his left. Sweat began to collect under his hatband. Two hawks circled high above, riding on an updraft from the vertical red-rock wall. A small, pink lizard scampered away. Buster didn't seem to notice. Roz saw a dead gopher the hawks hadn't found. It would be gone before nightfall.

The roadsides were dry. A thin layer of topsoil covered shale and granite-based gravel. The temperature rose, and he became concerned about finding the kind of land he wanted. He hoped he'd see better prospects when he crossed the high ridge on his left.

He stopped, got down from the saddle to consult his map, and noticed two dung beetles rolling a marble-sized ball of cow manure up a slight incline by his feet. One pushed with its back legs while the other balanced on top. They would bury it in a sandy spot and lay eggs. Larvae would live on the food source until they matured. Roz wondered how they knew how to do what they did. It seemed there should be easier ways to live, better soil, even for dung beetles. He spread the map on the saddle. Buster held still while Roz studied, then re-folded and put it in the saddle bag.

His map showed the gap in front of him as Owl Canyon. Just before the short canyon a weed-choked, abandoned farmstead sat forlornly on the dry hillside. It wasn't encouraging. He considered turning back, but decided to ride to Livermore for food and rest, and then decide what to do next. He clucked to Buster. "May as well go on, old horse."

They entered the short canyon in shadow. A cool breeze blew from the mountains beyond. Roz stopped Buster with a light pull on the reins. Cliff swallows darted in and out, and Roz saw their mud-daubed nests high on the sandstone walls. Buster stepped from one foot to the other and raised his head up and down. Roz gave the go-ahead signal with a slight squeeze of his knees.

Buster walked out of the canyon into sunlight. They passed over a small hill to a vantage point that took Roz's breath away. Owl Canyon was a gateway to verdant abundance.

Rolling, grass-covered hills led down to a dark line of trees indicating the North Fork of the Poudre. He could just make out the buildings of Livermore, four miles distant. Beyond Livermore were more grass lands and long, sloping, pine-covered hills, silhouettes layered one after another to snow-covered peaks which seemed to comb the sky. There were no fences in sight; no hay stacks. No one moved across the landscape. The breeze pushed wind-shadows across the tall grass. Roz left the stage road and let the horse crop in stirrup-high forage while he looked, as far as he could see, at the most pleasing place he had ever imagined.

"Lord, what a country," he said to Buster. "Eat up, and we'll go find a new home."

Buster sensed Roz's excitement, raised his head, and commenced a brisk walk. Roz liked the look of the country better with each step. Livermore showed a collection of stores, saloons, and cabins marking a junction on the stage road. The right fork continued on to Virginia Dale and Laramie. The left went along Lone Pine Creek to Red Feather Lakes.

Except for the branching of the road and the proximity of Lone Pine Creek, which led to the North Fork of the Cache la Poudre, Livermore seemed to have little reason to be there. However, a hotel was being built, and the sign in front proclaimed, "The Forks." Close by was Saint Luke's Episcopal Church, also being completed. Graveled streets connected a scattering of log cabins and small frame houses. At least half of the buildings appeared to be new. He reflected on the fact that wherever he'd seen the confluence of rivers or roads, people built residences and provided services to travelers like himself. He supposed it was how commerce and cities started, and the more travelers and residents needing services, the larger the city was likely to grow. He rode past the Elkhorn Saloon, a one-story log structure with a boardwalk across the front and a large rack of elk antlers mounted above the door. He thought about going in, but was anxious to move on toward the land along Lone Pine Creek and the Red Feather Lakes beyond.

He chose the left fork that headed due west toward the white peaks of the Medicine Bow range, and watched as the country changed from grass plains to lush mountain meadows and pine-covered hillsides. The creek sparkled between cottonwood and willow trees. Snow-capped mountains appeared between gaps in the wooded hills. Birds sang and chipmunks scampered across the road. The breeze alternately brought the smell of pine needles and meadow grass. Small clouds formed from the high peaks ahead and moved over him, growing as they went. Cloud shadows flowed across the meadows and raced up the steep hillsides.

He let Buster crop grass while he thought how far away and insignificant Mesa de Luna seemed. The danger and difficulty of the trip to Denver was behind him. He felt a growing warmth and excitement, complex and difficult to understand. It seemed both tentative and hopeful, as if he'd finally found a place where he might be satisfied. It took a while for him to think of a term for what he felt; *appropriate* seemed best. But it was better than that. He felt as though he might be coming home. He'd never had the feeling before, and was pleased to know he'd recognized it, even if he needed more evidence to be certain.

In late afternoon he stopped at a small log cabin and was met by a sleepy black-and-tan hound that barked once, sniffed his horse's front legs, and went back to lie down in the shade. A grizzled old man with pants and suspenders worn over ragged underwear came out and squinted at him. "Help ye?" he asked, folding his arms over his considerable belly.

"I thought maybe I could stretch, rest the horse a few minutes, and ask about the Red Feathers."

"What about 'em?"

"Well, how far are they, and are there a lot of people living there, that kind of thing?"

"They're too close, and there's too many people." The old man seemed to look far away. "I've been trappin' mink and marten around here for forty years. Didn't used to see nobody. Yesterday there was two go by, and now here's you. No offense."

"None taken," Roz said with a smile. "Nice cabin."

"Built her in forty-two, believe it was. Had a wife. She left. I didn't."

"I hear there is a lot of open land hereabout," Roz said.

"People keep comin'. I expect it will all be taken soon enough. That what you're after?" Roz nodded. "There's neighbors two miles up the creek. Others down. You probably saw some." Roz had, and had been pleased to note that there was good pasture and hillside grazing all along the creek. Most of it appeared to be available.

"Are you homesteaded here?" he asked.

"Nope," the old trapper replied. "Got no use for it. I'd just have to pay taxes. I'll run my lines in winter 'til they won't let me. Then I'll be out of here. Higher up the mountain, or maybe Idaho. Plenty of room there, I'm told."

Roz conversed for a few minutes without getting much useful information. He continued toward the Red Feathers. However, after talking to another settler who gave him a better estimate of the distance, he decided not to go that far. He looked for a sheltered spot to make camp, with good grass for Buster. He caught three brook trout from a small stream, rolled them in cornmeal, and fried them in bacon drippings. After supper, when the fire died to a bed of coals, he saw the gleam of eyes moving in the shadows. He couldn't tell if it was a large animal or a smaller one closer to the fire, but the horse didn't seem concerned as he would have been with a predator in the area.

Roz reviewed his options. He'd learned from his experience in Denver that he didn't want to live in town, but he thought it would suit him best if he was no more than a day's ride away from Fort Collins. He knew he occasionally liked to have a few drinks, laughs, and enjoy the company of women, and he wanted to stay in touch with Moose. He wished he was already building a home and starting a herd. He felt an urgency to be settled. That, too, was new. He slept fitfully while the big dipper wheeled around the pole star.

The following morning he crossed over the north mountain ridge and rode down to Rabbit Creek. It didn't look as promising for grazing as Lone

Pine Creek had. The water flow was less, and meadows were smaller. He followed Rabbit Creek downstream to where it converged with Lone Pine Creek, and turned west up Lone Pine once again. He carefully noted where settlers were situated and tried to improve his maps with a pencil so he could file on land that hadn't been claimed. By mid-afternoon he had three alternatives.

He'd claim 160 acres of bottomland where he'd build his home and out-buildings. The meadows would provide hay for winter feed, and he assumed he could graze stock on the un-fenced hillsides that others would not want to homestead. He graded the three sites from most to least desirable, but thought he could be happy with any of them. When he finished, he felt almost as if he had already marked and claimed one of the locations. He decided to have a final look the next day before hurrying to the land office in Fort Collins.

That night he heard wolves howling far away. It was chilling, but comforting at the same time. He didn't worry about livestock depredation, and wouldn't until the deer and elk population had been reduced by settlers. It seemed it would be a long time before that happened. A horned moon rose above a timber-covered hill. Buster made small resting sounds. Roz put his coat over his shoulders and watched the fire until embers winked out one by one. He slept better than he had the previous night.

The next morning he decided to talk with the old trapper one more time to see if he could get advice or impressions concerning the plots he had tentatively selected. When he rode to the cabin's yard, the dog didn't bother to get up. The trapper came out and said, "You again."

"It is," Roz replied. "I hoped I could ask you a couple of questions about some sites I'm interested in."

"Might as well," The trapper replied. "Looks like you're going to do it, anyhow."

Roz smiled and explained what he had seen. He asked if the old fellow had any advice.

The trapper waited for a full minute before he said, "Tell you what I'd do if I was in your boots. I'd forget about the land higher up. It doesn't get enough sun to make good hay. Now, that place downstream by the big split rock. The soil's deep. There's always elk and deer in the winter, as there's a spring that never freezes. Grass is better, too. Plenty of timber to build your house and barn. But you'd be neighbor to the crazy woman. Better go talk to her first. See what you think."

"What's wrong with her?" Roz asked.

"She's strange. You'll see. She's about a mile and a half down the road east. You can't see her house, but her gate has a frying pan wired to it. Go to the split boulder. After that, you'll see the pan. Now, you need to go, and I need to rest. Any other questions?"

Roz thanked him and rode east, down-hill, the creek to his left. Tree shadows indicated early afternoon. A grouse flushed beside the road and curved away toward the creek. Buster shied and hopped a few times but settled into his easy walk. A raven squawked from an overhanging ponderosa limb. Two deer ignored him from a nearby meadow. Roz found the house-sized rock with a tree growing in the cleft. Beyond the rock was the gate with the frying pan wired between the middle and top poles. On the inside of the pan was printed in chalked letters the words, "EGGS—HERBS" and below that, "GARDEN PRODUCE." He knew there had been no printing on the pan when he passed it the previous time. He opened the gate, led Buster in, closed it behind them, and re-mounted.

The curving wagon ruts gradually revealed a log barn, corrals, a large vegetable garden, and a log house with a metal-banded wooden water tank placed by the stone chimney and slightly uphill from the house. The tank appeared to have a woven-wire fence around it.

A woman stood in the garden and watched him from rows of corn that were nearly waist high. She leaned on a hoe or shovel handle. A large sunbonnet hid her face. Her hands were gloved, and she wore an oversized shirt and what appeared to be black trousers with suspenders. She seemed tall and slim, but in the strange clothing it was hard to tell.

Roz stopped by the garden and tipped his hat. She raised a gloved hand and peered at him. "So," she said.

"I beg your pardon?"

"Pretty picture, you and that fancy horse. Get down. Stretch your legs." She looked toward the barn and gave a quick, beckoning wave. A tall, blond-headed boy came out of the barn with a Henry repeating rifle in the crook of his arm. He'd been watching as Roz rode in. At such close range, he could easily have controlled any horseman who was giving the woman difficulty. He seemed relaxed, but watchful. "This is Ken Junior," she said. "I'm Karin Pedersen. What's your name?" She spoke with a lilting Scandinavian accent.

"Roz Wells. I was wondering…"

"Get down, Mister Wells. I'm getting a crick in my neck looking up at you. Then we'll talk." She smiled with perfectly spaced, very white teeth. The rest of her face was in shadow.

"That's better. Ken, take the man's horse. Is that all right with you, Mister Wells? Will he give trouble?"

"Buster? Lord, no," Roz replied. "He'll follow anybody."

"There are carrots in the barn. Ken can give him a couple of those."

"If you do," Roz said to the boy, "I'll likely never get him back. He'll want to stay and I'll be walking to Fort Collins."

"Well," she remarked as they moved toward the log cabin, "Your horse is well fed, your saddle's been soaped, and you look cleaned up. You haven't traveled far. Are you a politician, a drummer, or looking for land?"

"Land," Roz replied, "to settle on. I'm thinking about the piece just west of yours." Roz realized her direct manner made him somewhat uncomfortable, but she had a graceful, swinging step, even in the oversized clothing she wore. He still hadn't seen most of her face.

"In that case, Mister Wells, we can talk. We'll have dinner. Sit here in the shade. I'm going to bring you a dipper of water. I'll go put some food on the table. Emily, come out here! Emily's five. Thinks she's fifteen. Emily! Come meet Mister Wells." A small, pretty girl with long wheat-colored hair came out of the door and stood by her mother. She looked up at Roz with a shy smile, then down. "Mister Wells, this is Emily. Emily, Mister Wells. What do you say?"

"How come you're so skinny?" she asked softly.

"Emily! What's the matter with you? Mind your manners."

Roz laughed and said, "I don't mind. Would you rather I was fat?"

"No," she replied. "Fat people break things. And they aren't happy."

"Is that so?" Roz didn't quite know what to say. "I thought maybe they were happy."

"They aren't. They'd rather be thin, like you."

"Emily, go into the house and get Mister Wells a dipper of water. That girl, I swear she…"

"She's just fine. You don't have to wonder what she's thinking, I'd guess."

"Oh, no," the woman replied. "She'll tell you. She's like me. I don't like to beat around the bush. I'm going in. I'll call you directly."

When Emily returned with a drink for Roz, she said, "We haven't asked anybody in for a meal since the preacher came…and he never came back."

"Why is that, that he didn't come back I mean?"

"Oh, probably something Momma said," replied the girl. "Are you a rancher? Or a farmer?"

"Not yet," Roz replied, "but I plan to be. Do you like ranchers?"

"I don't care, as long as they are good to their animals. If they aren't good to their animals, they shouldn't have any. Dad used to say, 'A farmer is never hungry.' Anyway, I'm going to be a school teacher. They know everything. Of course, I have a lot to learn."

Roz had the impression he was talking to someone years older than she actually was, and he understood her mother's comment. "Do you go to school now?"

"We're waiting for one to be built. Momma teaches me. I can read and count to one hundred, two hundred probably, if I want to. Ken's ahead of me in math, but I'll catch up. Can you read?"

"Yes, I can," Roz replied, "And I know some arithmetic, but I don't use it much."

"Mom says things that aren't used get rusty," she said seriously.

Roz laughed and said, "That they do."

"Is she talking your head off?" Karin asked as she opened the door.

Roz caught his breath and tried not to show it. He realized he'd put his hat back on and quickly took it off. Karin looked at him with wide-set, gray-green eyes above a small, pert nose and a generous mouth that smiled again as she said, "Please, come in Mister Wells. Emily, go get Kenny. Tell him we're going to eat."

She turned. Roz followed her in. She had brushed long, honey-colored hair and tied it back with a blue bow. Her simple blue-and-white-striped dress showed a slim but supple figure. Roz realized she was nearly as tall as he.

"Now, Mister Wells, sit down here." She indicated a chair at the end of a rectangular walnut table that would have seated six or eight people comfortably. Apparently it had been brought from the East; Roz doubted furniture of such quality was made anywhere west of Chicago. The chairs matched the table. Four white porcelain plates and bowls had been arranged beside linen napkins. The knives, spoons, and forks were of more common quality, but all showed the same pattern. He glanced around the room and saw that the other furniture had been handmade, well done but simple.

The room size was generous and served as a kitchen, eating area, and common room, with a fireplace on one wall and a cast-iron Prairie Queen kitchen range on the opposite. It was clean. Two closed doors led to what Roz assumed were bedrooms. Open shelves stored pots, pans, and supplies. A zinc-covered sink apparently drained through the wall to the outside. There was no hand pump at the sink as he would have expected. Instead, a long pipe led from the wall by the fireplace and ended with a spigot over the sink. Karin turned a valve and filled four tumblers with water and brought them to the table.

"Is the water gravity-fed?" Roz asked.

"Yes. There's a spring up the hill. It feeds into the tank you may have noticed when you rode in."

"What keeps it from freezing in winter?"

"Cow manure. It gets some heat from the fireplace, but mostly cow manure. Same thing with the stock tank in the corral. We put wire mesh around them with room for about six inches of manure. The house tank is closed so we put manure on top of it as well as on the sides. We cover the stock tank top with boards, except for a place to drink. The manure decomposes and stays warm. It keeps the water from freezing. In the spring, we take the manure and put it on the garden. We don't waste it. Is that enough talk about manure? We're about to eat," she added with a grin.

"Well, all right, but I may want to discuss it later. Seems I can learn a thing or two around here about how to handle cold weather."

"We have plenty of that," she replied, "although it's a good deal warmer up here than out on the plains," and as the boy entered the room, "Ken, wash up. We're about to sit down."

As Ken washed at the sink, he said, "I unsaddled your horse, sir, and put him in with ours. I curried him. He liked that. I gave him some carrots. He liked those even better. I was about to leave when he stepped on my foot. It wasn't hard enough to hurt, but I couldn't get away. I think he wanted more carrots. I thought I might have to whistle for you to come and get me."

"That sounds like Buster," Roz replied. "How did you make him stop?"

"I could just reach the curry-comb, so I started to comb him again. When he closed his eyes, I got loose. He acted like he wanted me to stay."

"You can bet on it," Roz said. "He's probably the smartest, orneriest horse I've ever seen. Give him an apple someday if you want to make a friend for life."

"Let's join hands," Karin said. "Ken, would you like to…?"

"Give us this day our daily bread. Bless our family, our friends, our guest, and…"

"And his ornery horse," Emily concluded with a giggle.

"Amen," Roz said with a laugh as the others echoed the word.

"Now, Mister Wells," Karin said, "Will you help yourself to the potatoes?"

"Yes, but I wish you'd call me Roz. Then I'll know who I am," he replied.

"Not this time," she answered. "Maybe later."

Roz was puzzled. Something about the way she spoke seemed to keep him from his normal, social rhythm.

"Emily, pass Mister Wells the cabbage."

"Momma, why is Mister Wells using Dad's chair?" Emily asked. "You didn't let the preacher use that chair. Maybe that's why he didn't stay—or come back."

"Emily! Please. Mind your manners. Mister Wells, I think you should know the children's father died three years ago. It's all right. We talk about it. For a time, I didn't want to see anyone else sitting there at mealtime. As to the preacher, well, I'm as spiritual as anyone, but he was bent on telling me how much we'd all sinned and how he was the only one who could save us. I don't hold to that kind of talk. Fear and sin won't rule our lives. Not in this house." Karin's eyes flashed.

Roz searched for a response to the impassioned statement. "Do—you have a church to go to up here?"

"No, the closest one is in Livermore, and that's a bit far for us to travel, particularly in bad weather, but we read the Bible and we discuss what it means to us."

Roz was thinking of an answer when she asked, "Would you like to know what we decided?" She folded her hands and looked directly at him with a small smile.

"Uh, yes. Yes, I would."

"All right. We, the children and I, believe that God is everything, that Jesus was incredibly intelligent and showed us how to live, and that we are meant to learn and help each other and ourselves, and love every living thing. We have no room for blame or envy or, most especially, guilt. We have little tolerance for anger and none at all for hate." She looked directly at him. "Does that make sense to you?"

"Yes," Roz answered, "it does."

"Do I sound like a preacher? I don't mean to, but when I really believe something—well, I'd better stop. You'll be excusing yourself to leave, and I don't want you to do that. Ken, my husband, was always out of his chair and off to do something."

"Your husband, how…"

"...did he die? The doctor said it was some kind of intestinal problem." She said, more quietly, "People usually die when they are ready, Mister Wells. Not before and not after, no matter what they say."

Roz didn't respond. Karin looked at him and explained, "I know some say they don't want to die, but they do. They're confused and afraid. You can't blame them."

Roz was on unfamiliar ground concerning the philosophy of health and death, and the idea that preferences could actually cause one or the other. "But there are accidents, I mean—"

"Not really. If you think about it, you'll see what I mean. Take illness. I'm an herbalist. You saw the sign. People come to me for herbs, sometimes for cooking but mostly for illness, although some of them think I'm a little crazy. That's because I tell them what I know, and some don't like it. They come, anyway. I sell them herbs and it helps, but most of the illness is in their heads. They'll die if they really want to, and live if they don't. The only way to help is with facts and a positive attitude."

"I see," Roz said, keeping his doubts to himself.

"I mean, not all the time, but people usually experience what they want, or expect. So. Enough of that. Did you meet old Charlie Liner, the trapper up the road?" Roz nodded. "Well," Karin said with a laugh, "I have to let him think I'm a little strange, or he'd be here for every meal. He's all right. Incidentally, you should drink more water."

"I should?"

"Yes," she replied, and the children said in unison with her, "Because - you'll - have - more - energy - and - better - health." Momma always says that," Emily added. "Sometimes I feel like a fish. May I be excused?" Karin nodded.

"Me, too, Mom?" the boy asked. She smiled and nodded again.

When they had gone, she said, "I discuss genuine things with them. I don't want them to grow up too fast. We play together, too. But I want them to hear real talk, real ideas. I appreciate that you were here to help. It's better to not always be the only adult."

"I like them," Roz said thoughtfully, mildly surprised that he'd said it. He liked Karin also, in spite of her blunt ways. She seemed genuine. There appeared to be no artifice or false importance about her. "I enjoyed the meal and the conversation. I should be getting on."

"I did want to ask about your horse."

"Buster? He isn't for sale if..."

"No," she said. "I'd just like to know how he is, what he's like."

"Well," Roz said with surprise. "He's six years old. Healthy. Pretty good walker."

"Is he reliable?"

"You can rely on him to entertain you," Roz laughed, and said more seriously, "Yes, I'd call him reliable."

"How long have you had him? Did you get him recently or bring him with you from the south? I judge you're from Texas or Oklahoma by your accent."

"San Antonio, ma'am. I raised him from a colt…"

"Did you break him?"

"Not really. It was more like we learned together. I'm not much of a bronc rider. I'd had an old horse that was so slow I'd get off sometimes to see if he was moving. I figured I'd better get a good colt to train for when the old fellow couldn't go anymore. It worked out about right."

"Does he bite or kick? Has he ever hurt you?"

"Buster? Lord, no. One time we were running on slick grass. We fell and he pinned my leg. He looked all the way around at me before he'd move to get up. He wanted to be sure I was all right."

"He seems good with children."

"He hasn't been around them much, but I think he likes everyone, young or old. Why do you want to know?"

"I was just curious. Animals can tell you a lot about people, I've found."

"Well, I'd hate to hear what he might say about me. Anyway, I should get going."

"Let me tell you one more thing. The one-sixty you're favoring, west of this place, is a good piece of land. Ken, my former husband, considered which might be better, and it was a toss-up. But what I wanted to ask is, have you heard about a timber claim?"

"No, I haven't," Roz replied.

"There's a provision for claiming an additional quarter section. You've probably noticed most of the timber is on the north side of these mountains." Roz nodded. "Moisture stays longer on the shaded side. You can claim an additional plot across the road to the south, like I have, on the north side of the hill. It isn't worth a lot now, but it will be someday. One is supposed to plant and cultivate ten acres of trees in the bare places. We transplanted saplings. They're doing well enough. We'll show you how. But you'll have to ask at the land office. They aren't publicizing it. I'm not sure why. It may be they're saving it for friends or for themselves. Anyway, I wanted you to know, if you're interested. You'd better go file before someone else does." Again she looked directly at him and smiled. She extended her hand. It was slim, warm, and dry. "Mister Wells," she said, "it has been a pleasure."

Roz thanked her and agreed. He said goodbye to the children, and before he had saddled and brought Buster out of the barn she was dressed as she had been when he rode in. She waved from the waist-high corn and called, "Come back. We have more to discuss." He rode away with the odd sensation that he was moving without hurrying. He thought about the conversation and the unusual things she'd said. He passed Livermore in late afternoon without stopping or talking to anyone. He rode on through Owl Canyon as the sun turned the rim rock a rusty red.

He decided to stop for the night at the abandoned homestead. Bats flipped and twirled, hunting twilight insects. Once again, he had the feeling that his future was in the land behind him, and that east of Owl Canyon there was too little moisture and too much confusion. As night fell he thought about the people who had passed through the canyon by stage coach, wagon, Indian travois, and other means. It felt like a gate, and he thought maybe there were other such places where travelers, seekers like him, had known their journey was nearing its end.

Roz was back in Fort Collins by mid-afternoon of the following day. He hurried to tell Moose what he'd seen. "Tomorrow I'll go to the land office," he said. "Then I'd like you to come up there with me and have a look, once I file. You could help me mark the boundaries and then we'd tell the nearest neighbors what I've done. After that we can go back to Denver and wrap things up. How does that sound?"

"Sounds fine. It's good you found a place. It isn't going to be that easy for me. There are a few businesses available, but at very high prices. If I build up my own hotel or store I'm going to need credit, and that won't be easy, either. They don't know me. I don't have enough money to buy what I'd want, so I may have to work and save for a while. But I'll figure it out. Let's go have dinner."

After they'd eaten and returned to their room, Roz said, "Maybe you should homestead like I'm going to do. It's mighty pretty up there. And, uh—I want to tell you about the neighbor lady I met." Moose looked at him carefully. "No, not that way," Roz laughed, "although she is a widow and has a fine place. Maybe if we put hers and mine together." Roz laughed and tilted his hat back. "Fact is I don't quite know what to make of her."

"What do you mean?"

"Well, she's different. I don't know. I've been trying to figure it out."

"Pretty?"

"Yes, very, but…"

"But what?"

"She's—tall." Moose raised his eyebrows but didn't respond. "She's interesting, and I'd say—capable. But I've always liked to lead a woman, help her, and have her look up to me. You know, do things for her. I expect Karin—that's her name—can do about anything I can do. Smart. Has a couple of nice youngsters. She seemed more interested in Buster than in me." He rubbed his chin, "Anyway, why don't you file with me. If you don't like it, you could come back."

Moose looked thoughtful for a moment, and said, "No, I belong in town. I'm just not the farming or ranching type. Funny, isn't it? I always did the horse-work while you built things. Now you're going to farm and ranch, and I'm staying here."

"I don't plan to do much farmin'. I'll raise cows, mostly. I'll need a few horses I can handle; maybe old ones. I'll have to cut and stack hay, but the thought of too much farming makes me nervous."

"Now, that's something I'd like to see. You, nervous. You haven't been nervous since you were born."

"I had my mother with me and that was a comfort. But I might be nervous out in that back-country if I can't get to town now and then. I need company you know. By the way, if you decide to go into the hotel business you might want to ask Henry and Manuela to join you. I think they'd be interested"

They talked into the night. Each had the sense they'd found an area where they could stay and, with luck and hard work, prosper. Both had left areas that for one reason or another weren't suitable. Each planned to return and visit relatives at some future time, but neither knew when or if that would really happen. They thought, with some envy, of what earlier settlers and business people already had accomplished in Fort Collins. But they believed they, too, could build their futures, just as had the people who were already there. It felt daunting, but exciting.

"We'd better get some shut-eye," Roz said with a yawn. "Tomorrow comes early, and I need to get to the land office before somebody beats me to it."

Moose looked at his watch. "It already is tomorrow. Poke a log in that stove. I'll see you when the sun comes through the window."

Chapter Thirty Seven

LITTLE BIGHORN

"Moose, are you awake?" Moose's recumbent silhouette could be seen before the window. It didn't move. Dawn was breaking, with pink and gold clouds glowing in the eastern sky. Two mourning doves called softly. A mule brayed from the fort's corral.

"Moose, if you're awake, tell me."

"What? What do you want?"

"I want to find food. I'm hungry. I thought you might want to go along."

"Roz, it's dark out there. I'm not ready. Go ahead if you want to."

"Shall I bring something back for you?"

"I doubt if you can find anything open." Moose yawned. "Stores are closed. Restaurants probably don't open for an hour or more. But, if you can, sure. Now, I'd like to get a little more sleep if you don't particularly mind."

“You look like an old bear. I reckon if I skinned an old…”

“I’ve heard that before. Now, let me rest. If you’re so all-fired anxious to be up and around, please do it without me, for crissake.”

“I thought I’d go over to Gillette’s Cafe. Their cooks will be busy making breakfast. I’ll see if I can talk them into helping a hungry homesteader like me.”

“Well, as long as you’re up you might as well see if there are some coals in that stove. Throw in some kindling. It’s cold over here by the window. Goodnight.”

“Moose, it’s not…never mind. I’ll make sure you’re toasty warm.”

Thirty minutes later Roz burst through the door.

“Moose! Get up quick. Hurry!” Moose sprang out of bed and nearly went sprawling with a blanket wrapped around his feet.

“Sit down. I’ve got something to tell you,” Roz exclaimed as he removed his hat and rubbed his brow.

“Crissake,” Moose said, half-wondering if a posse from Albuquerque had found them. “Do you want me to stand up, or sit down, or what?”

“Sit. Stand. Hell, I don’t know. Now, listen. There’s a crowd outside the telegraph office. Custer’s men were wiped out! All of them.”

"What? How?"

"The telegrapher read the news to us. Custer's entire force was killed. Over two hundred. No survivors. Major Reno's men couldn't get there in time. "

"But El…"

"He's dead, Moose."

"He can't be."

"He is."

"But—dead? What about Miguel?"

"Killed, too."

"Jesus, Roz. That's hard to take in…"

"I know. It happened at a place called Little Bighorn Creek. Sioux and Cheyenne. Thousands of them. When Custer's force came after them, they decided to fight instead of run. Reno's troops were to meet Custer's men, but got stopped by Indians some distance away. Quite a few of Reno's men were killed, too. By the time they got to Custer, every man and every animal was dead, except one horse. They scalped every soldier and scout—except Miguel.

"Miguel?"

"They apparently honored him. He'd killed quite a few braves. Blood all around him. And spent cartridges. Seems he was carrying more than a bugle."

"And—El?"

"Not much to tell. He and two Arickaree scouts were killed. Their guns and equipment were taken, like everybody else's. If I know El, he made a good account of himself. That's all I know."

"What about that Lobo fellow?"

"I don't know. He wasn't listed, at least not by that name."

"Lord! There'll be hell to pay. The entire U.S. Army will be after them. I wonder..."

"Moose, that's not all. This is the...I don't know how to tell you this." Roz looked down while rubbing his hands together.

Moose couldn't remember the last time he'd seen Roz at a loss for words.

"I remembered that Colonel DuPree's name." Moose's head snapped up. "There's a list of survivors and family members. I asked about him."

Color drained from Moose's face.

"He's dead, Moose. Suzanne's a widow." Moose sat down heavily.

"I asked where Custer and his men had come from. What post. They were from Fort Abe Lincoln up on the Missouri in Dakota Territory. Mandan country.

"Oh, Lord," Moose said. His mouth stayed open. He stared through the wall. "Oh, Lord above."

"Moose, Suzanne was listed as one of DuPree's survivors, one of his family."

"One? What do you mean, one?"

"There's another. A little boy. He is listed as Royale Parker DuPree, age five. Now, Moose, hold steady. Are you all right?"

Moose nodded and swallowed. "I don't, I don't know what to, I mean, I..."

"I'll tell you what I think, Moose. You have to get over there as fast as you can."

"To ...?"

"To Fort Lincoln. That's where she'll be, for a while, anyway."

"God, Roz, I don't know if I can do that."

"Of course you can. And you ought to get started right away."

"But it's been five years. Closer to six. I can't just go bustin' in there. I mean, what if..."

"What if what?"

"What if she doesn't want me? What if she, oh hell, I don't know."

"Moose. Listen to me."

"But, what if…"

"Moose, hear me out. You're in no shape to make decisions. So listen to me for a change. She loved you once. Is that right?" Moose nodded. "She didn't want to leave New Orleans, did she?"

"No."

"She didn't want to leave you. She didn't think she had a choice. Did she?"

"I don't think, I mean, no…I guess not."

"And you told me you should have done something to keep her. That's what you said."

"Yes. I should have told her I wanted—wanted to marry her as soon as I could. I should have taken her away."

"Well, now you have that chance. Don't make another mistake."

"No, I…"

"This may be the best chance you'll ever have, Moose. I'd hate to see you waste it. You have to go."

"Yes, but how should I—I'm not sure what to do."

"That's why I'm going to tell you. Do you still have that book she gave you?"

"Yes, I keep it with me."

"Can I see it?"

Moose reached into his pack and gave the book to Roz. Roz opened it to the inscription. As he did, the folded sheet of paper fell from inside the back cover. "Mind if I read this again?" Moose shook his head. Roz read the faded letter. It was thin and nearly worn through where it had been folded. The corners were tattered. Most of the words were legible.

"What do you think she means where she wrote, 'You can never know what you have given me'?" Roz asked.

Moose shook his head.

"It might be the child, Moose. It might be yours. It has one of your names, Royale. Maybe that doesn't really matter, but you have to go find her. Bring her here. You can do it. I know you can."

Moose looked around the room, confused. He started to dress. He buttoned his shirt incorrectly, and the shirt tail was stuffed into a back pocket.

"I see I'm going to have to look after you for a while," Roz said with a grin. "Tell you what. Why don't you try that shirt again, and we'll go get some breakfast. I'll take a pencil and paper. We need to make plans."

Moose glanced at him, down at his clothing. He, too, began to smile as he straightened himself. "Okay," he said. "All right. You need to go to the land office, don't you?"

"It'll keep a day or two."

As they talked during and after breakfast Roz had to bring Moose's attention back, time after time. Roz finally convinced him to leave the following morning on the stage to Cheyenne, and to then take the Union Pacific train to Omaha. From Omaha he would go to Fort Abe Lincoln by steam packet boat.

Roz agreed to take care of Moose's horse and treat it as one of his own until Moose returned. He offered Moose the money he'd brought. Moose said he was sure he had enough. Moose also said he might have to go to New Orleans before he could return. Suzanne might need to settle things with her father. If that was the case it might take up to two years before he came back. That was dreaming, but still…

"I'd rather come back with her than return alone. No matter how long it takes."

"You'll need better clothes," Roz suggested. "What we have is all right for what we've been doing here, but you'll need to look as good as you can."

"Clothes aren't easy to get in my size."

"We'll see what we can find," Roz answered. "You aren't the only big fellow around here, and we have all afternoon. We'll find something. Also, I can send some of your things from LaGarde's if you have to go to Louisiana. Just let me know where you are."

"You'll need to tell Manuela what happened when you get back to Denver," Moose said. "We probably should tell her sister, too, while we're here."

"I'll take care of that tomorrow. She may want to go to Denver with me. I'll ask. I don't know if she ever met Miguel or not."

Moose shook his head and said, "I can't get over El's being gone. Somehow I always thought he'd be around, standing up in the stirrups, looking at things the rest of us can't see."

"I know," Roz replied. "I'll always, uh…" Roz swallowed, cleared his throat. "I don't think there was any place for him to go."

Moose gave him a quizzical look.

"I know he could winter over somewhere like in Estes Park, or go camping in the mountains, but that isn't the way he wanted to live," Roz said. "The buffalo are about gone. I imagine the Indians will be gone soon, even if they did win this battle. Settlers are starting to put up barbed wire. It's going to be everywhere. I don't mind it so much, but how do you keep someone as—I don't know—as *free* as El was?"

Moose nodded.

"And Miguel," Roz continued, "I think in a way Miguel died when his father did. I think he died the way he wanted to." Roz remembered Karin's words.

"But, tomorrow's a new day and you have a long way to go. You'll bring her back, and the little boy, too." Roz hoped he was right, and hoped his friend wouldn't be hurt.

Moose looked far beyond the walls. He remembered New Orleans. He imagined a rustic fort somewhere deep in Indian country. He began to piece together the way she looked, the images he'd buried under painful memories. The eyes, the hair, dimples he'd almost forgotten, the fair white skin. Such skin. The back of her neck where damp hair curled. Pretty hands. Images flooded back. It felt as if he was free to hope and, this time perhaps, to make it happen.

Roz waited for him to finish his thought, and then said, "Come back as soon as you can. We're in the right place at the right time. And we have a lot of work to do."

Moose smiled and nodded. "Yes. We do. We surely do."

I hope you enjoyed FINDING OWL CANYON. If you did I'd love to hear from you. rextolsen@gmail.com If not - - - well, you probably have better things to do.

Positive reviews are very helpful in promoting book sales, even if the review or comment contains only a few words. When you see the Amazon review system that follows this page, it is easy to make a few comments - whatever you'd like to say. Not necessary, but much appreciated.

And now - a few words about the sequel. The sequel, REDFEATHER ROAD, shows Moose starting toward Fort Abraham Lincoln by Union Pacific from Cheyenne, and then traveling up the Missouri by steamboat. Will he find Suzanne? Will she receive him? Roz, latent entrepreneur, earns enough money in Fort Collins to start his homestead. Then he - 'courts' isn't quite the right word - the beautiful Karin Pedersen, who seems always to be one step ahead of him. And more, but, you know - why give the story away.

Sincerely, I **Thank You** for reading FINDING OWL CANYON.

\- - - -

Rex T. Olsen lives on Bainbridge Island in Washington State, with his wife Elizabeth, and a parakeet named Charlie Parker who calls himself "bird". When Rex isn't writing, he is restoring or playing vintage saxophones, cooking vegetarian, or building model ships.

44937214R10248

Made in the USA
Charleston, SC
06 August 2015